CHRIST AT THE ROU

The 21st Century in Our Times Series

Series Editor: Anne Mathews-Younes, Ed.D., D.Min.
Associate Editor: Shivraj K. Mahendra (Ph.D. Candidate)

CHRIST
AT THE
ROUNDTABLE

Revised Edition

E. Stanley Jones

CHRIST AT THE ROUNDTABLE
by E. Stanley Jones

Copyright © 2019 by The E. Stanley Jones Foundation

All Rights Reserved.
No part of this work may be reproduced
or transmitted in any form or by any means, electronic
or mechanical, including photocopying and recording,
or by any information storage or retrival system,
except as may be expressly permitted in writing
from the publisher.

First published by Abingdon Press, 1928

Revised edition, 2019

Printed and published with permission by
The E. Stanley Jones Foundation
Email: anne@estanleyjonesfoundation.com
Website: www.estanleyjonesfoundation.com

Cover Design: Marc Whitaker
Interior Design: Shivraj K. Mahendra

ISBN: 978-1791766481

MADE IN THE USA

D<small>EDICATED TO</small>

BISHOP BRUCE R. OUGH

God's mission is contextual and invites us to the Round Table of Christ, where all are welcome and loved. Bishop Ough's bold visionary leadership expresses inclusive Christ-like hospitality. His ability to simplify and communicate the gospel shows others the "Way" to abundant and real life through faith in Christ Jesus.

- Editor

CONTENTS

Preface to the Revised Edition 9

Foreword by Mark Teasdale 13

Introduction 21

1. Beginnings 31
2. At Grips with Life 37
3. What Can We Gather from All This? 56
4. Conversion—Horizontal and Vertical 76
5. The Collective Redemption 94
6. The Growing Savior 110
7. The Trend Toward Experience 126
8. Almost 139
9. Where is the Place of Certainty and Authority? 151
10. Interpreters of Christ 165
11. Missions at the Round Table 177
12. Nations at the Round Table 194
13. The Most Sacred Round Table of All 210
14. The Cross—the Key to Life 224
15. The Way 243
16. Christ—the Universal 265
17. The Cosmic Round Table 284

About the Author *309*
Other books by the Author *312*
About the E. Stanley Jones Foundation *315*
Other Publications from the E. Stanley Jones Foundation................ *316*

PREFACE
To the Revised Edition

JONES' PARTICIPATION IN A "CLINIC OF SOULS"

MY GRANDFATHER HAD a unique approach to presenting Jesus. He nurtured this approach by listening to others carefully, in order to understand their stories and their needs. Jones strongly felt he had no right to teach (or preach) to others if he was not learning from them in turn. He writes, "I came to India with everything to teach and nothing to learn. I now learn as well, and I am a better man for having come into contact with the gentle heart of the East."

One of the ways Jones listened and learned about the gentle heart of the East was through his Round Table Conferences. Up to forty leading representatives of different faiths—including agnostics and atheists—were invited to share what their faith or lack of faith meant to them. Jones would ask, "Tell us what you have found through your faith—What does it do for you in your everyday life?"

Present day dialogues with non-Christian faiths have been heralded as something new, and they are surely important. E. Stanley Jones held these conversations 90 years ago.

In this Round Table context Jones asked himself whether the gospel of Christ had any certainty to offer. "Will it show itself capable of bringing to confused minds and distressed souls everywhere a new sense of reality and certainty under this awful scrutiny. If the gospel of Christ is founded upon Life will it, therefore, stand the shocks of life? Or is it a great and heroic guess at the solution to the riddle of life? Would the Round Table Conferences shed any light on these problems?" Jones continues his reflections,

> The more I think of it, the more I realize that the most dangerous thing the Christian Church ever did was to send us to India. Not dangerous to us. It matters little whether we live or die. But to start a moral and spiritual offensive in the heart of the most religious and philosophical people of the world, and that at a time when the weapons of modern criticism and modern knowledge are available for counter-attack, is too dangerous for words. For suppose it should be revealed amid that struggle that Christianity is only one among the many ways, that its claim to finality is untenable, that its sharp alternatives are not valid, that it is only a stage in the evolution of religion and it will be passed by, the final stage being a sifted amalgam from the whole. What would be the result of this? In looking back at the Round Table approach, I see now how daring and decisive this approach was: Here we were putting our cards on the table and asking the non-Christian world to do the same. Suppose our "hands" with which we were playing the game of life should turn out to be inadequate; and suppose other ways of life should prove more adequate. This was a showdown, and the stakes were high. In every situation the trump card was Jesus Christ. He made the difference. The people who followed him might be spotty and inadequate, but

Preface

they had hold of the spotless and adequate or better Christ had hold of them! (*A Song of Ascents*, 239-40).

Jones presciently speaks of the potential for the Round Table approach to address current, internal controversies in the church.

> The fact cannot be disguised that we as Christians have our internal controversy. It has largely partaken of the method of long-distance dueling. We have shelled each other's positions, or what we thought were the positions, but there has been much smoke and confusion and not a little un-Christian feeling. Why not sit down at Round Tables as Christian men and women and see what religion is meaning to us in experience? We would listen reverently to what the other man and woman would say it was bringing to them, and we would share what it was meaning to us. At the close we might not be agreed, but we would be mutually enriched, and certainly we would be closer to the real issues. And we would be on the right lines of approach in facing these issues and in finding their solutions.

Church and lay leaders could prayerfully give the Round Table dialogue the occasion to let the Holy Spirit guide us in listening reverently to our brothers and sisters, and allow us to be enriched by that experience.

I am grateful to Dr. Mark Teasdale, Associate Professor of Evangelism at Garrett-Evangelical Theological Seminary for his outstanding introduction to this book. His is the perspective of a 21st century professor, pastor and evangelist. He writes that E. Stanley Jones faced in twentieth-century India very similar challenges to those we face in the United States today, and how his evangelistic approach via the Round Table can be a powerful example for us. Dr. Teasdale affirms:

> In a world beset by acrimony and divisions, often exacerbated by religious beliefs, Christ is already sitting at the Round Table. He beckons Christians to join him there and to welcome all others who are willing to enter into dialogue. There, as we

speak and listen to each other, He will make himself known, allow us to know each other more fully, and lead us all into his grace.

This book could not have been reprinted without the assistance of the Rev. Shivraj Mahendra, whose publishing, editing, and theological skills were essential to this project's success. I don't know how Shivraj finds the time to move these E. Stanley Jones reprinting projects forward with his customary speed, expertise, and precision. I am deeply grateful to him. Nicholas Younes contributed his considerable editing expertise to ensure that the text is clear and doggedly pursued the needed annotations. Barbara Hubbard brought her years of experience as an English teacher to double and triple check the grammar and punctuation. I am surrounded by gifted people and am truly blessed because of them. I trust that in turn you will be blessed by this book.

ANNE MATHEWS-YOUNES, ED.D., D. MIN.

President, The E. Stanley Jones Foundation

May 2019

FOREWORD

WHILE JESUS CHRIST is the same yesterday, today, and forever (Hebrews 13:8), the context in which Christians serve Jesus changes over the years. Every generation brings with it new cultural norms, new ways for people to relate to each other, and new challenges undreamt of by their forebears. As a result, books written to help guide Christian practice have a notoriously short half-life. Their advice, no matter how excellent in their own time, often is insufficient to address what Christians face today. So, these texts are often left behind as historical relics, and new ideas are sought to help Christians with the new struggles they are facing.

This is especially true in reference to texts on evangelistic missions. To be effective in evangelism, Christians must articulate the fullness of the gospel in a way that is meaningful to people in their current social and cultural contexts. However, these contexts shift so fast that books hailed as having great insights a few years ago are now considered passé.

E. Stanley Jones has bucked this trend. In fact, for a man who was born in the nineteenth century and who did most of his ministry in India during the early-and-mid-twentieth century, his work has become more relevant to Christian missions in the United States as the years have advanced.

The primary reason for this has been the demographic and cultural forces that have moved the American population away from accepting the nominal Christianity that many took for granted through most of the twentieth century. Demographically, American Christians, especially Protestants, have been aging and not replacing themselves in their churches. As a result, between 2003 and 2017 the total percentage of the US population that claimed to be Protestant has dropped from 50 percent to 36 percent, while the total percentage claiming to be Christian of any sort has dropped from 83 percent to 72 percent.[1]

This shift is not only caused by the natural attrition of older Christians dying without sufficient births in Christian families to offset those deaths. It is also from Americans becoming more comfortable either exiting their Christian faith or never espousing a faith in the first place. The growth of those who claim to be religiously unaffiliated in the United States has been meteoric in the first two decades of the twenty-first century, increasing from 12 percent of the population to 21 percent of the population during the same time that Protestantism was declining.[2]

While Christianity is still the majority faith in the United States, it no longer has a privileged place in the nation. The result of this is that Christians in the United States must take seriously the plurality of religious and non-religious beliefs people hold. To share the gospel in this new context means developing new strategies for evangelism. These strategies must shake off any assumption that Americans are favorably inclined toward Christianity and adopt a posture of humility while still offering the full hope of the gospel.

---

1 ABC News/Washington Post and ABC News Polls, "Protestants Decline," May 10, 2018, < http://assets.pewresearch.org/wp-content/uploads/sites/11/2015/05/RLS-08-26-full-report.pdf >.

2 Ibid.

The need to change how we practice evangelism does not mean we have to abandon it. In a culture that has become unmoored from any specific faith tradition, there is a deep yearning people have for meaning. This means that even the "unchurched" are open to having substantive and respectful conversations about faith, if only Christians would engage them.[3]

It is at this point that E. Stanley Jones becomes an excellent guide for us through the wisdom he offers in *Christ at the Round Table*. The situation he faced in twentieth-century India is very similar to what we face in the United States today, and his evangelistic approach through the Round Table becomes a powerful example for us.

When Jones served as a missionary in India, he entered a country in which Christians made up a tiny minority of the population. As of 2001, approximately 2 percent of the population of India claimed to be Christian, contrasted to the largest religions, Hinduism at 80 percent of the population and Islam at 13 percent of the population.[4] While these numbers are reported from much later than when Jones was in India, they give us a good sense of what he faced. This was an even starker set of statistics than what we face in the United States in the twenty-first century. How would Jones reach people in such a pluralistic setting that had such low cultural credibility for the Christian faith?

---

3 Life Way Research, "Unchurched Report," 2016,<http://lifewayresearch.com/wp-content/uploads/2017/01/BGCE-Unchurched-Study-Final-Report-1_5_17.pdf>.

4 "Population by religion, sex and urban/rural residence – India," UNdata, 2001. <http://data.un.org/ Data.aspx?d=POP&f=tableCode %3a28%3bcountryCode %3a356 &c= 2, 3,6,8,10,12,14,15,16&s =_countryEnglish NameOrderBy:asc, refYear:desc, areaCode: asc&v=1>.

During Jones' career, there were two primary approaches missionaries used in their work. At the risk of generalizing, I will call these the monologue approach and the silence approach.

The monologue approach sought to win people's hearts and minds to the Christian faith, having that replace their current faith. As the term monologue suggests, this was done largely by the verbal proclamation of the gospel with little opportunity for response from the listener. Jones attempted this initially in his ministry, attending public debates with leaders from other religions in an effort to persuade his listeners that the Christian faith was superior to what they already believed. However, Jones found this unsatisfying and ineffective. It both ignored what was good and right in the beliefs that most Indians already held, and it often required him to defend Western cultural norms alongside of the gospel. He needed something that allowed him to offer greater respect and interaction with the existing religious beliefs in India, demonstrating the power and beauty of Christ apart from the baggage of Western culture.

The silence approach was made popular in the book *Re-Thinking Missions* (published 1932). Written based on the Laymen's Foreign Mission Inquiry that was commissioned to determine the effectiveness of Christian missionary work in the early twentieth century, *Re-Thinking Missions* recommended that Christian missionaries would be most effective by allying themselves with other religions. Together with the adherents of other religions, they could join in a common effort to throw off the deleterious effects of non-religious beliefs, especially materialism, secularism, and naturalism.

The missionaries would be silent in the sense that they would not speak about Jesus or Christian distinctiveness. They would primarily seek to be part of this broader coalition of religious people, subsuming their message to their common work.

Jones certainly agreed with the pressing need to deal with the problems of non-religious ideologies creeping into the human heart. He also agreed with the need to respect other religions, as seen in his deep friendship with Gandhi and his attendance at Gandhi's ashram. He describes all these things in this book. At the same time, he felt that this approach gave away too much by silencing the invitation for people to follow Jesus Christ. For Jones, Jesus was at the heart of Christian missions, as seen in how Jones pleaded with Gandhi to receive Jesus. Anything less was insufficient.

Since he could follow neither of these approaches fully, Jones developed a third approach that combined the best from both and rejected what was problematic. From the first approach, Jones kept the emphasis on inviting people to know Jesus Christ as their Savior and Lord. From the second approach, he took the deep respect he believed was due to the adherents of other religions and the desire to overcome corrosive anti-religious forces. What he rejected was the thinking that assumed Christians could only choose between 1) a monologue meant to proselytize adherents of other religions into culturally patterned Christian forms or 2) remaining silent on Christian distinctiveness in order to respect other religions and work for a common good. Jones contended that it was possible for Christians to share about Jesus explicitly while respecting other religions through a third approach to missions: *dialogue*.

The Round Table was the ultimate expression of this dialogue. Simply put, the Round Table was a gathering of a small group of people who were adherents of various religions. These people each committed only to speak of how their religious beliefs had guided them in life, avoiding any doctrinal or historical debate. Each person would have the opportunity to speak while the others listened and reflected on what was said.

By creating space for this type of dialogue, Jones provided a unique arena where Christians, Hindus, Muslims, and members of other religions in India could acknowledge one another as fellow human beings seeking truth. In doing this, he also created a situation in which the relative size and cultural support each religion had was unimportant. People at the Round Table heard and spoke to each other as equals who had a common desire for a meaningful life.

The Round Table allowed Jones and other Christians to show they honored the adherents of other religions by listening and weighing what they said even as they could speak freely about their Christian faith, especially their personal relationships with Jesus Christ. They could do this without any need to enter into a competition, feeling like they had to outmatch the other participants or argue for a Western version of Christianity. They could simply share their experiences of living as a Christian, even as they heard others share about their experiences of living as followers of other faiths.

Jones acknowledged that this was a dangerous way of doing missions, in the sense that it did not have a guaranteed result tied to it. There was always the possibility that the people who shared about their lives under the direction of other religions would be more persuasive, winsome, and powerful than their Christian counterparts. This contrasted with the other approaches to mission that had clear outcomes (i.e., conversions from those who heard the monologue or interfaith partnerships from the silence). As you will read, Jones never entered into a Round Table dialogue without some trepidation because of this. However, he also believed that surrendering human control allowed the Spirit to move in powerful ways among the participants, leading them all to recognize the unique blessing of following Jesus Christ.

This kind of dialogical ingenuity is what we need in the United States in the twenty-first century! In the face of the declining public place for Christianity, we can be tempted by the other approaches to mission, either doubling down in our attempts to proselytize people into particular forms of Christianity or allowing our Christian faith to be subsumed into a broader coalition made up of people of goodwill. Certainly, both these approaches can be seen in action today, often attended by the desire to reclaim the time when Christians held a privileged place in the culture.

However, our wiser route would be to learn from what Jones did and take a seat at the Round Table. By surrendering any claim to privilege and equalizing our Christian experience with the experiences of others who come from different religious, and even non-religious traditions, we open the door for several benefits:

1. We bypass the heavy skepticism about evangelism that so many people have whether they are Christians or not.
2. We grow in our Christian faith as we learn to articulate our experiences of following Jesus Christ even as we listen to the experiences of those who profess other faiths.
3. We offer those who are not Christians the opportunity to hear the full message of Jesus Christ without them feeling attacked or belittled because the process of sharing the message at the Round Table is as good as the message itself is.
4. We help develop a larger community of goodwill across religious lines, as we listen to one another and work toward the common desire to live into what is good, true, and beautiful.
5. We have the opportunity to see God appear in power and grace to accomplish great things in the lives of everyone involved, all in the name of Jesus Christ.

CHRIST AT THE ROUND TABLE

As can be seen from this list, when practiced well Round Table evangelism offers all the possible benefits of both the monologue and silence approaches. People are invited to follow Jesus, communities working for the common good are formed, and all of this is done even as Christians speak boldly about their experiences of Christ, listen humbly to what others say about their beliefs, and see the power of God break forth.

In a world beset by acrimony and divisions, often exacerbated by religious beliefs, Christ is already sitting at the Round Table. He beckons Christians to join him there and to welcome all others who are willing to enter into dialogue. There, as we speak and listen to each other, he will make himself known, allow us to know each other more fully, and lead us all into his grace.

MARK R. TEASDALE
June 26, 2018
Evanston, IL USA

INTRODUCTION

THIS BOOK HAS written itself. During the twenty years of intimate contact with the soul of the East, it has been slowly writing itself in the inmost depths of my being. In hours of innumerable personal conversations, in times of quiet but fierce clash of idea upon idea, in periods when I have opened my soul to the beauty and thought of India, in hours of prayer, in moments of brooding over the mind of Christ in Sacred Writ, and most of all in the Round Table Conferences where we have bared soul to soul, these pages have been written and these convictions formed. They have come to me almost irresistibly and now it seems that I do not hold them, rather these convictions seem to hold me.

Not that they are unalterable and fixed. If there has been one guiding principle which has held me these years, it has been this: No plans cannot be changed if they cease to be vital and real and no convictions cannot be altered if fuller light comes.

But if these pages have written themselves, the transcribing of them has brought heart-searchings. How can one bring back the atmosphere of these Round Table Conferences? Will not the beauty and delicacy of these hallowed moments fade and wither if plucked from their quiet surroundings? Can we be objective and fair in drawing our conclusions? Is the purpose to win a religious victory or to find reality? Is there a desire to justify a missionary movement or to help someone as we have been helped? Can we be loyal to the land of our adoption and yet loyal to our deepest convictions? How can we be free to speak of life as we saw it at the Round Tables unless we are free to face life as it is —its weaknesses and its strengths, its successes and its failures? Although I have held the principle that my chief concern should be to present my constructive message, leaving untouched in public address the religious systems that my hearers held so that they might be free to draw their own conclusions, can I now freely speak of life as I see it? Whether satisfactory answers to some of the above questions can be given, they must be judged as we go on our way through the narrative and to its conclusions.

My impulse has been not to quote directly what men were saying in the Round Tables, but to write of general impressions. I have felt this would be unfair, though, particularly to Hinduism. So much stress has been laid in the West on the lower phases of Hinduism, that the impression that the ordinary man of the West holds is that it is made up of caste, idolatry, child widows, and so on. This ordinary man thinks of religion as centered in the temple. Therefore, if I spoke of Hinduism in this book, I would be interpreted as meaning temple Hinduism. The fact is that the Hinduism of educated India does not enter in the temple but in the Upanishads and the Bhagawad Gita. The possible exception to this is South India, where temple Hinduism has a stronger hold. Even here, the Saiva Siddhanta, centering in the poems of the Tamil saints, holds the hearts of the educated rather than does the temple. You might wipe out the Hinduism centering in the temple, along with caste and corrupt social customs, and this Hinduism centering in the Upanishads would live on, perhaps with greater power. But it is not the ordinary man of the West alone who is laboring under this misunderstanding. I showed some of the statements made by the members of our Round Table Conferences to a highly intelligent Westerner who had been in India for forty years, and his comment was, "Well, I'm very glad to find that they are thinking about these things and not merely going blindly to the temple." Thinking about these things? Why, "there are more words for philosophic and religious thought in Sanskrit than in Greek, Latin, and German put together." India has thought on these things more deeply than any other people on earth, and if her philosophy has suffered from anything it has not been from under thought, but from over strain. Moreover, it is not educated India alone which holds these ideas of the Upanishads. They have to a very great extent percolated down into the masses so that the ordinary worshiper who goes to the idol temple goes there with a higher interpretation of life in his mind, and he explains his idolatry in the light of the background of the All of the Upanishads: If Brahma is the All, then why should not this idol be worshiped as a portion of him? This philosophic Hinduism is all-pervasive and not confined to the educated few.

I felt I would be unfair if I did not let these representatives speak and interpret their own faith. I could do it because these Round Table Conferences were not Round Table Confidences. They were open and frank, each man laying before us what religion was meaning to him. Each was given the chance to say the best he could about his own faith. Surely, no one could object to having such statements repeated. The presupposition is that he would be glad to have it done, provided it was done sympathetically and fairly. This, in fact, has been the attitude taken by those Non-Christians from whom inquiry has been made. But after full inquiry where any hesitation or objection to having his views repeated has been shown, in these cases we have refrained. In only two cases have there been objections.

Another consideration which now makes it possible to speak openly about things concerning which it would have been scarcely possible a few years ago, is the fact that Gandhiji[1] in his autobiography, entitled *The Story of My Experiments with Truth,* is showing the way to a new frankness. Week by week he bares his soul and discusses freely his attitudes toward Christianity and other religions and his reasons for deciding upon the religious life he now leads. The door for frank discussion is now open— opened by an Indian hand.

I found myself not particularly interested in the victory, as such, of one religious system over another. That might take place and we still could be far from the goal. We were after truth and reality and spiritual freedom, and we knew that it was possible that one religious system might conquer another and these questions remain untouched, or worse, be lost in the struggle. The crusaders conquered Jerusalem and found in the end that Christ was not there. They had lost him through the very spirit and methods by which they sought to serve him. Many more modern and more refined crusaders end in that same barrenness of victory. Mere proselytizing partakes of these methods and shares the same barrenness of results. We wanted something deeper and more fundamental. The fact is that the final issue is not between the systems of Christianity and Hinduism or Buddhism or Islam, but between Christlikeness and un-Christlikeness, whether that UN-Christlikeness is within the non-Christian systems or within Christendom. The final issue is between Christ and other ways of life. If in the opening chapters we have had occasion to deal with un-Christlikeness outside, before we are through we face it within Christendom.

Moreover, our problems are not Eastern or Western problems, but just human. Human need and human sin are not geographical. Materialism, greed, moral failure and spiritual yearning are in the East and in the West. They are found wherever man is found. Can we not,

---

1 I refrain from using the term "Mahatma" because of his declared dislike to it, reserving to myself the right, however, to hold him to be a "great soul." "Ji" is a term of respect.

then, sit down at the Round Table of Life and face our problems, not as Easterners or Westerners, but as men, and see if there is a way out?

As to being scientifically objective in coming to conclusions, I might as well confess that I probably will not be. Not that I do not want to be, but that, first of all, I have not had that intensive training in scientific methods, so necessary if one is to be objective and scientific; and, second, I have brought too much of subjectivity to these Conferences to be absolutely objective. Religion has meant too much to me during these years to be able to stand off and view it apart from that fact. That may be a disqualification—and it may not. At any rate, this book does not pretend to be written in a detached, judicial manner. I am an evangelist recording impressions that have come to me in the midst of my evangelistic work. These impressions compel me to become an advocate. This fact will cause what I say to be discounted in the minds of some. This is inevitable and to be expected. Moreover, dealing with religious values, in the nature of the case, the impressions recorded will seem subjective. This too is inevitable.

> Our problems are not Eastern or Western problems, but just human ... Materialism, greed, moral failure and spiritual yearning are in the East and in the West.

Another consideration weighed with me. We as Christians find ourselves in a very serious crisis. A number of things have brought it on. The scientific mind, with its demand for the attitude toward life of open mindedness and for conclusions based on the facts, and its handmaid historical criticism of the Scriptures have challenged many claimed infallibilities in many realms. This is a world-shaking movement. The full force of it has not yet struck the Non-Christian faiths. That will come, but we are in the throes of it.

Another factor making for disturbance of mind has been the discovery of Sanskrit literature. It has opened to the West an amazing world of philosophical and literary treasure. Schopenhauer voiced the extreme wing of appreciation when he said: "The Upanishads have been my consolation in life; they will be my consolation in death." At first the church was indifferent or hostile toward this storehouse, but Christian scholars have been sifting out the finest from it, and what was the property of the scholar is now becoming available for the ordinary Christian. Through comparative religions the rank and file are now seeing that God has not left himself without witness in any land, and that truth and lofty thinking are not the exclusive possession of any race. Human intercourse is getting closer every day and we are discovering that worth and ability and goodness are not confined to particular geographical areas or to special tints of skin. The ordinary Christian is being compelled to relate his Christianity to these facts.

Other elements making for disturbance have been the disillusionment following the war and the deep questionings of the soundness of Western civilization and the bitter criticisms of it from both East and West. They have contributed to the vast uncertainty.

Unsympathetic attitudes and contempt toward foreign cultures and religions and national aspirations have in large measure given way to appreciation and sympathy. This is to be welcomed and cultivated, but the fact must not be overlooked that this has a tendency to cut under exclusive claims and to undermine evangelistic passion. It was easier to be evangelistic when the issues were more fiercely defined. Finally, Theosophy steps in amid the resulting bewilderment, waves its hand and says: "All religions have the same underlying truths. The differences are in the details—at the center they are one." The tendency of all this is to wipe out distinctions, tone down superiorities, and have everything end in a diffused kindly feeling, or, as someone has put it, "in a mush of amiability." All these things put together are disconcerting and disturbing.

The more I think of it, the more I realize that the most dangerous thing the Christian Church ever did was to send us to India. Not dangerous to us. It matters little whether we live or die. But to start a moral and spiritual offensive in the heart of the most religious and philosophical race of the world, and that at a time when the weapons of modern criticism and modern knowledge are available for counter-attack, is too dangerous for words. For suppose it should be revealed amid that struggle that Christianity is only one among the many ways, that its claim to finality is untenable, that its sharp alternatives are not valid, that it is only a stage in the evolution of religion and it will be passed by, the final stage being a sifted amalgam from the whole. What would be the result of this? Certainly, the missionary movement would, at least as now carried on, wane and die. And it is questionable whether, with the conviction of finality gone, Christianity could hold continued sway over the mind of the West.

Amid this vast uncertainty has the gospel of Christ any certainty to offer? Will it show itself capable of bringing to confused minds and distressed souls everywhere a new sense of reality and certainty under this awful scrutiny, yea, even because of it? Is it founded upon Life and will it, therefore, stand the shocks of life? Or is it a great and heroic guess at the solution of the riddle of life? Would the Round Table Conferences shed any light on these problems?

We had not gone very far with the conferences with the non-Christians before we saw that here was a method of discovering reality that would be valuable for us as Christians. The deepest things of religion need sympathetic atmosphere. In an atmosphere of debate and controversy the deepest things, and hence the real things of religion, wither and die. In order to discover what is most delicate and fine in religion, there must be an attitude of spiritual openness, of inward sensitiveness to the Divine, a willingness to be led by the beckoning spiritual facts. We felt the conferences tended to bring this. The sense of battle seemed to fade out and common spiritual quest and sharing took its place.

The fact cannot be disguised that we as Christians have our internal controversy. It has largely partaken of the method of long-distance dueling. We have shelled each other's positions, or what we thought were the positions, but there has been much smoke and confusion and not a little un-Christian feeling. Why not sit down at Round Tables as Christian men and women and see what religion is meaning to us in experience? We would listen reverently to what the other man would say it was bringing to him, and we would share what it was meaning to us. At the close we might not be agreed, but we would be mutually enriched, and certainly we would he closer to the real issues. And we would be on the right lines of approach in facing these issues and in finding their solutions.

But this controversy and the Round Tables as a possible method of approaching it was not in our minds when we began to have them for Christians only. The purpose was to face the questions of how religion was working, what it was doing for us, and how we could find deeper reality? Under this quiet but searching scrutiny some missionaries and Christian workers, with a great deal of restrained emotion, have told the group quite frankly that it was not working except in outward phases, that the deepest things were not there. But often before the conferences were over, lives have been renewed and new depths found.

The valuable thing for us as Christians in the Round Table Conferences with non-Christians lay in the fact that we were compelled

INTRODUCTION

to rethink our problems in the light of the non-Christian faiths and in the light of the religious experiences of non-Christians. So, while these Conferences have been valuable in our approach to the non-Christian faiths, they have proved of even greater value to us in facing our own problems, spiritual and intellectual.

They have given some answers to the problems now facing us in the crisis we have mentioned above.

But the most difficult question of all had to be faced before I could go on: Dared I try to see life and see it whole and tell what I saw? The answer came back: "Yes, provided you are willing to face what you hold in the same frank way." And I found myself willing, even eager, for I felt that if

> Why not sit down at Round Tables as Christian men and women and see what religion is meaning to us in experience?

any adverse appraisal must be given, I would do it with as much tenderness as I would point out the fading health on my mother's cheek.

Moreover, I knew that, if criticism was considered necessary in the Indian situation, none of it would be directed toward the Indian people, whom I consider one of the finest and most lovable peoples on earth, but only against yokes that need to be lifted to let this great people go free.

If there is a conclusion running throughout this book, it will probably be found to be this: Christ represents Religion. Organized Christianity, mixed as it is with the mind of Caesar and the mind of Christ, is a religion. Religions must be judged and evaluated in the light of Religion. I feel free, therefore, to evaluate or criticize or commend non-Christian religions as well as the present organized Christian religion in the light of Christ who is Religion.

Until a few years ago the usual attitude toward other faiths and cultures was criticism and lack of appreciation. Now the pendulum has swung back the other way to an attitude on the part of many of unqualified approval or to the attitude that all faiths are more or less the same. The time has now come for an attitude between these extremes, namely, an attitude of appreciation with appraisal. But this evaluation must not be merely intellectual, it must he deeply experiential. What does religion bring in experience? What is its value for life?

I think I have noted a change in emphasis during these twenty years. At first it was a battle of Civilizations. The attitude was that we must find defects in Indian civilization in order to establish our own. Along with this was the "Battle of the Books" — which book contained the truths that we could call revelation? Then it shifted to personalities, the ones who embodied these truths—was Christ or Krishna the Way? Now I find the emphasis going straight toward experience. The question of the books and the personalities is still there and will be there, but the evaluation is more and more resting on experience. Where can we find God? Where can we get a dynamic for spiritually victorious living, release from what we are, a saving from sin and evil, a renewed character? Where can we catch a passion to help our fellow men? How can we realize the brotherhood of our common humanity, and bring the kingdom of God on earth? Does religion work? What does it produce in experience? This is the direction in which things are now going. It is the direction of the demand of the scientific outlook on life in relation to the facts. This made our Round Table Conferences inevitable.

While the Round Table Conferences form the basis of the book, nevertheless we do not confine ourselves to them, but go beyond them. The convictions recorded have grown out of the wider contacts of the years.

Chapter 1

BEGINNINGS

INDIA HAS OPENED many great things to me and to that indebtedness I must add another, for it was a Hindu who unknowingly opened the door to these Round Table Conferences. He had voluntarily associated himself with the Christian Committee to arrange for our public meetings. He asked if he might have a tea party at his home and invite the leading men of the city so that I could talk to them in a more intimate and personal way than was possible in the public meetings. We sat in a group and soon the untrammeled Christ was before us. I had asked what their reception of Christ would be if he came disassociated from Westernism, if he came in his own person and made his appeal direct to the soul of India—would it make any difference? I was speaking thus when the mayor of the city, a non-Christian, interrupted me and said, "I hear you speak about finding Christ. What do you mean by it?"

The question was penetrating and sincere. Here I saw a deeper demand than the one for an objective Christ—however untrammeled he might be. *They wanted to know about this Christ of experience.* I paused a moment, for here was a penetrating demand. I replied that I could only tell him what it meant to me. So, I told him how I had found him. I shared the joy of the found treasure. He then made it more personal and said, "Now tell me how I could find him."

I did. Here we sat with the leading men of the city, talking in this intimate personal way about how to find Christ.

Our eyes were opened to the possibilities in the small selected group. But we could not hope to find all groups as responsive as this, for some would be sullen and uncommunicative and some argumentative and hostile. How could we approach them when the atmosphere was not friendly and the situation was filled with misconceptions and misunderstandings? As in many another perplexity, it was "given in that hour." It came this way.

A few weeks later we were holding a series of meetings in another city and I told Canon _____ about our selected group meeting in the other place. He suggested that he invite a group of the leading men of the city for a garden party and I proceed with them at the close in any way I thought best. But that was not as easy as it sounded. As I slowly walked through the garden on my way to the group, thinking of what I should say to them, the thought occurred: Why not turn the whole thing into a religious Round Table Conference, asking each man to tell what religion is meaning to him in experience?

I am quite sure that if I had had time to think about it, I should never have ventured upon it. Could one get highly educated, cultured men to open their souls in this intimate way? It is easy to talk of religion and to debate religious concepts, but would they say what religion was meaning to them in experience? Or would they close up like sensitive plants and the whole thing end in failure? But I was too close to the group to have time to think it through, so I ventured and it worked—amazingly. The Inner Voice does not fail.

We have had scores of Round Table Conferences since then, and while our first procedure "given in that hour" has been elaborated, it has not been substantially changed.

As we sit around in a circle we suggest to them that we take a new approach to religion—new when we think of the ordinary approaches in common use. We suggest that we have had the controversial, the comparative, and the dogmatic approaches to religion. There is another approach possible. Let us come at it by the method more closely akin to the scientific method—a method so gripping to the mind of the world today. This method has three outstanding things in it: Experimentation. Verification and Sharing of Results. I suggest to them that we try this method. We are all religious men, some more and some less, and we have all been experimenting with this matter of religion over a number of years. We have tried it as a working hypothesis of life. As we face the problems of life —its joys and its sorrows, its perplexities and its pains, the demands of duty, the moral struggle with sin and evil, the upward call to higher life, the desire to help our fellow men and to be of use, the craving for God and for redemption—what has religion brought to us? What has it brought to us of light, of moral dynamic for personal and social life, of inward peace and harmony, of redemption from sin and from the power of this world, and of God? What have we and what are we verifying as true in experience? Will you share with us the results of your verification?

We suggest, therefore, that no one argue, no one try to make a case, no one talk abstractly, and no one merely discuss religion, but that we simply share what religion is meaning to us as experience.

We can almost hear the inward gasp that goes on in the souls of the group when we suggest this. We assure them that we recognize that this is not easy to do, that it is not easy to put into words what one realizes in these deepest moments of life, so that we do not want anyone to feel that he has to speak, that if he so desires he may simply ask to be excused when his turn comes.

We also suggest that we do not want them to feel that the friendliness of this atmosphere must cause them to iron out differences, or to put it in other words, to reduce everything to a least common denominator; that if religion centers for them in Rama, or Krishna, or Buddha, or the Vedanta, or the Koran, or Christ, to say so. Let everyone be perfectly free, for we are a family circle; we want each one to feel at home and we will listen with reverence and respect to what each man has to share.

We know how facile our talk about religion may be, so in order to bring an atmosphere of deeper reality, we suggest that perhaps some will find that religion is meaning nothing to them, that they will be like a leading nationalist in our Round Table Conference, who, when his turn came, said, "I have dismissed God and religion from my life. So many things are done in the name of God and religion that are revolting to me that I have simply dismissed them. I am asking what is my duty to my country. If that is being religious, I am religious; if it is not, then I am not."

This is the air of sincerity that we crave. We suggest that, as in the case of this nationalist, there is often more faith in an honest doubt than in a great deal of easy, meaningless believing.

I have noted the change that comes over the group in the first ten minutes. Many have come fortified and ready to enter a battle of wits and to uphold their religious system against all comers. But immediately the atmosphere changes, a deep seriousness comes over them, for here the battle drops to levels deeper than a mere battle of words or of ideas —drops down to where we meet life—we are at grips with life. Others who have come languid at the thought of further verbal controversy or long lectures are immediately galvanized into attention and interest, for here is something different—religion is to speak out of life. Has it any adequate answer to give to life? Or is it a series of mental and social left-overs, out of touch with life and its meaning, and contributing little to its solution? We were to report results of the Great Experiment, we were to tell of verification, if any: deep was to speak to deep.

I must confess that I never approach these Round Tables without feeling my heart beat a little faster, for here before us sit members of the most religiously inclined race of the world, men who belong to a people who have persistently searched for God and reality, as no other people on earth have searched; sons of a philosophical and cultural past that stretched back millenniums before Europe awoke from barbarity. What answer would they bring from that hoary past and this heaving present? Would it be an adequate one?

> **Was our gospel a broken light from God .... Or was it God's adequate answer to man's need—intellectual, moral, spiritual, social?**

And we Christians who came with what we call a gospel—would it sound like a gospel here? When we had stripped our religious life of overgrown verbiage, how much fact would we have left? Would our gospel ring true to reality? Would it move amid these problems of life with assured poise and conscious power? Would it face life and answer it? Was our gospel a broken light from God, illuminating patches and portions of life but leaving life as a whole unilluminated? Or was it God's adequate answer to man's need—intellectual, moral, spiritual, social?

Count Keyserling, disappointed with his European researches and experiences, starts on his long quest in other lands. One of the compensations in being a missionary lies in the fact that you are forced to rethink your religious life in the light of other faiths and cultures and ways of life. All the old shibboleths and modes of expression and accepted outlooks on life are challenged and one begins to see where the relevant lies. Some years ago, when in southern California where there seems to be plenty of leisure to discuss religious doctrines, I was approached by all sorts of people asking what I thought of their particular and pet doctrine. I told them, or at least I showed them in some way, that I was not particularly interested. I am sure I was set down as not being zealous in religion, and hence, scarcely fit to be a missionary, but I had been forced to come to grips with the big, relevant issues of life in contact with other faiths and other ways of life. This feeling has come over me again and again in these conferences. Which is the way of life?

I think all of us breathed a little faster as we closed in with this question.

Did I say that a Hindu had opened the door into these Round Tables? I am convinced that the nail-pierced hand of the Son of man, through this son of the East, opened this door and bade us enter. It was a searching, dangerous adventure to which he called us. Would this door of approach to religion lead to life?

Chapter 2

AT GRIPS WITH LIFE

WE USUALLY INVITE about fifteen members of other faiths and about five or six Christians to compose the Round Table. We desire this large preponderance of the members of other faiths not only because it gives wider range to the views expressed, but also in order that they may not feel that we Christians have packed the meeting. Moreover, we try to get them at their very highest level, asking only those non-Christians who are really religious, the best representatives of the faiths we can find. The majority of these are highly educated, but we also get representatives of other faiths who have been untouched by Western education and speak only the vernaculars—pundits, sadhus, Muslim maulvis, and Buddhist monks. Of the Christians, the majority are usually Indian.

To keep the conferences from being wordy, we remind them that when Swami Vivekananda was on his quest for God, he used to ask men two questions: "Have you found God? Can you tell me how to find Him?" If the man who was questioned started on a long lecture about the attributes of God, or something of that kind, the swami would turn on his heel and walk silently away. He knew he had not found God, for if he had, he could have said so clearly, and could have put his finger upon its meaning for life. The conferences have been remarkably free from wordiness.

We have carefully noted what each man has said, and the rest of this book could be filled with these statements, but we can give only a selected few of those most typical.

We find the statements arranging themselves roughly in the following groups: (1) The followers of the Vedanta, the philosophy that posits the Supreme Being, Brahma, as impersonal and the world as Maya, or illusion, the supreme effort of the seeker being to throw off Maya and realize his identity with Brahma. This is the most far-reaching of the philosophical systems in India. (2) The followers of Bhakti, or devotion to the personal God or gods. (3) The followers of Karma Yoga, or the way of works. (4) Those who are skeptical. (5) Those deeply influenced by Christianity. (6) A group holding miscellaneous views.

The conferences are on. We enter them with a prayer for reality, for God, for an answer to LIFE.

(1) The followers of the Vedanta.

A Hindu Chief Justice speaks: When a man thinks about religion he thinks about a goal. My ultimate goal is the elevation of the soul to such a pitch that it merges into the Universal Soul.

Hindu: The realization of God and of self may take several births. I can only realize it from within whenever that Ideal wants to reveal itself to me. I must wait for that revelation.

Hindu teacher: I feel God in all things and I worship him alike in Kali and Rama and Krishna. This seems to me to give a sense of satisfaction.

Principal Sanatana Dharma (Orthodox) College: Religion to me is Dharma. It will lift man to the fullness of life. It develops man on all sides, physically, intellectually, and spiritually. There are eternal laws according to which men can be developed on all sides. Belief in a Deity is essential. Intellectually, I am convinced of the Vedantic thought, but I know intellect is different from Anubhav [experience]. I feel that the abstract Deity as taught in the Vedanta is not practicable for a man circumstanced as I am. I wish to please the Deity and we can do it by serving humanity.

Hindu student: Ultimately, we find that all is illusion. To get out of illusion into the Universal is religion. There is a certain order in the universe and to get along with that order is my religion. In this connection, I have to believe in a personal God. I am yet hesitant and do not know what to believe.

> Intellectually, I am convinced of the Vedantic thought, but I know intellect is different from Anubhav [experience].

Hindu pundit, learned in Sanskrit lore: I cannot realize God in the worldly affairs I am engaged in. I believe in the way of Vedanta, but I cannot say I have realized God. I should be telling a lie if I said I had. One has to give up all worldly pursuits if he is to realize God.

Hindu teacher: I have the end of life as the realization of the Universal Self. All my trouble will be ended when that is realized.

Hindu shastri—one learned in the Hindu sacred books: I believe that we will obtain deliverance by the process of elimination of the senses till they are at an absolute minimum. But this cannot be done in a day. It may take ages.

Christ at the Round Table

A Swami of the Ramakrishna Mission defined religion as a development of inherent powers. There must be no invasion from without; there must be development only from within. I am peaceful and I have a sense of brotherhood that is real. I am ready to embrace all religions, but I must confess I am not yet a realized man. I have not found God.

Hindu headmaster: I see outside of me a larger self. I sit outside of God in pain and misery. I want to throw myself wholesale into God, then all my trials would cease.

Hindu professor: I am in revolt against all forms and ceremonies and objective prayer, and a personal God and against Scriptures—though they may be useful. I have no dependence on outside power—it is all within. I am a Vedantist.

Hindu: I started in at Vishnuism, then I went to Brahmoism, now I am in Shaktism, but I find myself relapsing into Vedantism.

Sadhu Nanakpanti (follower of Guru Nanak): We must know ourselves first, then we can know God. Ahankar [egotism] must be rooted out. This is the most important. As the air in the football is uneasy until the bladder bursts and loses it back into the air, so we are uneasy till we merge into the All.

Hindu: Man is a microcosm of the macrocosm, but just as frosted glass keeps out the light, so we must get rid of the glass and perceive our unity with our Universal. I believe in many lives and in one of them I shall find. I have never seen one who was a Jiwan Mukta [one who has found salvation], though I have read of two, Swami Rama Tiratha and Rama Krishna Paramahansa.

A Hindu Swami who had lectured much in America on Vedantism, began by pointing out the failings of Christianity versus Christ and said that he had respect for Christ as one of the Incarnations. I suggested

AT GRIPS WITH LIFE

that he was hardly speaking according to the purpose of the conference and would he mind sharing with us what he had found in religion. He replied: That is a hard process and to find God takes a long time and it would take a very long time to explain it to this group.

(2) The followers of Bhakti or devotion to the personal God or gods.

A Hindu lawyer: Religion may be communion with God or faith in God. There are many theories. Rama is my guru and my worship is only trying to imitate him as far as I can. We have simply to go on in the path. The result may be communion with God, or it may be that my soul will merge with the Universal Soul. I do not bother myself about the conclusion.

Bengali devotee: I sometimes doubted God and sometimes believed that he was. My father gave me a copy of the Gita and I read it for seventeen days. One night, whether I was awake or asleep I cannot tell, I had a vision. It was light, and I have never forgotten it. I have tried to have the vision again, but it has never come again. Now I have the same love for men, animals, and even plants. I cannot put my mind to work. I sometimes read, but I cannot remember anything. All religions and gurus are to me the same. I hope to get to my goal through the religion of my father.

Bengali Goswamy (head of religious order): I believe in Sri Chaitanya. I practice both bliajan [singing] and kirtan [religious devotional procession and dance]. When I am alone in my house and my wife and my children are away, I feel God is very near me. I have this experience almost every time I have kirtan in the morning. The name of Hari gives happiness.

Hindu devotee: It is difficult to express. The dumb cannot tell the taste of a laddu [sweetmeat]. Religion is my *isht* [my choice]. I believe in faith. A son was born to me, and when he died I did not feel the least sorrow for him. That was due to my faith.

Hindu: I am a Saiva Siddhantist. I think of God all day, the whole twenty-four hours, so I do not care for money, or for my family or for the fleeting world.

(3) The followers of Karma Yoga or the way of works.

Hindu: To me the whole of religion is contained in the well-known text of the Gayatri which means right action.

Hindu lawyer: The ideal may not be realized at once. In the meantime, we have to do what we can, namely, follow our Dharma. I find I get a certain amount of comfort when I perform my religious ceremonies. I count that a happy day when I have performed my ceremonies correctly.

Hindu: Strong scientific men can do morality for morality's sake, but the ordinary man must have religion to make him moral. But religion is not necessary for further advanced souls.

Pundit of the Servants of India Society: God's laws are unchangeable. Karma must have its course.

Hindu: I believe in disinterested work. I believe in life as Lord Krishna explains in the Gita. I believe in devotion for the sake of devotion.

Nationalist: Religion can only be followed by the educated. The illiterate know nothing about it. My religion is to do good to others and not to hurt anyone.

Hindu nationalist: I have had nothing of the emotional experience which the Christians term conversion. Religion stands for the proper ordering of life and consolation in sorrow. Karma gives every man a hereditary status in society. It promises each man the possibility of a better place in the next life and it eliminates competition in this life.

At Grips With Life

The conception of duty keeps one unmoved in joy and sorrow and it gives a varying standard of conduct to suit every situation. But this religion of duty lacks joy. The Christians seem to have joy. That feature is lacking in my life.

Hindu teacher: I believe that we can realize God through love, service, and inward purification—through action and not by mere meditation. I have not seen God nor do I know him, but I am his servant.

Hindu: My religious life has been entrusted to my guru. When I am in difficulties I go to him and follow his instructions. Karma is the most important. It directs me to do good. God is the totality of the universe and this forms a link between me and the universe.

> **I have had nothing of the emotional experience which the Christians term conversion. Religion stands for the proper ordering of life and consolation in sorrow.**

Hindu barrister: If to be religious is to realize God, then I must say that I am irreligious. I want to realize God in the aspirations of my country. To serve my country is to serve God. I am not discouraged, for I feel God must be back of me in service.

Hindu teacher: I think we can find God not by religion, but by character.

(4) Those who are skeptical.

Hindu judge: I was a skeptic and wandered through various phases, Theosophy among them. I am not very religious. I am not sure about finding God, for I do not know whether I would want him after I had found him. I once heard of a man who wanted to see God, and he was revealed to him in the form of Kali with a hundred heads. He laughed. When he was asked why he laughed he replied, "I was just thinking of what would happen to you if you caught a cold." I am not sure I want to see or know God.

Hindu: I am uninterested in religion, but the doctrine of Karma and transmigration seem to me to embody the explanation of life.

Hindu Oxford graduate: There are times when I feel that religion has some value for life and other times when I feel it has no value. If it has any value, it consists in morality more than anything else.

Electrical engineer associated with one of the great men of India: Life is a stream. I do not find a place of anchorage, and I do not know where it will lead or whether I will find God or not.

Hindu lawyer: I think of God when I get more clients and am prosperous, but when troubles come I think my Karma is visiting me. Then I do not care for God. I think of him only as a schoolmaster then.

Hindu deputy magistrate: I am in a wilderness of bewilderment. Religion should mean strength. I want to respect Rama and Krishna, but I cannot exactly do it. In examination, I tried "action without desire for fruit" and I got "plucked." I tried the second time and desired fruit and I got through. So, I do not know what is the meaning of religion.

Hindu doctor—a shastri: I think of a good many men; who can teach the gods a great deal, for instance Gandhi, Tolstoy, Jesus, and Buddha. If God ever has to create the world again, he should call some of these people to consult. Religionists doubt nine hundred and ninety-nine gods and cling to one. I doubt that one more. I am stronger since I have stopped praying to gods and have depended on myself. The aim of life should he summed up in the words, "Do unto others as ye would that men should do to you." Give this religion of doing unto others as you would have them do to you a chance and in five hundred years it will revolutionize the world.

Hindu: I am not very certain about religion. I have been an agnostic, but I have now a feeling of faith in the Motherhood of God.

Sikh: Religion really means nothing to me except perhaps prayer, and I am not sure but that this may be auto-suggestion. The thing to do is to replace God by humanity, replace religion by morality, and develop your own personality.

Hindu nationalist: I am almost blank. I have no personal religion. The society in which I have been born is religious, but I have drifted from my moorings. I have prayed, but I do not feel any better. I do not know whether there is a God. I try to be moral simply because there is a craving for it, but I fall down. I am like Saint Augustine when he prayed, "Make me pure, but not now." I wish there would be something to give me light. I am not strong enough to lead a moral life.

(5) Those deeply influenced by Christianity.

Hindu principal of college: The whole of life is to me regulated by our ideas of religion. My idea is that I should establish intimate relations with our Creator, the one Universal Spirit. I try to join myself with God. The supreme medium is service to his creatures. My particular service which I have chosen or rather God has chosen for me is education.

Hindu justice of the high court: After my college course, I was driven into skepticism. I read Haeckel.[1]

---

[1] Ernst Heinrich Philipp August Haeckel 16 February 1834 – 9 August 1919) was a German biologist, naturalist, philosopher, physician, professor, marine biologist, and artist who discovered, described and named thousands of new species, mapped a genealogical tree relating all life forms, and coined many terms

I then began to study the life and teachings of Jesus. There was a sense of belief in God restored. I have studied Theosophy and have been a Theosophist, but what I found strangely enough made me interested in and attached to the teachings of Jesus. To me now, service to all creation is the goal of religion.

Hindu nationalist: I was uninterested in religion and did not care for it until Mahatma Gandhi came on the scene. I felt that through him religion became once more a living reality. He was interested in Jesus and in his life embodied his principle, so I became interested in Jesus and in his teachings.

The end of religion now seems to me to be expressed in the words, "Do unto others as you would that men should do unto you."

Hindu: At one time, I came very near being a Christian. People thought I would be. Then I went into Theosophy. I feel that religion should save me from sin—that is what I crave through it. Jesus and the Mahatmas that hover around one are the inspiration to service. I feel discouraged at times that so little is done, but I am trying to cut off some sins by doing good.

---

in biology. Haeckel promoted and popularized Charles Darwin's work in Germany and developed the influential but no longer widely held recapitulation theory ("ontogeny recapitulates phylogeny") claiming that an individual organism's biological development, or ontogeny, parallels and summarises its species' evolutionary development, or phylogeny. (https://en.wikipedia.org/wiki/Ernst_Haeckel, Accessed, June 16, 2018)

Hindu teacher in government training school: I began to study the Bible through someone saying that the best English was found in the Bible. I read it for that purpose, but soon found myself forgetting about the language, for its message gripped me. The miracles of Jesus are different from the miracles of other religions—they are superior and more real. The character of Jesus is superior to the character of any other. [Here I stopped him and suggested that he should not argue but tell his experience of religion. I thought he was a Christian. Here I was, suggesting to a Hindu not to be too pugnacious against other faiths and not to be militant in favor of Christianity!] All right, he replied, I can speak from experience. I find refuge in prayer. In difficulty, I find consolation in Christ.

Hindu doctor interested in psychiatric care: I am a Christian, but I have not taken baptism, for I feel no need of it. The thing that strikes me about Jesus is that he connected sin and the cure of disease— the two went together—this is sound.

Hindu sub-judge: I believe all religions are equally good, but my religion is "Do unto others as you would be done by."

Hindu language teacher: I heard some Christian lectures and asked Mr.——— and others to pray with me. This made a deep impression on me. I am now between Vaishavism and Christianity and follow a mixture of both.

Sikh doctor: Religion to me is to free humanity from suffering, and I do that by attending to patients. This is my religion.

Hindu barrister: My father was a strict leader of the Arya Samaj (Members of the Arya Samaj believe in one God and reject the worship of idols). I believe in God without being convinced that there is one. I think in this country, religion has been responsible for our degradation. Religion has exercised greater tyranny than anything else. I would welcome Christianity because it would bring brotherhood and social and political emancipation. I feel that India will not rise until there is one religion. Islam has lost its grip and Hinduism is decaying. I wish India would be Christian tomorrow morning from the Himalayas to Cape Comorin. God can be reached only by self-sacrifice and service.

Elderly and thoughtful Hindu doctor: I have been an agnostic, but I have worked my way from agnosticism to faith in a personal God. Christ has been the path along which I have traveled to this faith. He is the supreme revelation of God. His teaching concerning the using of sorrow is a workable philosophy of life.

Hindu: Prayer is my religion. Through it I have communion with a personal God. My religion is a simple religion, but I have reality in it. Christ is prayer and Christ is God. I do not want to study philosophy for fear of disturbing this satisfying experience. We Hindus hate to admit it, but Christ is transforming all our ideas.

Hindu professor: I am still groping in the dark. Religion does not mean to me dogma, ritual—it means under heaven one family. I have rejected caste from my heart. If I am born again, I want to be an outcaste in protest. The Jesus of dogma I do not understand, but the Jesus of the Sermon on the Mount and the cross I love and am drawn to.

Hindu teacher: I found myself falling down a precipice and I fell into the arms of the Divine. God has become real to me now.

Hindu: I am asked to speak. I will remove my cloak and reveal my shallowness. I have not arrived at any intellectual conception of religion. I am following my instincts and I am not sure my instincts are right. When a sage was given the privilege of a boon, he asked for the privilege of vicarious suffering. That to me is the greatest thing. I want to keep before me the scene enacted on Calvary. I wish I had power to take on myself the sufferings of others.

(6) *A group holding miscellaneous views.*

Hindu doctor: Religion raises such questions as: where we have come from and where we are to go to, and the meaning of life, and how the spirit works through the body. I am on the verge, but have not found anything.

Hindu professor: God is our creation. It is a question of being willing to believe. The human being is so credulous that he will believe what he has a will to believe. We have a great reverence for the inspired writings of the Veda.

Hindu head official: I have no time to be really religious. I sympathize with the Buddhist idea that we cannot bother ourselves with God and realization. We must give ourselves to the threefold path of Sangha, the Buddha, and the Law. The Law is our Dharma. I must fulfill that.

Islamic leader: The great prophets did not count much—Jesus, Buddha, and Mohammed. It is God who really matters.

Brahmo leader: Religion comes to me not as a continuous thing—sometimes God seems to me to be real and sometimes not.

Hindu professor: Religion is not a belief but an expression of life. Religion is an all-pervading influence in my life. It is an endeavor to lift me to God. I have not been able to reach God. The best way to realize God is prayer. Prayer touches my soul, and I feel that the soul has been touched. I then feel divine grace and I wish to have it always. I wish to live a life of purity, service, and usefulness. But all these things I consider secondary. The primary thing is to see the light. I very often find that the light is not present.

Nationalist lawyer: I do not know whether I am a religious man. I thought I was a religious man until yesterday, but a rat fell into a tub and I wanted my house sanitary so I turned two dogs on it. A Hindu friend saw me doing it and said, "You call yourself a religious man?" I have been very troubled in mind since, as it has struck at the whole of my religious life.

Islamic sufi: I have found something. It is light and joy and strength. It is surrender to the will of God.

Hindu: I have a path prescribed by my guru, and when I walk in that path I have consolation. I am not at liberty to tell what that path is.

Hindu lawyer: When I sing hymns to gods and goddesses I feel a sense of satisfaction.

Hindu inspector of schools: I have had no deep sorrow. I feel the need of some great sorrow or calamity to make my religious life normal. In fact, I am eagerly looking for it.

Parsee professor: The finite cannot grasp the Infinite. I cannot grasp God intellectually, but I hold on to God spiritually by an inward conviction or faith.

Hindu: Religion is not an intellectual concept but an inward realization, but I have not realized God yet. I may do so in this life; it may be in the life to come. All students who finish their M. A. are agnostics or atheists. I was, but I have some faith in God.

Head deputy magistrate: Religion is a growth. I am feeling after it. I cannot say that I have found it. I am hoping.

Hindu professor of education: Among the fourteen ways of Hindus to obtain Moksha [deliverance], ten are without God. It does not matter which one you take to obtain the knowledge of the Self. You may meet God on the way in any of them, but that does not matter in the realization of the Self. I have no experience I can share with anyone except to one who is in the same process.

Hindu shastri: I obey the Sanatana Dharma [old Orthodox] which is ahimsa [harmlessness]. This ahimsa includes not only animals, but vegetables as well. The only thing we can eat and practice this ahimsa is dried leaves that fall from trees, for they have no life within them. I must see God in trees and stones and even in a serpent.

Hindu pleader: There is a kind of hero-worship in me. I must see God in some eminent person. Mahatma Gandhi is now my ideal man.

Hindu honorary magistrate: I have not realized God as yet. It is difficult to know him. But I believe in a Creator and I feel no harm should be done to anyone.

Buddhist monk: I have nothing to express. I did not come prepared.

> All religions are the same, but Jesus is the Son of God.

Hindu: Religion does not mean much to me. I have never been bigoted. All religions are more or less alike; they all have their good points. No religion should say, I am the way. I have never been able to find out where God comes in in actual life. Only when life is needy do we need God.

Hindu principal of college: I do the Shastric duties prescribed for me—whether I shall discover God or not I do not know.

Hindu: If God is impersonal and perfect, he is of no use to me; he will not hear my prayers; he will be supremely indifferent and let nature's laws work. If he is personal, he is imperfect, but that is what I want him to be. I want him to set aside his law and forgive me. I want him in the imperfect state. When one takes refuge in the lesser ones—

Mohammed, Krishna, Jesus—he is taking refuge in the personal and imperfect, and I think it is a sin to disturb him.

Buddhist: God and religion to me are one. Religion sharpens the moral conceptions and is thus of use, but religion really is doing ethical things.

Hindu government official: All religions are the same, but Jesus is the Son of God. However, Theosophy has taught me that some of the things I had given up as untrue are true.

We have refrained from giving more Islamic and Arya Samaj statements. The former lacked inwardness, being usually a claim for the finality of the Koran; and the latter scarcely knew how to fit into our conferences. Their native air is debate and they were not quite at home in this atmosphere of quiet search for truth and reality through sharing.

We can give only a few statements from Christians at this place, as others will be found scattered throughout the book. The first three are from those outside organized Christianity — "unauthorized Christians," as they have been called.

Hindu graduate: My father died and we lost all our money. This hardened me and I determined to be as wicked as I could. I became a very bad man. During that time misery set in and my sister said that God was angry with me because of my life. I began to think and to try to turn around. I went to a sadhu and gave him the little money I had left. He spent it on Canabis Indica [marijuana]. He gave me nothing. I began to wonder if there was anyone who could sympathize with a poor, sinful man such as I am, and then the thought dawned on me that there is life for a look at the Crucified One. I gave him my life. I try to follow him, and I suppose I may be called an unbaptized Christian.

Hindu professor: I went to England for study and gave up my belief in dogmatic religion. On my return I preached agnosticism, not because I was atheistic, but because I wanted to find reality. There was one thing amid the conflict of ideas that held me steady—the personality of Jesus. But I needed something to concretize it. I saw Christianity attempted on a wide-spread scale in the Non-Cooperation Movement. It gripped me when I saw it in Gandhi and George Lansbury. I may live and die a Hindu, but my attachment is to Christ. He has become my center and my joy. My soul has been unfolding to him like a flower to the sun.

Hindu professor: The personality of Jesus began to be very attractive to me through the personality of Doctor M. He was a very great man, yet so approachable. He was so strong and yet so humble. I fell in love with Christ. I felt rebellious with Doctor M. when he said the college was not there to make converts. I felt it should make converts, for I felt that everyone should love Christ. I feel now the difficulty of adjusting my faith in Jesus with the old religion. How can I be loyal to Jesus and respect Rama? I feel that there must be a center and all things must cluster around that. Jesus to me is that center and all other characters must cluster around him. My capacity to blunder led me to Christ. It was not an intellectual approach, but a moral approach.

> I may live and die a Hindu, but my attachment is to Christ. He has become my center and my joy. My soul has been unfolding to him like a flower to the sun.

These three perspectives represent a large and growing number of persons who have not seen their way to come into organized Christianity, and yet announce themselves as followers of Christ.

Some of the statements from within organized Christianity were inadequate and halting, as for instance these:

Indian Christian professor, graduate of a Western university: Religion is the emotional background of economic values. I have come to think of religion as morality. I think religion is the background of morality, but I have not got any further.

Burmese Christian: I had Christian parents, but have had no real conversion. Hence after my training in England and return to my homeland, broadness led to a mixture. There has been a loss of, or rather lack of, any personal relationship with God.

Burmese Christian government official: I am a Christian and I am not. I am a Buddhist and I am not. I have a religion of my own. I believe in God —that is about all.

One European Christian lady doctor was frankly skeptical about prayer, about God, but found in Christ a model for service to others.

Apart from these, the Christian participants were amazingly uniform in saying "Christ has brought God to me."

"I have not found God, but God has found me in Christ. If Christ cannot save me, I feel I cannot be saved; but Christ is saving me."

"I cannot bear to think of a God who sits in awful and isolated perfection above the world and its tragedies and takes no part in it. But I can love God if he is the Suffering Companion of my life. In Jesus God seems to be that to me, so he has my heart."

"I came to Christ through the mind—an intellectual love of God—and now Christ gives me an orderly world for the mind and a resting place for my soul."

"In the fierce battle of my passions I was failing. I laid them at His feet and He stilled the tempest and gave me deliverance from myself."

"My life was broken and he came and made it whole."

"Now God has become to me intimately real, closer than breathing and nearer than hands and feet."

"I find a norm for conduct in Christ and a dynamic for service."

"Nothing less than a new birth came to me when I became his bhakta."

"An indescribable sense of rest and deliverance was mine when I came into contact with him and trusted my sinful soul to him."

"I have tried to serve, but found I needed to be saved from myself. I gave my heart to him and now for me to live is Christ."

"Christ to me is life—life abundant."

"The cross has become the center of my moral universe. Here I see light and find life."

"God saw something in me that I did not see in myself. He won't let me alone. In that is my salvation."

One feels as he listens that men are not quite able to tell the full content of what is in experience. But as the Chinese proverb puts it, "Words are the sounds of the heart," so one could detect the sounds of the heart in the words if he listened with sympathy.

One could feel that some of the statements meant less than their face value and others meant more. Gathering up the sum total of impressions one can come near the facts involved.

To that we come in our next chapter.

Chapter 3

WHAT CAN WE GATHER FROM ALL THIS?

WE HAVE BEEN deeply privileged. We have been in a clinic of souls. Here the ages have been in travail—what has been brought forth? Here systems built up through millenniums, by prayer and tears and austerities and pilgrimage and thought and aspiration, have let their devotees speak. What has been the voice? Is it that word for which we have been listening - that healing word?

What impressions write themselves upon the mind and heart as one listens in at these conferences?

1. In the men who took part was a very great deal of intellectual and spiritual culture. They were men of whom any nation might well be proud. I never sat and listened without a feeling of deep joy that my lot had been cast with them and that India was my home. There was a delicate sense of spiritual appreciation. When a spiritual note was struck, one felt that they were not dull and indifferent—they were responsive and keen to note it. The Indian has a highly sensitized soul. He talks about religion more naturally than does a Westerner. Although we suggested that no one need feel that he must speak and that anyone

could say that he preferred to "pass," yet among the scores of Round Tables scarcely ten persons availed themselves of the privilege. Many times, I found myself deeply disappointed at the poverty of the finding, but the words of a modern philosopher would ring through my mind over and over again as an antidote: "I am seriously interested in the world's possibilities, not in its actualities." The spiritual possibilities in India are surely the greatest of any race of the world, for here religion seems natural and unaffected.

2. Again and again, I felt no one has a right to teach others who is not learning from them. I came to India with everything to teach and nothing to learn. I now stay to learn, as well, and I am a better man for having come into contact with the gentle heart of the East. I think I know now the meaning of Ezekiel's going to the captives by the river to speak to them out of the "heat and bitterness of his spirit." As he was about to speak, God said: "No, Ezekiel, not yet. Sit down." And "for seven days I sat where they sat," said Ezekiel. For seven days, he entered into the problems, the pains, the temptations of the captives—for seven days, he learned sympathy and understanding. At the end of that time, God said, "Now you may speak," and when he spoke there was the undertone of understanding sympathy in his words. In these conferences, we have tried to understand sympathetically the viewpoint of the other man—to sit where he sits, and I have been enriched through them. Life can never be quite the same again.

3. Although there was naturalness and willingness to speak, the impression one gained was that we were all being called upon to face religion and life in a new way. "As I sat here awaiting my turn to speak, I felt it was like an approaching Judgment Day," said a thoughtful Hindu. "I have never faced my life under this scrutiny before." "It was very searching and sobering," said another. We all felt that we were entering a new stage of religious inquiry in India. The traditional attitude toward religion is beginning to give way to the experimental

and experiential. Men have taken things for granted, for it was all handed down. It was the "unexamined life" of Plato. Now things must be put to the test of life and examined experimentally. "These conferences would have been impossible ten years ago. There was no mentality for them," remarked a thoughtful friend. True, this attitude is not widespread and it is only in the beginnings, but the fact that it is there is significant for the future.

4. People are incurably religious. Religion put out by one door comes in by another. A great many in our conferences had lost their faith under the impact of modern life, but had regained a faith of some kind or other, however inadequate it might be. The soul, as well as nature, abhors a vacuum. Even if in some lives faith is in eclipse, there is no rejoicing over the loss, but a wistful yearning that it might be real. This wistful yearning is itself religious. Religion cannot be wiped out of the human heart by materialism or a plunge into the present, for when the soul comes to itself it says, "I perish with hunger; I will arise and go to my Father."

5. Humanity is fundamentally one. I can no longer think of a man as simply a Hindu or Muslim or Parsee or Christian. He is a brother man facing the same problems and perplexities which I face. The question of our skins being brown, white, yellow, or black makes no difference when we drop down and face life and God. We *are* one. This distinctly points to the fact that, since we are one, and since we are incurably religious, we should finally be united at the place of religion. There will be a deep sifting of religions to find Religion, but we shall find it, for humanity cannot be finally separated at the deepest place of life.

6. The fundamental need of the human heart is redemption. Life is not what it ought to be. The "ought to be" stands over against the "is" and will not let us rest. That answering response within us is religion.

What Can We Gather...

And as long as men want to be better —not merely wiser or happier or more comfortable, but better—religion will remain. The fundamental problem of religion is to bring us to the "ought to be"—it is fundamentally redemptive.

7. There was not a single situation that I can remember where, before the close of the Round Table Conference, Christ was not in moral and spiritual command of the situation.

There was no drawing of contrasts between the different disclosures of the adherents of the various faiths, no pointing out of superiorities by a clever summing up. We left the statements to speak for themselves, to be their own witness by their own worthwhileness. Nevertheless—and I do not overstate when I say it, for no one could escape the impression—at the close, everything else had been pushed to the edges as irrelevant and Christ controlled the situation. As men listened to what those who were in touch with him were quietly saying, they instinctively felt that here was something redemptive at work at the heart of life, redeeming men from themselves and from sin, putting worth and meaning into life, giving an unquenchable hope to men, lighting up the inward depths of life, bringing them into fellowship with God in beautiful intimacy and furnishing a dynamic for human service. The living freshness of it struck us all. Here was life catching its rhythm and bursting into song. Here was God, not an absent Deity or an abstraction, but God tender,

> Religion cannot be wiped out of the human heart by materialism or a plunge into the present, for when the soul comes to itself it says, "I perish with hunger; I will arise and go to my Father."

available, opening the sources of divine love to the healing of human need and entering into fellowship with the human in an intimacy too close for words to express.

I do not mean to say that God is realized in this redemptive way by all those who are inside the organized system of Christianity. There are large numbers of "Christians" to whom this would not apply. It would be easy, if one picked his facts, to duplicate, inside of organized Christianity, the same barrenness of results which he finds in the other faiths. But wherever men are in fellowship with Christ in a personal way, this realization does happen and it happens with almost mathematical precision.

Very striking was the fact that the raw human material upon which the redemptive forces were at work often seemed to be of the type which men would call unpromising. But here were men, some of them from the lowest rungs of human society, who were spiritually at home, unabashed before the inheritors of the spiritual culture of the ages; they spoke quietly and masterfully of the redemption they were finding.

For instance, we sat in a group of highly cultured men: judges, government officials, doctors, lawyers, a head of an Ashram for spiritual culture, devotees of the various cults—as highly trained a group of men as one can sit among. Before we began our conference, one of the Hindus passed around a paper filled with keen objections to the Christian faith. He had written a book which was a savage attack upon Christianity with the latest weapons drawn from the armory of the Rationalistic Association of Britain of which he was a member. He thought the conference would be precipitated on the points raised in the paper he had just passed around, but it went to deeper levels and to things more fundamental. He was disconcerted and dismayed and when his turn came to speak, he tried to come back to the surface level, saw it could not be done, said a few halting things and closed. He did not know how to get to grips with this new challenge. In the midst of this group sat an unassuming, retiring youth with bare feet, dressed in simple homespun. He was an M. A. student, a convert from the aborigines. There were millenniums of spiritual and social culture between the rest of his group and this youth. But as he began to speak, every eye was soon fastened on him, for he was evidently speaking out of reality as he told of what Christ meant to him. It was simple, direct and real. Christ's touch was upon his life, and lo, he had leaped beyond the group around him and had gained life's secret and meaning. As men sat listening they instinctively felt that he had found the way of life and that they had missed it. At the close, my combative friend, moved to his depths by the impact of the whole upon him, came up to me and limply said, "He speaks well, doesn't he?" Yes, he had spoken well, for he caught the accent of the lips of Him who spake as never man spake. An aborigine in a few swift years becomes the teacher to the Brahmans and the highly cultured. The next day, as he sat with me and told me of his plan to turn his back upon the prizes that university education was offering him in order to go back and live as a sadhu among his people in the hills, to share with them what Christ was meaning to him, I knew that the passion of the cross had caught fire in his heart. Life was under redemptive influences.

Or to take another: We were in one of the sacred places of India and sat in a group made up of the Brahmans of the Brahmans, the religiously *elite*, along with men trained at universities, both Indian and Western. A man is speaking. He has the quiet dignity of a statesman; his words are well chosen; he moves amid spiritual things with poise and with the sense of being at home. He said: "Religion can be summed up in three simple words: Get. Grow. Give. I got from Christ all that I have and am. But it is not a static redemption I have received, for I find that my life is growing in moral victory and in fellowship with my Master. And I find that I have something to give to others. The wonder of it is that I who had nothing, have something to share." As he talked on, this group before me seemed to fade away and in mind I watched another group of the lowest of the low castes carry out the carcass of a dead animal to feast upon it with rejoicing. There is a boy among them. The boy grown to manhood is now speaking and we are hanging on his words. We feel that he has got something, that he is growing and that he is giving to us all. The miracle has happened. A power, not ourselves, working for righteousness and redemption, was at work.

> Men find God through Christ—not merely hope to find him, but actually find him.

While a number of these striking cases could be cited, yet it was not from them that our deepest impressions came. They came out of the fact that on a widespread scale—in fact, wherever human life touched Christ—there was a steadying of the mind amid the clashing currents, an enforcement of the will to goodness, and the setting afire of the heart with a new love for God and man. Christ was meaning life to men.

But most impressive of all was the fact that where men come into vital contact with Christ, the God consciousness becomes real and living. God has become reality. He is present in the heart in intimate clearness. Men find God through Christ—not merely hope to find him, but actually find him. The Hindus have noted this and have spoken of it again and again.

At the close of a conference a Hindu magistrate asked for another Round Table conference the next day. It was hard to fit in amid the public meetings, but he was so urgent that it was done. After we had assembled the magistrate said: "The conference yesterday was very wonderful and surprising. I wanted another one today because, as you saw yesterday, our discovery and realization of God was indefinite and uncertain. That of you Christians was definite and certain. I suggest that we do not speak today but that we simply hear more of the content of your experience. Tell us more minutely what it means to you, how you found it, and how we might find it." He saw what was obviously a fact—that men in Christ were finding the realization of God, and that this was lighting up their whole lives.

Another discerning Hindu said at the close of a conference: "Today eight of us have spoken and none of us has found; five of you Christians have spoken and all of you seem to have found. This is very extraordinary. You apparently find this through Christ. If he should come to me as he has come to you, I would receive him. Why does he not do it? What do I have to do before he will?" I was not quite so sure that he was as willing to be led where that Light would lead him, as his words would imply, but he did see that God was coming to man through Christ.

In one place at the close a thoughtful Hindu said: "You Christians have thought about these things so you can express yourselves with facility, but we have not thought about these things, so we speak with difficulty. It was a terrible thing to ask myself the question: What does religion mean to me in experience? For the first time, I realized how serious it is." But was there not something deeper than facility of expression?

Another Hindu who had been attacking what I had said in the public meeting the night before, said in the conference the next day: "This fact amounts to a mystery to me. I find Christians, who have not gone through any greater discipline and moral endeavor than I, are apparently finding the realization of God. This puzzles me." And well it might.

Christ at the Round Table

Sometimes the acknowledgment of this fact of finding God through Christ on the part of his devotees takes a dramatic form. At the close of a conference when the melting sense of the Divine was upon us and every heart was moved, a Hindu lawyer arose, took the flowers from the table, walked over and laid them at the feet of one of the group, touched his feet and said: "You have found God; you are my guru." All felt that it was not a personal tribute, but India doing obeisance to the thing she has desperately yearned to find through the ages, the realization of God.

No one could sit through these conferences and not feel that Christ was Master of every situation, not by loud assertion, or through the pleading of clever advocates, but by what he is and does—because he is doing something for human life that we cannot do without. That conclusion was irresistible. Through it all, one could feel that there was no boasting of spiritual attainment, which would have made the whole thing intolerable, but grateful hearts laying the tribute of their love at the feet of the Redeemer.

8. I wish I could let the matter rest there and that I were not compelled to turn to the other side and ask questions concerning the results found in the non-Christian faiths. One is reluctant to turn to the other side, since if shortcomings are found, it is very liable to produce attitudes of superiority and complacency in our own midst. And nothing is more deadly and un-Christian. It would not be a Round Table, though, if we looked at only one side of things. One could not escape the impression that the non-Christian faiths seemed to be proving inadequate for life. I cannot help confessing to a deep disappointment in regard to what the non-Christians seemed to be finding as an outcome of their faith. I had thought that the results would be greater. All those thoughtful and sympathetic Christians who listened day after day shared that disappointment.

What Can We Gather...

One could see scintillations of truth as they spoke from experience or quoted from sacred books. One also found that caste morality and the doctrine of Karma had often kept life on a higher moral level than that of a good many professed Christians who had taken the outward customs, but had not assimilated the morality of the gospel. And one could feel that the non-Christian faiths had kept alive in the soul of India a thirst for God and reality far deeper than that found in any other people. A wonderful capacity for self-renunciation, the love of simplicity and a sensitiveness to the spiritual have to be set down to the credit of these faiths. Nevertheless, the results were meager and disappointing.

Let us look at the outer movements for reform and the inner movements of the spiritual life. There are many fine movements for reform going through India, and Hindus and Muslims are carrying them on. Caste is being challenged and modified, the low caste is being raised, widows' homes are being established, widow-remarriage is beginning to take place, hospitals are being established, orphanages set up, and woman is being emancipated. It is a glorious list. But the disturbing thing is that their religions do not seem to be backing the finer movements going through the soul of India. These movements seem to be carried on in spite of them. They are a drag on the situation. Does the patriot want to do away with caste and untouchability and lift womanhood and have widow-remarriage? Then Manu must be explained away. Does he call for service? Then Brahma must be quietly replaced, for he is the non-serving. Does the patriot believe in non-violence? Then Krishna's attitude in the Gita where he urges Arjuna to fight and proves to him why he must do so, must be got rid of by a species of exegetical legerdemain. Religion says that the inequalities of life are the result of a previous birth, while the patriot feels that they are the result of the wrong organization of human society and that they should be tackled here and now. Religion says that the world is

Christ at the Round Table

Maya, or illusion, while the patriot feels that conditions can be changed and that the kingdom of God should come on earth. The country should be united, but religions seem to be keeping it divided.

One was constantly impressed with the fact that the power of religion was, on the whole, not with reform but against it. Of course, this would also be said about organized Christianity. It, too, has often blocked reform. Whenever it has turned to its Fountainhead Christ, though, it has been awakened to reform. Herein lies the difference. The non-Christian faiths carry on reform as they move away from their base, the Christian faith as it moves toward its base. "We sincerely desire to help the low castes, but we must be mindful about our religion," said a Brahman in a conference in which the raising of the untouchables was discussed. In a conference of Muslims, one of them called the Hindus "brothers." Immediately there was a protest, and after a great deal of heated debate, it was decided to appeal to the Koran to see if it were allowable. "We will never make any progress until we drop all the pundits into the midst of the Ganges," said a Hindu patriot to me one day. It is true that Hindu reformers have arisen again and again and have done noble service, but the mass of Hinduism has remained more or less inert.

This reactionary and blocking tendency of religion is generally admitted, but the reply is made that the contribution of religion is in the higher realms of the spirit, in the realization of God. I asked one of the greatest living leaders of Hinduism what, in his view, was the

What Can We Gather...

greatest contribution Hinduism had to make. He replied with eagerness, "The greatest contribution will be the knowledge and realization of the Self as found in the Upanishads." In other words, it was the realization of one's identification with that Universal Self, God. Here he touched Hinduism's central thought—its sole concern. If, however, the realization of God is the supreme contribution of Hinduism to life, then it seems to be failing in that contribution.

It is certainly true that there is a kind of God-consciousness in India, but it is held in a vague diffusion, a sense of the intimation of the Divine. To put it in other words, it is held in solution, ready to be, but not yet precipitated into crystallized realization of God. There is a vast diffusion of this sense of the Divine, but along with it is a vast uncertainty.

In our Round Table Conferences, we have anxiously listened for this note of finding on the part of non-Christians, for would we not be happy if men were finding God? But while there was sensitivity to the spiritual and a wistfulness of search, yet the note of finding seemed to be absent.

Out of the scores of conferences, only five or six men impressed us as having found something comparable to what the ordinary sincere Christian is finding through Christ. Three of these were Hindus who were inwardly saturated with Christian ideals and were living in fellowship with Christ. Another was a Islamic sufi who seemed to have found inward peace and harmony and light. I learned that he was a teacher in a Christian school, and he told me privately that when he read the Sermon on the Mount he could not keep back the tears. Another was a poet whose background I could not discover; and the final one was a Sikh doctor who said: "I started out as a Vedantist, but could find nothing in it. I went to the Sikh scriptures and there I found peace. I found it through devotion and service." He impressed us as having found some reality through religion. That he had found God, of course, he did not say.

The above is the sum total and it is meager. And this is not at its lowest place, but at its highest place where Hinduism is supposed to make its supreme contribution.

While we believed that we had a cross section of the religious life of India in our Round Table Conferences, I did not feel that we were justified in drawing too large conclusions from them. Thinking that we were possibly not getting the ones who were finding, I began to make careful inquiry throughout India, asking Hindus if they knew of anyone who had found Jiwan-mukti, living salvation, and the realization of God. I asked the great leader who mentioned the supreme contribution of Hinduism whether he had seen one who had realized, and he replied after a moment's silence, "No, I have not." Then I asked him whether he expected to find salvation before he died, and the reply tinged with wistfulness was this: "I do not know whether I will or not. I do not know how far I am along." And he is one of the finest and sincerest Hindus I have met. But the uncertainty!

It is quite true that there is a difference in definition regarding the meaning of the realization of God between the Vedantist and the Christian. To the latter it means a personal saving fellowship with God issuing in eternal life in the midst of time, to the former it means the realization that one is Brahma. This difference must be taken into account. But if the respective ends are realizable, we would expect them to be working. This is the point at issue. And this is the point at which I find Vedantism failing. It does not seem to be working.

A sadhu, a Sanskrit scholar, was asked whether he knew anyone who had found, and he replied: "We know the theoretical Vedanta philosophy perfectly, but the practical Vedanta very little. You might have found Jiwan-muktis twenty or thirty years ago, but now you will

What Can We Gather...

not find any." But why not now in this period of the Hindu Renaissance?

At a place where Hinduism was at its very highest and had flowered into its finest forms, I asked the leading pundit the same question and the reply was a simple "No." Another put it in these words: "There may be some man in India who has worn down his passions and has found release." A Hindu judge in one of the most sacred places of South India replied in this way: "India has produced saints and realizers of God in the past, but none now. I hear, though, that there may be some found in the Himalayas." I am now in the Himalayas and a few days ago I visited a famous ashram and asked the American swami, who has been up here for twenty years seeking through the Vedanta to find "spiritual freedom," whether he expected to find through the impersonal or the personal. He replied, "It does not matter to me whether there is a God or not, whether he is personal or impersonal, just so I find freedom." After twenty years search it seemed very remote.

Throughout India the names of two men are mentioned as having found—Rama Krishna Paramahansa and Swami Rama Tiratha, and sometimes a third, Chaitanaya. None of these is living. Are there no living witnesses? I am reminded of the remark of a Hindu: "We are like men who go around showing the bankbook of our forefathers and boasting about how much they had on deposit, while there is very little in the bank today to our name." It sounded harsh to me then, but ...? But suppose these three men had found, could this be called a redemptive movement when out of the hundreds of millions now living devoted to a faith and ardently following it, only three have found—and these three not now living? What hope is there for these seeking millions? Moreover, when I look closely at these three I am further perplexed. I find Rama Krishna, among other strange things, offering flowers before himself as to God. Chaitanaya, in the madness of his devotion to Krishna, thinks the moon his spirit-lover and rushes into the sea and drowns himself. These two seem hardly balanced: they are erratic and non-imitable. The third is the joyous attractive Rama Tiratha. Our hearts warm to him. He seems to have caught the secret of joyous spiritual living and preached it throughout the world, especially in America. And he seems to have found it through the Vedanta. But looking a little closer, I find that he was a student in a mission school, a professor in a mission college, and was saturated with Christian ideas and his Vedanta was not Vedanta. The pundits of Benares saw this, twitted him that he knew nothing of Sanskrit, and hence, nothing of the Vedanta. He took up their challenge, began to study Sanskrit and to learn the real Vedanta. The result of this study, as his biographer and disciple, Puran Singh, makes perfectly clear, was to plunge Swami Rama into a sea of doubt, destroy his blithe spirit, and change him into a moody and pessimistic philosopher.

Here are the three always pointed out as the finders, and yet... and yet ...? But I was not satisfied, for while I was convinced that Vedanta, the real philosophy of India, with its pessimism and illusion, was not giving what it promised, that its verbal currency was inflated and that its cash value was small, and that it was falling like a blight upon the fine soul of India as it fell upon the radiant soul of Swami Rama Tiratha, I thought perhaps I could find more among the Bhakti schools, devotees of personal deities. So, while at the central place of the Bhakti movement, I inquired for the greatest living devotee. All agreed on a certain man. At his feet rajas had sat and it was known that some of them had offered him lakhs of rupees which he had spurned. He lived in his rags in the hermitage and came to the town once a day to beg for his food. Even that he would not take if what was offered was not the simplest. Here was a bhakta in deed and in truth. So, I sought him out in his hermitage, found him seated in the sun, in the dust of the pathway. He had reduced his life to an absolute minimum, his food, his sleep, his clothes, his desires—all reduced that he might pour everything at the feet of his lord Krishna. We sat down in the dust with him anxious to know what he had brought back from his ardent devotions. In answer to my query about what he had found, he said: "The Bhakti Marg [the way of devotion] is the most difficult of all. In other ways, you may know whether you have received and attained something, but in this you never know. The more you give up, the more you have to give up. Sometimes I feel as if I had found something and sometimes I feel I have not." Here was the most ardent and sincere of devotees, and yet the dread uncertainty was here, too.

> [B]ut the real jungles seem to be within the human heart and men are trying desperately to cut their way through the tangled underbrush to get to Light and Freedom and Home...

But perhaps these men might know of someone else, not here, who had found. I inquired of the head of a religious monastery, a Goswami. He replied: "Yes, we believe in Jiwan Muktas in Vaishnavism and we all hope to attain someday, but there are none here. There may be some in the jungles."

Yes, I know that through the jungles of India, men are fiercely trying to wring from the universe her secret, and by austerities are trying to make God answer the need of the up-reaching heart, but the real jungles seem to be within the human heart and men are trying desperately to cut their way through the tangled underbrush to get to Light and Freedom and Home, but...?

And worse than all, men everywhere, outside of these devotees who still fiercely knock, have settled down to a dull acceptance of the idea of not finding. They would continue to do their duty, perform their ceremonies and the future—well, that would be seen. Immediate expectation is given up and men are content to live in what Lecky calls "the land of the unrealized and the inoperative."

It is good to remind ourselves that this process of the upward struggle toward redemption and release has been going on, according to Hindu and Buddhist thought, for untold ages. It is not in its beginnings. This tree with its roots so far in the past should be bringing forth fruit in released souls who have arrived. Why aren't they arriving?

Buddha began his movement with an "illumination" here and now, and we would expect that something of the same would be reproduced, but there is a dead hand of non-expectancy upon the Buddhist world. A Burmese scholar told me that he had inquired for thirty-four years to find anyone who in the near future, either in this birth or the immediately succeeding ones, hoped to find Nirvana, but no one either among the pongyis (monks) or the laity even remotely expected to find Nirvana. An abbot in a monastery, a great and celebrated man among the monks, was surprised when the scholar asked him, while he was on his dying bed, whether he hoped to attain. "Oh, no," he replied; "that is afar off."

The layman feels that the best he can do is to lay the foundations in this life that he may be a religious man in the next life and begin to prepare for Release.

A great Buddhist preacher, speaking in reference to the chances of being reborn as a man (not the question of attaining Nirvana but of being reborn as a man), pictured the vast ocean with a blind turtle and an ox-yoke floating aimlessly about in it, and he said that one has as much chance of being reborn as a man as that blind turtle has of diving and by chance putting his head through that ox-yoke. Could hopelessness become more hopeless?

What Can We Gather...

One is amazed at the persistence of the human heart as it knocks at the gate of heaven and receives so little response. But one is reverent, too, in the face of the Vast Persistence.

Again, and again in public meetings, I am asked if one cannot find God in some way other than through Jesus Christ. My reply is that we cannot settle the matter by an argument or by a statement. The only way to answer that question is to go out and find God in some other way and then come back and discuss the matter. The crowd invariably laughs. That laugh is the most revealing and startling thing I have ever heard. It means that the idea of immediately finding God does not seem to be practicable. It does not seem to be in the realm of the immediately realizable. I have often thought what I would reply if such a challenge were put to me. I think I could reply at once that I know where and how anyone, the wise or the ignorant, the worst or the best, can find God if he is willing to pay the price, and he can find him now.

But one more place of inquiry remains, and if clear light can be found anywhere, it will be found here: Gandhiji, the saint and patriot of India. This last year I stayed eight days with this great soul in his Ashram at Sabarmati. These wonderful eight days left deep impressions upon me: Here was simplicity yoked to national service and to the service of the poor; here was a deep voluntary sharing with the unprivileged, for cultured men wearing only a loin cloth, dug in fields, turned the charkha (spinning wheel), and, *mirabile dictu*, did scavengers' work, Brahmans among them. The three scavengers of the institution when I was there were a South India Brahman doctor, a German lady, and a Hindu pundit! Here was a national struggle going on on a stupendous scale—a struggle for inward and outward freedom, but there was no hate and no bitterness; a quiet friendliness pervaded all. The soul of it was Gandhiji, a charming noble character, who compels my respect and admiration. It was a Spartan regime. The rising bell

Christ at the Round Table

sounded at 3:45 when I, with the rest, would arise and go to prayers on the river bank, under the stars an hour before dawn. As I sat there listening to the droning of the prayers, the quaint, half-sad, but attractive music and the quiet voice of Gandhiji as he expounded the Gita, I could not help but be strangely moved, nor could I get rid of the thought that ran through my mind: In both ways, it is pre-dawn. I will tell you why that thought kept persisting.

I told Gandhiji about the Round Table Conferences we had been having throughout India and I suggested that we have one between us, with his sharing with me what religion was meaning to him in experience and I doing the same. He assented. I cannot tell of those great hours we spent together as we sat upon the floor in his little room. These things must remain unspoken. But two things I mention, permission to do so having been asked and granted. He said that there was a time when unjust criticism made him writhe within and caused resentment, but now, through religion, he was conquering it and was no longer resentful. This was a beautiful victory and one well worthwhile. Here was a real contribution to life through religion. Then we faced a deeper question: God. He said: "The more I empty myself the more I can discover God. The world is a well-ordered machine and we may discover God in obeying its laws, but no miracles are to be expected, and it may take ages." And then he quoted Shankara, who said: "He who would find God must have as much patience as the man who would sit on the ocean beach and take up a drop of water on a straw and put it aside and thus empty the ocean by carrying away one drop of water at a time." As I sat there and pondered Gandhiji's words, I remembered he had said that he had not found as yet, but when I glanced up and looked at his face, I knew that he was determined to continue his search though it took as much patience as Shankara had indicated, and though it might take ages of time in many births. And he would strive to empty himself to the utmost.

But as I walked slowly back to my little room off the weaving shed, those words came to me over and over, "No miracles are to be expected, and it may take ages." And they have haunted my mind ever since.

Is that the answer the best that the highest and noblest living and striving, apart from Christ, can give to the ultimate problems of God and redemption: There are no miracles, and it may take ages? If that is the final answer, then some of us will have to be left out of God and redemption, for we need both desperately *now*, and we know that if we are to be saved, a miracle must be performed.

Was Gandhiji right or did there echo through his words that Noble Despair so characteristic of life lived apart from the Way?

As I walked home that morning, something else welled up in my inmost being. I remembered that twenty-five years before, when I gave my bankrupt soul to Christ, a miracle was performed, and it did not take ages either. God has been the supreme reality in experience ever since.

I told Gandhiji of this the next day. Our eyes grew moist and our hearts warm and tender as we talked.

Chapter 4

CONVERSION—HORIZONTAL AND VERTICAL

IN OUR ROUND TABLES, those in fellowship with Christ spoke again and again of "conversion" having occurred in their lives. It was always spoken of with gratitude and usually with a sense of wonder. What did they mean?

The author of *Mirrors of Downing Street* (p. 112) finishes the characterization of Mr. Churchill in these words: "General Booth once told Mr. Churchill that he stood in need of conversion. That old man was a notable judge of character." But Winston Churchill is not alone in his need of conversion—it seems to belong to our human nature as such.

When Jesus says that "except ye be converted ... ye cannot enter into the kingdom of heaven," he is not laying down an arbitrary rule, but is putting his finger upon a necessity inherent in the facts of life. One of India's greatest statesmen frankly acknowledged this need when he said to me: "I am not religious, but I am not irreligious. Religion isn't real to me. I wish it were. I have often felt the need of it. There are ashes in my heart and it is cold. The fact is what I need is conversion for myself, or else I must warm my heart up against someone who has found it." In this great statesman, the "ought to be" was standing over against the "is" and he knew the passage from one to the other was by conversion.

There are five great kingdoms representing five stages of life. The lowest is the *mineral kingdom*, above that the *plant* or *vegetable kingdom*, the next is the *animal kingdom*, then the *kingdom of man*, and fifth and highest the *kingdom of God*. We stand between the kingdom of the animal on the one side and the kingdom of God on the other. The kingdom of the animal, although lighted up with gleams of altruism, stands for self-assertion—the weakest go to the wall and war sounds through it. 'The kingdom of heaven stands for self-sacrifice, the renewal and regeneration of the weak, and peace, harmony and brotherhood pervade it. We are in the stage between, and life seems to mingle both of these kingdoms. The selfish and the sacrificial struggle within us for mastery. We feel the pressure of this higher kingdom upon our souls, and it awakens us to higher aspirations. This pressure gives birth to religion. We feel our real life is in the higher, in the kingdom of God. So, we feel the need of a vertical conversion. Vertical conversion is that spiritual change wrought by Christ that lifts us from sin to goodness,

> **Vertical conversion is that spiritual change wrought by Christ that lifts us from sin to goodness, from discord to harmony, from selfishness to sacrifice, from ourselves to God, and gives us a new sphere of living, the Kingdom of God.**

from discord to harmony, from selfishness to sacrifice, from ourselves to God, and gives us a new sphere of living, the Kingdom of God.

Some are skeptical about such a change being possible. Among the Muslims is this proverb: "If thou hearest that a mountain has moved, believe it; but if thou hearest that a man has changed his character, do not believe it." Schopenhauer voices the same thing when he says that a leopard can change his nature sooner than a man may change his. And a Hindu said to me, "A man may change his acts, but not his character—this is fixed."

But there is nothing more fluid and unfixed than human nature. Water with temperature raised turns to vapor, lowered it turns to ice. But human nature is even more convertible. It is capable of almost anything. Vertical conversion is possible.

But conversion may be merely horizontal. It may be a mere change from one religion to another, leaving the person on the same level of character and life. It may involve no change of character. It is in this problem of horizontal conversions that most of our religious difficulties are found. Conversion in India has become a national problem. It has assumed such proportions that it is upsetting the whole national life. Since there is communal representation in the Reform Scheme, conversion is being used to swell communal numbers and so add to communal political power. The Hindus have organized their Shuddi Movement and the Muslims their Tabligh Movement for purposes of conversion from other communities. Numerous riots have taken place as a result of these activities. The Hindus of Aligarh raised ten thousand rupees to fight a court case over the conversion to Islam of a sweeper woman. None of them would come near her, for she is untouchable and she would not be allowed in the temple, but she must be saved to Hinduism. A Muslim came to a Christian friend and said, "I hear that funds are being cut off from your mission work, and that you must close a good deal of it. Why don't you come to us? We will contribute and help you rather than see this work closed, for if it is closed, many of the Christians will go back to Hinduism, and we Muslims don't want that." When force was not available because of police protection, Muslim maulvis have lain down on the doorstep of their co-religionists, so that they would have to walk on their prostrate bodies in order to go and be reconverted to Hinduism.

Conversion has sunk very low—to the merely horizontal. But Christianity is also not blameless. Many of our conversions have been and are horizontal conversions. Europe was largely converted on this level. Many historians have called attention to the fact that European conversions on a national scale were not infrequently matters of political or economic expediency, or both. European and consequently American Christians are "mass-movement Christians"—horizontally converted, but for the most part still in need of vertical conversion.

> But conversion may be merely horizontal. It may be a mere change from one religion to another, leaving the person on the same level of character and life. It may involve no change of character.

But in India, also many of our conversions have been and are of the same type. To the credit of missions let me say that, on the whole, they will not baptize unless there has been Christian teaching over a considerable course of time, and unless there is evidence of a changed life, so that conversions are usually on a far higher level than those mentioned above. Nevertheless, there has been too much of the merely horizontal, too much stress on statistics, and too much of the using of the rite of baptism for legal and communal purposes. The fact is that baptism has fallen very badly in India and needs to be redeemed to its New Testament position. Some of us have said very little about baptism in the last few years because we wonder if too much has not already been said about it. We have tried to throw the weight of emphasis over on the vertical, for the horizontal has far outrun it. In Paul's day, the question was acute as to whether circumcision was essential to being a Christian. Paul threw the emphasis upon the new creature: "Neither circumcision availeth anything nor uncircumcision, but a new creature." I am quite sure that if Paul were here today and found a rite being made the deciding factor as to whether a man is in the kingdom of God or out of it—he is in if baptized, he is out if he is not—he would again throw the emphasis upon the new creature and would again say that spiritual character, and not external rite, is basic in Christianity. For the simple fact remains that great numbers who do undergo the rite are not in the kingdom of God—their whole lives show that. The conversion is very horizontal indeed.

Some of the most spiritual bodies of Christians in the world, as the Friends (Quakers) and the Salvation Army, have reacted to this and have eschewed external rites entirely in order to witness to the spiritual character of the gospel. We can sympathize with their underlying feeling, while not being able to agree with their position, for we believe in Christian baptism. But there is no doubt that it needs to be lifted to higher levels and restored to the New Testament position. Horizontal conversion should not take place, unless it involves a vertical conversion. I agree with Mr. Natarajan when he says, "The more we think of it, the less do we believe in religious conversions which are brought about by any consideration except that of being brought nearer to God."

Only that which is happening inwardly should happen outwardly. "Why do you put labels on people?" asked a Hindu in an audience.

I replied, "I do not put labels on anyone. I ask each man to put his own label on. If he is inwardly a Hindu, let him put his Hindu label on. If he is inwardly Christ's, let him put his Christian label on. Let him be inwardly and outwardly the same."

A label corresponding to what is on the inside of a package is a good thing, but proclaiming what is not there is worse than useless; it is an evil. A Christian rite, not proclaiming an inner Christian fact, is un-Christian. But proclaiming it is one of the most beautiful of things.

Who, then, is a Christian? Luther says that a man never is a Christian; he is only becoming one. Another says that "a man is a Christian who is responding to all the meanings he finds in Christ." A Christian is one who, through faith in and fellowship with Christ, is becoming Christ-like in character. He represents nothing less than the emergence of a new species of being. He is as different from the ordinary man as the ordinary man is different from the animal. He is a new creature, for old things have passed away and all things have become new.

Jesus says, "Except ye be converted [a new direction] and become as little children [a new spirit], ye cannot enter into the kingdom of heaven [a new sphere of living]." Here is a man, then, with a new direction, a new temper of spirit, and a new sphere in which to live.

This vertical conversion may mean different things to different people: It may mean a saving from sin, the slaying of the beast within a man, the gathering together of discordant forces of the soul into harmony, the cleansing of a stained conscience, the calm of conviction to an unquiet mind, the opening to more abundant life, or the inner sense of fellowship with Christ. Conversion need not be cataclysmic to be real. There are those who cannot point to the definite moment of decision, for they have grown up under such fine Christian influences that they have never known the time when they did not belong to Christ. They have opened to Christ as a flower to the sun. While they cannot tell the exact time of conversion, nevertheless they witness to the fact of it. While this is true of many, nevertheless, most of us, having wandered away, need a definite break in the return. In all these, the phenomena change, but the underlying facts are the same: new life, Christ, God.

It is impossible to describe—one must know. Paul tries to describe it again and again, but as Glover says, "The Holy Spirit disorganizes his grammar." Words break down under new weight of meaning, so he has to coin others—a new man, a new creation!

It is this stepping forth of a new man—a son of God—from ordinary dull and defeated human nature that is the astonishing thing that comes with the impact of Christ upon life. It is as much a miracle as the calling forth of Lazarus from the dead. Dean Church speaks of the joy and exultation that throbs through early Christian literature as one of the most solemn things in history.

In his book entitled, *Conversion, Christian and Non-Christian*, Alfred C. Underwood says that the future of religion lies between Hinduism and Christianity, for these are the two religions where conversions seem to occur. I wish I could be as sure that conversion was taking place in Hinduism as the literature he examines would imply. In the Round Table Conferences, we did find men coming to a kind of conversion through the Non-Cooperation Movement with its demand for self-sacrifice and simplicity. But within Hinduism itself, that joyous note of finding conversion seemed to be absent. Men seemed to be depending on indefinitely long periods of time to do something for them. Immediate expectation of conversion was certainly not there. "Our religion is not living, or conversions would occur among us," said a prominent Hindu. W. E. S. Holland tells of a Christian student who was given to secret immorality. He was introduced to a missionary and, in a few months, came back transformed. Several months later, there was a Hindu student in the same immoral condition. There was no use to talk to him about Christ, for he was uninterested. So Holland went to the best Hindu he knew, the head of a reforming sect, and told him of the two cases.

"Now tell me," he said, "of a Hindu saint or teacher to whom I can take this lad: a Hindu home, or institution, or influence where there is good hope of his being reformed. I want him saved this week." He shook his head.

"What," said Holland, "can Hinduism do nothing for the case?"

"No," he said, sadly.

"Then what am I to do?" asked Holland.

And the reply came: "Can you not take him to your chapel, pray with him, read the Bible to him, lend him the lives of the Christian saints?"

Here was bankruptcy confessed.

Again, and again, in the Round Tables when some young man was asked to speak, the remark would be dropped by someone, "Oh, he's too young to know anything about religion," or "He is inexperienced, so he does not know." Religion seemed an old man's business and time was the great factor. There was not an expectation of immediate revelation of divine grace in giving immediate conversion. When I heard such remarks, I could not help thinking of a letter I have in my possession from a Chinese girl, daughter of wealthy Confucian parents. She was converted in one of my meetings, but she was not allowed by her parents to be baptized. Shortly after her conversion, her father lost all his money and from being a millionaire was reduced to absolutely nothing. At the darkest moment, a multimillionaire Chinese gentleman came into the room of the despairing man and placed on the table a check for a million dollars. He told the father that it was his if he could have his daughter as a secondary wife, a thing perfectly proper according to Chinese social etiquette. The father looked at the daughter. What would her answer be? It was a great strain to put on the conscience of this girl so newly a Christian, but it did not take her a moment to decide.

How could she do this and be Christ's? The daughter walked out and left the man with his check. Her allegiance to Christ had cost a million dollars. But as I read her letter written shortly after this event, I felt that the price was cheap, for she had found the pearl of great price, life's secret and meaning. This is what she says:

> In your first talk to us about the Christ spirit and the Cain spirit, you brought home to us so clearly the difference between the two that it was the first time I ever realized that I had the Cain spirit in me, so when I knew that there was a choice for me, I chose to have the Christ spirit. Therefore, at the close of the meeting, I fully surrendered to the Lord Jesus and was never sorry for it afterward. So, then I turned over a new leaf and took my stand as a Christian. When I went home, I did not tell my people about it, for they were all non-Christians. I was so afraid that they would know it, but thank God we cannot hide true Christianity, for it tells in our very lives. So very soon my parents found out I had taken my stand as a Christian. Then began my persecutions from big and small, from old and young, among my own people, but God gave me his grace to face out all these squarely. There I lived Christ in my home for more than two years without being baptized, but on the third anniversary of my surrender to Christ, I was baptized.

Conversion ...

No words can express what Christ means to me now. You know it and all true Christians, too. I am the only daughter and, being a spoiled child, I was never satisfied with what I had, no matter what it might be; but now I am satisfied in Christ and Christ alone. Of course, we all have our temptations to meet, and our earthly troubles and burdens to bear, but we can carry our cross with a smile, which the world knows not how to do.

But this is not all. I know I am saved, but my heart can never be at rest without winning my people to Christ, for Christianity must be able to stand the test of the home life. I have touched a few lives and they have taken their stand as Christians in the same way as I did. I have not been able to win my people to Christ yet, but I can tell you that down right in some of their hearts they are Christians; only it takes time to throw off the old inherited religion and conservative customs and practices. Gradually, I can see that they are yielding to the influence of Christian living...

> **When the church loses its power to convert, it loses its right to be called a church.**

As I read this letter which breathed not a word about her sacrifice—I heard that from others—I was seated in the General Conference of the Methodist Episcopal Church, surrounded by a thousand picked churchmen from all over the world with the bishops upon the platform. As I brushed away the tear of joy from my eye and looked up at the bishops, I found myself saying: "This Chinese girl, just out of Confucianism, knows as much about real religion and the meaning of life as any of us, including these bishops. Conversion has revealed it to her. Conversion is a fact."

This is the vital fact that the church must bring or fail. When the church loses its power to convert, it loses its right to be called a church. Unless it is making bad men into good men, weak men into strong men, uncertain men into certain, selfish men into unselfish, and men lacking the God-consciousness into men radiantly realizing God, it is failing as a church of the living Christ. And nothing can take the place of this fact of conversion.

Through psychoanalysis, you may come into the kingdom of the somewhat relieved mind; through social emphases, you may come into the kingdom of a better and more just social organization; through education, you may come into the kingdom of interesting facts; through systems of mental suggestion, you may come into the kingdom of improved health; through self-culture, you may come into the kingdom of refinement, but if you come into the kingdom of God, you must be converted. When Jesus, Son of Fact, uses the word "except" in connection with conversion, then there is no exception to that "except." The church will never sophisticate itself away from this need of conversion. For the strong man of affairs knows that, after all, these are only "affairs" with which he deals. He knows that they do not touch the inmost need of his heart overlaid with ashes. He needs conversion as deeply as "the down and out." For "Conversion," according to Paul Sabatier, "is a creative and inaugural experience," loosing untold possibilities in human personality and inaugurating life into adjusted and spiritually authoritative living. It brings to life "a solid happiness." "You have found God. By your energy and happiness, you show it," said a Hindu to a Christian at the close of a Round Table. He had, for conversion is that "inward happy crisis by which human life is transformed and an issue opened up toward the ideal life."

Through it, men find power to live by, for it is not so much a doctrine as a dynamic. Sin, worry and defeat drop off from the life like the clinging dead leaves of the tree before the rising sap. According to

Saunders, "It is the birth of a new dominant affection by which the God-consciousness, hitherto marginal and vague, becomes focal and dynamic."[1] God upon the margin! Something else at the center—self. God vague! Just real enough to disturb the life, now and then, flashing into it like a lightning flash that leaves things darker than before. But the living Christ brings conversion: God comes in from the margin to the center; he becomes focal and he becomes dynamic. Things that were impossible now become the normal. God becomes the Light by which we see, the Joy of our joy, the Peace of our peace, the Love of our love, and the very Life by which we live.

And moreover, it is "an irreducible fact of experience." You cannot reduce it into "mob contagion," for some of us found it in the quiet; nor into nervous overstrain, for it acted like balm upon the soul; nor into "adolescent phenomena," for some, like Cabot, can say, "I was a rationalist until I was fifty, and have been a mystic since;" nor into "an uprush from the unconscious," for the source seems to be the divine, it has the feel of the heavenly upon it; nor into "an emotional spasm," for it gives a clear eye and a world view; nor into "suggestion," for other suggestions would kill it. The more it is suggested against the more it shines. "I'll knock that out of you in two weeks," announced my companion in the law library when I told him I had been converted. At the end of two weeks, he had turned to the defensive because he had inwardly collapsed. No, it cannot be reduced to outside factors, for "it is an original and unborrowed experience." It is a new birth to life, to Life Itself.

In his talk with Nicodemus as they sat upon the roof under the stars and the patriot asked about the coming of the Kingdom that would free his country from its yoke, Jesus lays his hand upon the heart

---

[1] K. J. Saunders, *Adventures of the Christian Soul* (Cambridge University Press, 1916), p. 61.

as the means to all freedom of every kind. "Except a man be born from above, he cannot see the kingdom of God." Startling figure (alas!) grown commonplace, but to think of it: a man when he is "old" in hope and moral vigor, can have a new birth within this birth, a new life within this life. It is the gospel of a second chance. It makes irrelevant the necessity of the round of rebirths to which the Hindu and the Buddhist look to find deliverance, for the cure for rebirth is new birth. Here we are lifted above birth and death and have eternal life now in the midst of time.

> **I feel deeply about this matter of horizontal and vertical conversions, for I have known both—the moral and spiritual disaster of the one and the wondrous renewal of the other.**

I feel deeply about this matter of horizontal and vertical conversions, for I have known both—the moral and spiritual disaster of the one and the wondrous renewal of the other. The first happened this way: When a youth I heard that a minister from England was to preach in the church I attended. My curiosity was aroused, for I heard that he pronounced English very strangely (you see it works both ways), so I went to hear him. But as I sat in the gallery listening, I soon forgot all about his pronunciation, for his words were falling like a trip hammer upon my heart. I was never so shaken before. I felt the foundations give way from under my life. I knew I was all wrong. And when he pointed his finger toward the gallery and said, "Young men, Jesus says, 'He that is not with me is against me,'" it was the finishing blow, for I knew I was not with Christ—my whole life proved that. But I hated desperately to feel that I was against Him, for amid my wildness, I still held an inward reverence for Him. But I was against Him: that thought made me ready for any suggestion that offered a way out of my misery, so when we were asked to come forward and kneel at the place of prayer, I did so. I felt very miserable, but I did not know what to do, nor did those in charge tell me. They dealt with us en masse: no personal word, no telling me how to take Christ as my Savior. At the close, the leader said that if it was alright with us, we should stand. I supposed it was alright and stood. They asked me to join the church which I consented to do. The next morning, my mother came into my room before I was out of bed and kissed me to show how glad she was that her son was converted. But I was not. I felt religious for a few weeks and then it simply faded out and I was back exactly where I was before, the sum total of the result being that my name was upon the church record. The springs of my character were uncleansed, no old habits were broken up, no new center of life formed. Religion had simply skimmed the surface, leaving the depths untouched. I was horizontally converted.

For two years this went on. I prayed sometimes, but was half afraid that God would answer my prayers, for I was not ready to commit myself to goodness, to God. At the end of that time, I heard another man who awakened a desire to find what I did not find before. It was fanned into a flame. I sought. For hours, they prayed with and for me, but it was all dark. This time, I would not be put off with the repetition of catch words and phrases. I wanted Christ. I wanted this sense of inward burden and guilt taken away, but I seemed to speak to "the Dumb Silences." The third night of this crisis, just before going to church, I went aside in my room, knelt and said: "Oh, Christ save me tonight. Here I am. Take me." It was a dim prayer, but profoundly meant. The tiniest ray of light stole down into the darkness within. I leaped to my feet. Hope had come! On my way to the church, I found myself running: if I could only get to the church, He would meet me! I think I understand now why these weary pilgrims eagerly press on and on up into these sacred places in these Himalaya Mountains: "the ripple in the mind" makes them hope to meet Him there. I, too, "with the ripple in the mind" was a pilgrim running that mile to the church, fleeing from what I was, to what I wanted to be. In my eagerness, I went straight to the front seat—a thing I had never done before—and yearned for the minister to stop speaking so I could seek and find. I was sure I would. As I look back, I see that Christ had met me in my room and that ray of light was the silken cord that bound my heart forever to him. I had been taught, though, that the public place of prayer was the method and I felt I must fulfill this if I were to meet him. And I did! I had scarcely bent my knees when my whole heart was flooded with a sense of the healing Christ, of peace, of release, of life. All barriers were gone. I knew him! I walked out into a new universe. The next day when I came out and looked upon the world, I had never seen such sunshine, or such greenness in trees. With my heart bursting with joy, I went up to an old companion, slapped him on the back and said, "My, this is a d** fine day!", using the old vocabulary to express my newly found joy. Of course, that langauage dropped away like everything else belonging to the old. There was no effort. It was all gone.

Too much emotion? No, nothing short of this could have broken up my old habits and swept me out of what I was to a new center of life. The emotion is not the important thing—the new center is. If one can get to that new center more quietly and on "dry faith," it does not matter, provided he gets there.

My first public statement about my conversion experience was this: "There is only one thing better than religion and that is more religion, and I want more." At the heart of my satisfaction was a dissatisfaction. It has been there ever since. This first public statement has become a kind of life motto.

Conversion ...

I find my spiritual life getting on by a series of crises, each lifting life to a higher level, and each the precursor of larger demands on me. In a few months after my conversion, I found my hunger for more so intensified that it burst into a flame as I read a book that told of the full, victorious life. Here was what I wanted: a life inwardly cleansed of secret mind sin and outwardly victorious and full. As I was eagerly reading the book, a Voice seemed to say, "Now is the time to find." I protested that I did not know what I wanted, that the book was telling me and that I would read on. But the Voice persisted. At last I saw that I was in a controversy, closed the book, dropped on my knees and said, "Now what must I do, Lord?" And the Voice replied, "Will you give me your all?" I answered without hesitation, "Why, yes, Lord." Then the Voice very softly said, "Then take my all." I did! I arose from that hour with a sense of inward refining and of the fullness of the Divine that I never knew before. The deeper surrender had brought a deeper adjustment to Christ's mind and purpose and had opened to me deeper Resources.

> "There is only one thing better than religion and that is more religion, and I want more." At the heart of my satisfaction was a dissatisfaction.

But this deeper experience did not end in itself. It was immediately followed by the conviction that the study of law was to be dropped and that the ministry was to be my life-work. I gladly assented. There was no struggle—none for me, but my mother's first exclamation was, "What, a poor Methodist preacher?" She was willing for me to be converted, but not too far!

I went to college to study. While I was there, I met another crisis—one concerning which I seemed to have nothing to do with and which seemed to me to be sovereignly thrust on me. I could not understand it then, but I do now. One night I was in a student's room in a prayer meeting. I was asking nothing for myself; in fact, I was nearly asleep when suddenly I was spiritually swept off my feet. I did not sleep the rest of the night. I paced the floor, my heart too full of joy to sleep.

I wondered what it meant: I had asked for nothing, and nothing was asked of me—it was just given. But again, the experience did not stop with itself, for soon the Voice was quietly saying, "I want you across the seas—will you go?" I assented at once; there was no struggle, none for me—but for mother? The call to the ministry was a hard blow to her, but this news that I would go to the heart of Africa crushed her. I saw by her letters that she was pining away and I received the dreaded telegram from my doctor brother: "Come home, mother dying." I sat in the train to go on the long journey and the Accuser seemed to sit beside me: "Now, this is your call to the mission field—you've killed your mother." Then my struggle began: Would I bend to her will? If so, she would live. Would I go on with the fulfillment of what seemed God's will for me? If so, she would die. I loved her more than I loved life, and yet I seemed to be killing her.

She was just alive when I arrived, had been twice reported dead, so low had she sunk. What was the matter? My brother said he did not know—she was just refusing to live and was dying. But I knew. I also knew which way I should have to take whether mother died or lived. It was the hardest thing I ever told God, but I told him. When I made the decision to follow at any cost, to the amazement of everyone, God raised up my mother. Not only brought her back to physical life, but brought her into a new spiritual life and outlook. Instead of trying to keep me back, she was proud to send me. The next few years of her life were so radiant that when she did die, it was not death. "Do not put a crepe upon the door, put a bunch of white flowers instead; and do not lay me out in black, dress me in white, for it will be my coronation day—the happiest day of my life, for I shall be with Him," she said before she slipped away.

Christ had not failed me. He never has. The failures have all been mine. I came on to India and after eight years was in broken health. I have written elsewhere how Christ became health and life to me. But this Touch, too, did not end in itself, for immediately afterward Christ opened the door of evangelism among the educated classes of India and bade me enter. Each crisis has led to a further call. The last one came just before the Round Tables began when he asked for a deeper surrender, saying, "If you will make the surrender, I will walk with you through Asia." And he has done it. I have stumblingly tried to keep up with him. There will be many more crises to come, each leading to a higher conversion and call. Life with Christ is a beautiful adventure. "It doesn't take much of a man to be a Christian, but it takes all there is of him." But then, we get all there is of Him.

Chapter 5

THE COLLECTIVE REDEMPTION

IN THE CONFERENCES we did not often hear the note of hope and faith regarding human society and its ability for redemption, but when we did hear it this note was always struck by those who followed Christ. Others did not seem to strike it.

Jesus believed in life and in its redemption. Not only was the soul to be saved—the whole of life was to be redeemed. The kingdom of God coming on earth is the expression of that collective redemption. The entrance into the kingdom of God is by personal conversion, but the nature of that kingdom is social.

The kingdom of God is the most astoundingly radical proposal ever presented to the human race. It means nothing less than the replacing of the present world-order by the kingdom of God. It is the endeavor to call men back from the present unnatural, unworkable world-order to a new one based on new principles, embodying a new spirit and led by a new Person.

As Jesus announces this new kingdom, we find some things begin to rise into prominence as essential elements. God is our Father, and trust in him with its rest and poise is to replace the present order based

The Collective Redemption

on self-centeredness with its worry and inward frictions. Men are brothers, and the brotherhood of our common humanity is to replace the present order based on race, color, money, and class distinctions. Human personality is of infinite value, and this conception is to replace the present order based on the exploitation of others. Service is the only sign of any way to greatness, and is to replace the present order based on conceptions of power through command of the service of others. Self-renunciation is the way to self-realization and must replace the present order based on self-assertion. The cross is its manifestation and symbol. Love is to be the working force of the new kingdom and is to replace the present dependence upon force. The seat of this new kingdom is in the heart—the kingdom of heaven is within you—and it works from this center to every human relation. This is to replace that in the present order which organizes life in things outside of the man.

> **Jesus believed in life and in its redemption. Not only was the soul to be saved—the whole of life was to be redeemed. The kingdom of God coming on earth is the expression of that collective redemption.**

These are some of the things that stand out and grip our attention and our hearts. But while these are sufficiently astounding taken by themselves, they become more so when determined by Jesus. He puts content into them by what he was and did. In one place Jesus identifies the Kingdom and self-sacrificial, heroic moral action. He that puts his hand to the plow and looks back cannot fit into (literally) the kingdom of God (Luke 9:62); in another place, he identifies the Kingdom and truth as one (John 18:36, 37), and then identifies it with life (Mark 7:43, 47— "enter into life" and "enter into the kingdom of God" are used synonymously). The kingdom of God, then, is right, sacrificial Action, Truth, and Life, or in other words, Ethics, Philosophy and Religion. It is summed up in Jesus who is the Way (action, ethics), the Truth (truth, philosophy), the Life (life, religion). The kingdom of God cannot be understood apart from Jesus who is its illustration and meaning. Life, lived in all its relationships according to Jesus, is the realization of the kingdom of God. It is the final spiritual and social order.

When Harnack was asked by a group of us what was the Christian solution to a certain question, he said: "Christianity provides no solutions—it provides a goal and power to move on toward that goal." The goal is nothing less than the realization of the kingdom of God on earth. And Christ provides not only the goal, but the dynamic to move on toward that goal.

All other programs for human living, except the kingdom of God, are misfits. All endeavors to live in any other way are an attempt to live against life. They break themselves upon this final order. They carry within themselves the seeds of their own dissolution. A group of heroic thinking Christians expresses it in these words: "The Fellowship sees in the characteristic methods of the present social order a contradiction to the law of the universe which is the spirit of Jesus, and summons men to create in place of this decaying society one which expresses the brotherhood of all men" (*Reconciliation*, Jan. 1927). While the kingdom of God expresses the brotherhood of man, it is wider and more thoroughgoing, for it means nothing less than building the mind of Christ into human society—replacing the mind of this age with the mind of Christ.

How the Kingdom will come, I do not know. It may be through the steady conquest of the mind of this age by the mind of Christ; it may

The Collective Redemption

be apocalyptic; it may be, as Alfred George Hogg thinks, through a combination of both—gradual victory until the line between that heavenly kingdom, waiting to descend on us and this kingdom approaching it from this side, gets so thin that the kingdom from above bursts upon us in victorious completion.

We do not realize how radical this conception of the Kingdom is until we contrast the outlook of the other faiths in regard to the redemption of human society and the making of a new world. There seemed to be no note of this from other faiths in our Round Table Conferences. Where it did come in it was an importation from Christian sources. It did not come up out of the heart of the non-Christian faiths. Redemption seemed to be individual release. I know of no program in the non-Christian faiths corresponding to the kingdom of God. The influence of religion is not toward a new world, but an escape from this one. Hinduism teaches that "there is no escape from the grinding out of an age (Kalpa) doomed to steady deterioration till the final crash and the abyss. It is futile to seek to alter or improve." The dead hand of hopelessness about the present world is on everything. It is this that lies at the root of the stagnation that has been on things. If India is awake today and is progressing, it is because she has become less under the dominance of hopeless ideas about the world and is more and more coming under the dominance of other ideas, namely, Christian ideas, which embody the conception of the kingdom of God.

Because it believes in the identification of existence and suffering, Buddhism says, "Whatever is, is wrong." Because it believes that present conditions of all life are the result of past Karma, Hinduism says, "Whatever is, is right." Because it believes in life and its ability for redemption, the Gospel says, "Whatever is can be made right." In one of my meetings, a Hindu asked this question: "Why do you cure a man suffering from disease? We should let his fever run its course, otherwise we are interfering with the law of Karma." It is seldom put so baldly as that, but that this underlying attitude is there no one can seriously question. The inequalities of life are explained on the basis of previous Karma. If one is born blind, it is because of wickedness in a previous birth. The disciples facing some of the same questions that have been occupying the mind of India for ages asked Jesus, "Who did sin, this man or his parents, that he should be born blind?" And Jesus gave the puzzling answer that his blindness came "that the works of God should be made manifest." We are just now beginning to see the meaning of his answer—the laws of heredity, with the possibility of passing on blindness to others through the operation of these laws, or "works" of God, are now being made manifest. We are now discovering why blindness comes—syphilis and smallpox account for a good deal. We do not need to go back to a previous birth; we can lay our finger here and now upon the laws that operate and bring it. Previous to the discovery of these laws, men said sickness and death were either the will of God or the result of the law of Karma. But since the discovery by medical science of these "works of God," the length of life has changed amazingly. In Europe, the average length of life in the sixteenth century was twenty years, by 1850 it had gone to forty, by 1870 to forty-five, and now the average is fifty-eight years. In India, the average length is about twenty-three. Has India, therefore, been the most wicked in a previous birth? I cannot believe it. India holds the previous-birth theory and says that whatever is, is the result of that, and therefore, right. It has been the most costly idea that ever settled on the soul of a great people. Religion explains physical evils and leaves them as they were, for the endeavor is to get out of it all through Moksha [salvation].

Gandhiji, seeing the need of some program in religion for the renewal of human society, began to talk a short time ago of the coming of "Rama rajiya" [the kingdom of Rama]. I asked a follower of

Gandhiji what he meant by it and what content it held, and he replied, "I asked Gandhiji the same question and he replied, 'It will never be realized, so what is the use of talking about it?'" The idea seems to have been stillborn. There wasn't enough soul in it to keep it alive.

No, the non-Christian faiths do not seem to have any program corresponding to the kingdom of God on earth. But if they haven't it, on the other hand, the followers of Christ have been painfully slow to realize the implication of this program of Jesus. As soon as we took hold of the gospel we began to render it innocuous. It demanded a new creature and a new world. And the very heart of the kingdom of God was a losing of oneself in order to find a larger self.

> As soon as we took hold of the gospel we began to render it innocuous. It demanded a new creature and a new world.

In many ways, we are not unlike the Brahman who attended an evangelistic meeting where the Christians were glowingly telling how Christ had saved them. He felt he could stop it, so he got up and said: "You people say you are saved. So am I. As Christ has saved you, so Krishna has saved me." The missionary in charge of the meeting was wise, so he said: "I am very glad to hear that you are saved—very glad indeed. Now we are going down to the outcaste quarters and are going to see what we can do for these poor people. We will sit on their beds and in their houses and will share their lives to help them. Will you join us?" The Brahman thought a moment and then said, "Well, sahib, I am saved, but I am not saved that far." Some of our Christianity, like the Brahman, is individually saved as far as the mind of Christ. It goes only part way. It is not socially applicable.

We have shifted the kingdom of God to another sphere—to heaven where it will be innocuous as far as this world and its present order are concerned. The Pharisees sat at the table with Jesus. He watched them choose out the chief seats and he astounded them when he gave a call to these religious leaders to forget about chief seats, to step down from religious pedestals, to cease giving complimentary dinners that could be returned, but to throw themselves into the service of the poor and to lose themselves. This was Jesus' great call to the Pharisees to throw in their lot with the Kingdom by self-renunciation for the sake of others. There was a tense moment as the reality of his words fell upon their hearts. They were meeting the supreme call. There was an embarrassing silence. A polite gentleman who hated these upsetting things at dinner parties tried to smooth things over by the pious interjection: "Blessed is he that shall eat bread in the kingdom of God." He met the challenge with this commonplace. The call to share bread now was met with the explanation of what joy it will be to eat bread in the kingdom hereafter. This gentleman is with us still! He takes the edge off Christ's challenge, he explains away its rugged meanings, and he tones it down to suit things as they are. He is the greatest danger that the gospel has today.

In order to support a state that may be graft-ridden and animated by greed in its foreign policies, he unctuously says: "But did not Jesus put his stamp of approval upon Caesar and command our support of the state, no matter what its character may be, when he said, 'Render to Caesar the things that are Caesar's'?" No, for Jesus never said that. What he did say was, "Render to Caesar the things that are Caesar's, and to God the things that are God's." This passage is one of the most quietly revolutionary things ever uttered. Alongside of the principle of rendering to Caesar the things that are Caesar's, he put the principle of rendering to God the things that are God's, and then he went on to enlarge the things that belonged to God, until in his teaching of the kingdom of God he says that all life belongs to God. As he enlarged

The Collective Redemption

this side of it, soon there was no standing room for Caesar. And Caesars have been going ever since. All Caesarism that will not fit in with the kingdom of God is doomed.

But we do not believe that Jesus' way is workable. If we believed that, nothing would be impossible. The real skepticism is just here. A British prime minister recently said that the state could not be run on the principle of the Sermon on the Mount. The Christian Church took the statement very quietly, but one who styled himself a "hardened old agnostic" replied, "One would have thought that after two thousand years of Christianity such a statement from such a quarter would have raised such a storm that would have made it impossible for the speaker ever to represent this nation again, but not a voice was raised. How different would have been the indignation of the church had the premier threatened to deduct one half of one per cent from their stipends! While differing from the standpoint of the ordinary Christian, I feel that what the prime minister ought to have said would be that a state can only be run on the lines of the Sermon on the Mount." (Quoted in, *Christian Revolution*, Hodgkin, p. 38.)

The "hardened old agnostic" was right, for everything else is doomed to fail. The present creaking machinery of industry and social organization and political life comes out of the fact that life can only be run along the lines of Jesus and the present society is organized on other lines, hence, it creaks and groans and breaks down. It is an attempt to live unnaturally, to live against life. At first sight, it seems the other way around—the Kingdom seems impossible and the world way the reasonable and workable way. Jesus, knowing that men would feel that his way is impossible, says, "I send you as lambs in the midst of wolves." It looks as though the principles of Jesus have about as much chance of success as lambs have of getting through a pack of wolves. What can humility do in a world where it is considered weakness? What chance of success has a business man if he should take the way of the Sermon on the Mount? Would not his competitors tear him to pieces, as wolves do a lamb, if he attempted it? And a nation that built its collective life upon the principle of love and of turning the other cheek—would not other nations make short shrift of it? They would be lambs in the midst of wolves. So, it seems, but when John saw the final end of things in the Apocalypse, the Lamb was on the throne!

> "Why didn't Jesus strike back when he was struck on the cheek at the Judgment Hall? ... if he had done so, I would not be talking about him tonight. He turned the other cheek and where did the blow fall? On your heart and mine.

"Why didn't Jesus strike back when he was struck on the cheek at the Judgment Hall? Didn't he have a legal right to do so?" asked a Hindu one day. I replied that I supposed that he did have, but if he had done so, I would not be talking about him tonight. He turned the other cheek and where did the blow fall? On your heart and mine. This is power. The Lamb is on the throne. Everything else is weakness. This way is power.

Jesus said that the greatest among you shall be the servant of all. Hitherto, those were greatest who had the greatest number of servants, but now that man is greatest who serves the greatest number. Those who will not serve will be pushed to the wall. I went through thirteen empty palaces in Europe last year. Why were they empty? Those who had occupied them wanted to be served; they would not serve, so they broke themselves upon this law.

The Collective Redemption

Two classes are losing themselves in India today —their place is slipping: the holy men and the Brahmans. Mrs. Sinclair Stevenson, in *The Rites of the Twice-Born*, tells this story:

> The terrible experiences through which many parts of India passed in the autumn of 1918, scourged by famine, plague, and pneumonic influenza, gave to ascetics of every type, and school their opportunity of proving their value to the commonwealth. They had a debt to repay, for they had been supported by the alms of the people; they had passed beyond all fear of death, and had severed every tie which might have made it difficult or undutiful for them to hazard their lives.
>
> One night the present writer happened to be in an outcaste quarter of a town, where the people were dying in terrible numbers. Some of them drew her attention to an unknown stranger, whose friends, seeing that he was stricken with disease, and fearing infection, had got out at the station hard by and deposited the dying man on the veranda of an empty house; then, abandoning him there, they had themselves slipped away unseen in the darkness. The pitiful derelict was literally rotting in his own filth; it was impossible to get food or medicine between his clenched teeth, nor could men be found strong enough to carry him to a hospital.
>
> On a bridge above, two sturdy, powerful ascetics were sitting, intoning sacred verses in the quiet starlight. The writer asked them who they were. "We are holy men," they replied. So, she suggested that they should leave off hymn-singing for a little, and come and help her carry the unknown sufferer to the hospital. Never will she forget the astonishment and blazing anger with which they enunciated the foundation truth of the Way of Asceticism, that Road to which the Path

of Works and the Path of Devotion ultimately led. "We!" they cried. "We are holy men [Sannyasi]; we never do anything for anyone else."

They do not serve and, as a consequence, they are falling in estimation. Only those sadhus who have caught the spirit of the new day in India and are serving are holding the hearts of the people. The same thing can be said of the Brahmans. Many Brahmans are truly serving. They have stepped down from Brahmanical privileges to the people. One section has called themselves "Tiyagi Brahmans," those who have "renounced" Brahman privileges. They are leading by renouncing. But those who stand upon Brahmanical privileges are becoming ridiculous in public thought. In Travancore, (in the Kerala region of India) the Brahman still holds to distance pollution. A procession of low-caste Christians was going along the road when they met a Brahman at a place where there was water on both sides of the road. The low-caste people formerly would have gone off the road to let the Brahman pass by, but not now. They had the road. The Brahman could not retreat, so the only thing left was to get out into the water. There he stood up to his neck in the water shaking with anger, but his rage was impotent, for the low caste persons had the road. That picture of the Brahman up to his neck in water shaking with rage is the picture of all Brahmanism of every country and type and kind. If it will not serve, it may rave, but it will be ridiculous.

Employers must step down from Brahmanhood to brotherhood or else fail. A frank employer said to me: "We are willing to do anything for the laboring man—anything except to get off his back." It reminded me of a scene on the banks of the Jumna at Muttra, a holy city. The worshipers come down to the river and throw grain on the banks for the monkeys and into the water for the turtles. The broad backs of the huge turtles come up out of the shallow water as they pick up the grain from the bottom. The monkeys are clever. They pick up their share from the bank, stuff it into the pouches of their cheeks, and when the bank is cleaned up they leap onto the backs of the turtles and reach down into the water to get the grain intended for the turtles. Clever? Very. But the Nemesis comes. The patience of the patient turtles sometimes gives out and they grab a grasping arm and when turtles once take hold they do not know how to let go. And sometimes the patience of the patient people gives out, for when the monkeys become too much of a nuisance they are caught through their greed in huge crates and then shipped off to mountain jungles where they are no longer sacredly fed, but must find their own food.

It is a parable and the meaning is plain: Everyone who stands on the back of another, everyone who will not serve and will not share, will sooner or later find himself in jungles of difficulties. Whoever shows the jungle spirit to the jungle will go. Many white men in the East are worried at the present time— things are not going the way they used to, and the way they would like them to continue. Their anxiety is being caused by the beginning of the operation of this law of the Kingdom. They have been exploiting weaker peoples, have commanded service instead of giving it, and now jungles of isolation and suspicion seem to surround them.

Nor will it compensate to preach fine doctrine and to give forth fine sentiment—we must share or fail. An Indian evangelist told me that he and his colleague started on an evangelistic tour through the country districts. They hired a Hindu coolie to carry their luggage. They overloaded him. They were feeling rather conscience-stricken, so they began to preach the Gospel to him. The coolie listened patiently for some time and then he suddenly stopped, threw down the load and said, "You pile such a load as that on me and then you preach such things to me!" The evangelist and his colleague knew the coolie was right, divided up the burden among them, and then as they walked along sharing common burdens, they could share a gospel for the heavy laden.

Self-renunciation, in order to reach self-realization, is the deepest law of the Kingdom. When Jesus said, "He that findeth his life shall lose it, and he that loseth his life shall find it," he put his finger upon the greatest thing in our moral and spiritual universe. It does not become arbitrarily true because Jesus said it, but he said it because it was true. And this is true for God and man. Jesus announced the same principle in the words, "Strait is the gate and narrow is the way that leadeth to life"—if you want to find life, not heaven but life here and now, you must find it through a narrow gate of self-renunciation. This is true in every realm of life. The athlete, who puts himself under a stricter and stricter regime of training, denies himself what others feel free to indulge in, finds physical life and freedom, for he enters by a narrow door. The student who burns the midnight oil, gathers up spare moments, and denies himself many things finds himself free at last, at home with the ages—he has found intellectual life by a narrow door. The musician who goes through years of self-denying practice, setting up higher and higher standards, is at last free and at home in the land of harmony and can make us feel the depths of classical music, or make us sit pensively by the seaside, or hear the roar of the storm. He has found this freedom by a narrow door into musical life. But if I should say, "I do not believe in all these laws of harmony; I believe in being free, and I shall strike any notes on the piano I like," I would find at the end that the life of harmony would not open to me. I should be trying to enter by the broad way. The mango seed lying upon the ground unburied is lost, for it refuses to lose its life in the earth, to find it again in the growing tree. There is only one way to life, and that is through a narrow gate.

The Collective Redemption

Jesus took that way. Why is it that he has so much authority and redemptive power over our spirits? It is no mere chance; it is not fortune's fling. He obeyed his own law. He lost himself to the limit, and he finds himself. He entered the narrowest of gates and found the fullest of life.

There is one way that Jesus can be surpassed. It will not be by propaganda or by advertising—it will only be when someone with purer and richer character will go to deeper depths, go through a narrower gate, toil up a lonelier Calvary and give himself more completely than Jesus did. Then, and then only, can he be surpassed.

And I am sure that the God and Father of our Lord Jesus Christ will have the hearts of men for the same reason. He wrote this law of greatness by service in the universe, and he obeys it himself. The Hindu thinkers saw this Narrow Gate, but they said, "This is not for Brahma." So, they placed him in a Garden of Quiet apart from life where no desires ever beat across his spirit and where all is calm. He is in the Nirguna state, that is, without relationships and without bonds. Brahma does not give himself. The Islamic thinkers saw this Narrow Gate and they said, "This is not for

Allah, so they put him on a throne high and lifted up above the world. He never serves; he is served. He never gives himself. He rules. But Jesus came and showed us a God whose very nature is self-sacrificial and who entered this Narrow Gate. For this reason, God knows Life. The Father will have our hearts because he took the Narrow Gate, and obeyed his own Law. For God and man, the Law works with precision and there is no other way. The kingdom of God is the final social and spiritual order because it embodies the final laws of living.

Everything that fits in with this survives and everything that does not will be broken.

I have written elsewhere of how Jesus is being naturalized in India in an amazing way. The Kingdom is slowly but surely entering the hearts of the people everywhere. It is stealing down into the crannies of their thinking and taking charge of their mental processes, and going further, is taking charge of their hearts by its own inherent trueness to life. Jesus is being naturalized. There is a sense in which Jesus, though, cannot be naturalized in any situation either in East or West, and our salvation depends on his not becoming naturalized. He does not fit in with things as they are. He meets them with "an abrupt challenge." It is this challenge that stabs our souls and our civilizations awake. As long as little children toil in factories under inhuman conditions, as long as those who have exploit those who have not, as long as stronger nations suppress weaker ones, as long as might is the arbiter among classes and nations, as long as priest-craft exploits credulity and fattens upon it, as long as woman is treated as a chattel and the tool of man's lust, as long as one of these little ones is caused to stumble, as long as the Father is not known and realized and the brotherhood of our humanity not a working fact, as long as the Kingdom has not come, and as long as men need to repent for anything, Jesus stands with his abrupt challenge. That challenge is our salvation.

The Collective Redemption

There are places here and there where it would seem that Jesus is naturalized, where the Kingdom has come, and where the challenge has turned to a communion.

I have been in such places in India, and among them one stands out. As we went in to see the institution, we were taken first of all into the little chapel for quiet prayer. There was something in the place that could be seen only through prayerful eyes. The three hundred children lived in cottages, each cottage under an Indian girl with about a dozen tiny children in her charge. "How much do you pay these young women who care for all these children?" I asked. The lady replied, "It is very expensive work, for they have to be up at all hours of the day and night—it is too expensive to pay for, so none of us get a salary, we all do it through love." And love had begot love, for one could feel it in the very atmosphere. And love in turn brought forth joy. I have never seen such joy on the faces of people. They shone. There was more joy here to the square inch than there was to the square mile outside. Here I felt that Jesus was at home and naturalized. You could feel his gracious presence everywhere.

As we walked out of the place in reverent silence, my professor friend broke it by saying, "The kingdom of heaven is like unto Dohnavur,"(the name of this orphanage and child development center).

Chapter 6

THE GROWING SAVIOR

THERE IS A Redemptive Purpose running up through nature. Healing forces are at work everywhere. If a bone is broken, forces set to work to knit it together again. If a wound is received, the tiny corpuscles hurry to the distressed part with their healing. If a hillside is scarred by the torrential rain, nature will hasten to fill the ugly scar with flowers. Wherever there is a loss, nature tries to provide some compensation. There is a healing purpose everywhere.

These intimations of redemption burst forth into full meaning in Christ the Savior. They are the signposts that point to him.

This Savior has been growing upon me. He has been the same, but I have been catching further glimpses of the wideness of the redemption he brings. I have known him as Savior these years, but I did not know how big a Savior he was to become. Max Muller was right when he said that you do not know the worth of your Christian faith until you have compared it with others, and one may add, until you have subjected it to life. The wonder of it dawns upon me. The deeper the scrutiny I have subjected it to, the more I have put it under the test of life, the more it has shone.

As I have sat in these Round Table Conferences and have listened to what men were saying about life and destiny and God, I have watched my Savior grow before me. I had not realized what he had saved me from, what he had saved me to, and what he was saving to me. He is a Savior from sin, first and foremost, but that is not all—he saves my universe. He saves everything that he touches and he touches everything.

As I listened in to the statements of these fine men, felt the impact of their cultural past upon me, I found myself deeply grateful that Jesus saves to me the Indian heritage. When I first came to India, I knew that he had come to fulfill and save that wondrous line of preparation running through the Jewish people, but what about this line represented here? Would it all go for naught? Is this line of quest to be wiped out or would he preserve all that was fine and noble in the past of the Hindus? All that is not good, not beautiful, not true in that past will be wiped out. Jesus is a Savior, and this means that he not only saves us from the evil, but that he saves the good to us. Believing in the gospel as I do, I would yet have my moments of hesitation if I felt that all that was noble and great in the Indian outlook on life should be lost or destroyed by the presentation of that gospel, but it will not be. Jesus stands on the peak of Life, not merely fulfilling this incomparable path that rose upward to him from the Jewish people, but also those upward reaches running to him from all sides of that peak. He is not the Son of the Hebrews; he is the Son of Man. Not one jot or tittle of that law written and graven in stones, or of that law written, as Paul says of the Gentiles, "in their hearts" will pass away until all be fulfilled.

"Hitherto, the roots of our life have been in the East, now they will be in the West," said the Indian minister of education to us. "We have pointed our youth to the sitting gods of the East; now we will point them to the standing gods of the West," he added. I am not sure that I want India to do the same. It may be only an exchange of gods for gods. I want the Indian woman to retain her sari, not merely because it is Indian, but because it is the most beautiful dress of the world. More deeply, I want to see India retain those fine touches in her life so attractive and worthwhile: her love for simplicity, her sensitivity to the spiritual, and her deep belief in its reality. Jesus, the simple, the spiritual, the sadhu, the Bramachari, holds steady these ideals of the past and preserves them in himself.

How grateful we are that he preserved all that was fine in the past of the Greeks, and we shall be grateful and enriched because he saves all that is good, beautiful, and true in the past of the Indian. As I sat in the conferences and listened, I knew in my heart of hearts that I was not a lurking enemy of India's heritage when I presented my gospel, but a friend presenting a Savior—a Savior of all that was fine in that past.

Again, as I listened, I felt that there was an utter confusion about the material universe. Men seemed to oscillate from one extreme to the other. In the midst of it, I found Jesus saving *the material universe* to me. It is difficult to find a balanced view of the material. We of the West know that to our confusion. We have given ourselves to the material until it has become materialism. And materialism has become a blight upon us. India too has never had a sane, balanced view of the material. She has oscillated between its denial and its deification. Sometimes the attitude is denial, as in the philosophy of Maya working itself out in such forms as Rama Krishna Paramahansa shivering in fear and horror at the touch of money, and sadhus holding aloft their arms until they wither away. On the other hand, India has swung to the deification of the material—showing a crassness of materialism that the West never dreamed of showing. Tagore, with rare courage and insight, puts his finger upon this fact in these words: "Materialism? What could be more material than thinking that bathing in a river could wash away one's sins?" And we may add, that pilgrimage to places can induce the God-consciousness, that the stars can influence human destiny, that present prosperous physical conditions are a sign of goodness in a previous birth, that bargaining with good deeds can counterbalance bad action and one can "lay up" merit, that physical birth in a Brahman house makes one necessarily holy, that food renders a man holy or unholy, that physical touch makes a man unclean, that Surya the sun is God, that Agni the fire is God, that money should be worshiped on certain festival days, and so on.

It looks as though the material universe put out as Maya, comes back deified. This is the nemesis that always takes place from exaggeration.

But Jesus, so balanced in his outlook on life, puts the material in its rightful place. He seems never to have been interested in "sacred things" as such. He was interested in the ordinary occupations and the ordinary things—the farmer sowing his seed, the housewife kneading the bread, the children playing in the streets, the lilies blooming on the hillsides and the birds among the trees: all life seemed holy and all things a sacrament. He repudiated the idea that a man was rendered unclean by what went into his mouth—it was what came out that mattered. He brushed aside ceremonial purifications as irrelevant. He taught that if life became pure at the heart, then all things were pure to him. Material things were an entrustment. The command was, "Lay not up *for yourselves* riches upon earth." Riches are a curse when selfish purpose is behind them, but there can be a laying up for others, for the service of humanity. Then the material is no longer the material; it is the spiritual, for its power has been broken by its dedication to spiritual ends. You cannot serve God and Mammon, but you can serve God with mammon, as someone has suggested. Jesus, therefore, does not stand for its deification or its denial, but for its dedication. This is workable. He thus becomes the Savior of the material universe for me.

Again, as I have sat and listened to men recounting things that seemed to them miraculous, I have found myself inwardly turning away from it. The miraculous was the weird, the mere showing of power, an intrusion into the universe with its laws and order. I knew in my inmost soul that religion, if founded upon intrusion into nature, would soon be looked upon as an intrusion. This scientific age has been rather hard on miracles. It has such a deep sense of the continuity of natural law and of an orderly universe that miracles seem out of place and an intrusion and hence impossible. Certainly, one has a good deal of sympathy with the idea that religion should not be founded upon wonders and isolated interrupting phenomena. I have a note in my New Testament: "I do not ask for fleece to be wet—this is periodic. I rely on the consistency of the character of Jesus. I do not ask for signs, but for a Savior upon whom I can rely day in and day out." While this is the attitude I find myself taking, nevertheless, I find the miracles of Jesus holding steady amid the storm and stress of things. *Jesus saves the miraculous to me.* He does this because his miracles are not an unnatural intrusion into a universe of dependable law, but a calling back from the unnatural to the truly natural.

There are three things which are intruders into life—sin, disease, and death. These three things have become the accustomed, but they are not the natural. They are not rooted in the real universe, but have come in as the result of moral beings living against the universe—in other words, sinning. Jesus' whole offensive was against these three destroyers of life. His miracles were a calling back from the unnatural to the truly natural. They are not the irresponsible putting forth of mere power.

They are, rather, like the sovereign Lord of Nature moving amid his creation and working along the lines laid down in the Constitution of the Universe.

A leper disintegrating with leprosy looks in the face of Jesus and forgets all about the law that would keep him at a distance lest he defile others. He forgot about the law, for he had seen LOVE. He fell at Jesus' feet and implored him to cleanse him. Jesus put his hands on the head of the leper, for his is not a protected goodness but a purifying force; he was not rendered unclean, but the leper rose to health. Which is real nature—the man disintegrating in his leprosy or the man now going back with health tingling in every portion of his being? Health, not disease, is real nature. The man by the wayside begging, with sightless eyes turned upward and seeing nothing, now follows Jesus in the way, rejoicing in the normal functioning of his eyes. Which is real nature? Sight, not blindness, is real nature. Trace all the way through his miracles of healing and you will find the Great Restoration at work calling back life to the normal and the natural.

> You cannot serve God and Mammon, but you can serve God with mammon... Jesus, therefore, does not stand for its deification or its denial, but for its dedication.

While this is certainly obvious in regard to the healing miracles, it is not quite so obvious in regard to the other miracles. Even here we see the Responsible Lord of Nature working in line with universal laws and trends. On the mount Jesus glows in transfiguration glory—is not this in line with the fact that we see at work, namely, that evil darkens the soul and puts shadows across the countenance while goodness shines within and makes the face light up with a quiet glow? Suppose, then, you could find the perfectly pure, would it not break forth in unearthly light? It would, if back of it were unearthly purity and goodness. This is not an irresponsible happening, for it is in line with what we see at work.

Take even the nature miracles: Jesus knowing that his disciples were in distress comes down the mountainside and walks straight out upon the water to their relief. Is not this in line with that whole upward march of progress which more and more shows the conquest of matter by mind and spirit? The victorious spirit conquers matter. The perfectly victorious spirit perfectly conquers matter. Jesus was perfectly victorious.

Then, again, when Jesus multiplies the loaves, is it not what God is doing in nature, namely, multiplying the single grain into the many? Here is the Lord of Nature hastening the process by his sovereign touch, but always working along the lines he uses in nature. The turning of the water into wine is in line with the thing he does elsewhere, for in the chemical laboratory of nature the water is transformed into the juice or wine of the grape.

Only two of his miracles were miracles of destruction—the withering of the fig tree and the destruction of the swine. In regard to the first, we must remember that he had given the parable of the barren fig tree in words, warning the Jewish nation of their barrenness, and now he would give the same parable, this time in act, to a nation drifting to its doom. Surely, when we see this purpose pulsating through the act, we can understand that this is in line with nature which does not hesitate to sacrifice the lower for higher purposes. The fig tree never served a higher purpose than when through its own withering it would speak to men to be made whole. The same redemptive purpose runs through the healing of the demoniac and the destruction of the swine. The account says that the keepers "fled into the city and told everything and what happened to him that was possessed with devils." Everything and! How revealing that is! "Everything" to them was swine and the healed man counted little or nothing. Their values were twisted. Jesus let the world here see that in the redemption of a man, no price is too dear to pay. Swine never served a higher purpose than here where, through their destruction, they would startle men's souls, empty of all save the idea that swine are everything and a redeemed man an afterthought. Surely, this age, when thinking more of dividends than demon-freed souls and more of money than of men, needs most desperately this vivid lesson. The redemptive purpose runs through this. Jesus never destroyed except to build something finer.

The miracles of Jesus, then, are different. He was no mere wonderworker, for all his miracles show something more than mere power—it is redemption at work. And they also show that sense of responsibility that we would expect from the Lord of Nature, in that, in the exercise of divine power, he calls men back from sin, disease and death to the truly natural—goodness, health and life. Jesus is supernatural, but he is also supra-natural—over nature, its Lord and Master. His miracles are in line with that fact. He therefore, saves miracles to me.

> The miracles of Jesus, then, are different. He was no mere wonderworker, for all his miracles show something more than mere power—it is redemption at work.

But more, he calls on us to join his offensive against sin, disease and death, the unnatural. In doing so, he tells us that we may depend on miraculous power to accomplish this redemptive purpose. We are expected to do miracles and not merely believe in them.

Akin to this, is the fact that Jesus saves religion to *the sane and the balanced and the truthful and the accurate.* As one listens in to the religious life of India, so beautiful in certain things and yet so unbalanced in other areas, one yearns for that quiet sense of truth that Jesus brought. He brings "a stern sense of truth into an approximating world."

A member of one of our conferences said that the thing that had been outstanding in his religious life was the fact that he found when he read a book the letters would fade out and yet he could still keep on reading. He naively suggested that the doctors said that it was an optical illusion, but he held on to it as the big thing in his religious life. It was the out-of-the-ordinary, the weird, and therefore, the religious. But this is tame compared to what our friends of the Theosophical Society pronounce as religion.

I sat and listened while a leading Hindu Theosophist of South India unfolded to me things I had not hitherto known: There is a distinction between Jesus and Christ. Christ was incarnated in Jesus in Palestine. This time, he came for the poor and the oppressed. But through too much attention being paid to them, the poor and the unprivileged began to get out of hand, so to counterbalance this, Christ was incarnated again as Apollonius of Tyana, a rich man. He will come again in Krishnamurti, Mrs. Besant's protege. Jesus was incarnated as Ramanuja, the South Indian teacher of Bhakti, and he now occupies a Druse body in Lebanon. Proof of all this? Occult means! He must have felt the amazement and inward revolt of my soul, though I said nothing, for he remarked at the close: "This probably sounds to you like a cock-and-bull story." It certainly did—and worse. My inmost thought was, "Oh, for a breath of the realism of Jesus!"

The Theosophists have a great deal to their credit —they have served, taught human brotherhood, and have helped India to a new self-respect, but their predilection for the strange made me quite understand what a prominent Theosophist meant when he said to me, "We are the congregation of the weird."

It would be laughable if it were not so serious, for there is no doubt that Theosophy has set back the progress of real reform in India for decades. There was growing up a type of mind that demanded reality and reform when Theosophy appeared and took mental charge, and then the collapse. The member of the Round Table who said, "But Theosophy has taught me that many things I thought untrue in my religion are true," was expressing a widespread tendency. By what method are things proved to be true? This: Idols are "magnetized centers," and hence, not so foolish as they seem; each one of us has "an aura" around him, extending six feet, and one may be made spiritually unclean if an unclean person gets within that space, hence "untouchability" is reasonable. And so on. I sat in the train with a Theosophist Brahman lawyer. I asked if he was going to have his meal in the compartment with me, as I was ordering a vegetarian meal from the Brahman refreshment room. "No," he replied, "I must have mine in the Brahman refreshment room."

"Why," I asked, laughingly, "are you afraid of the evil eye?"

"No," he replied, rather haltingly, "but they tell us that different people emit different kinds of electricity, and if the one who sees you eat has a different kind of electricity from your own, it will stop your digestion. It is especially effective in children."

This attitude of Theosophy reminds me of the time when I was in Paris in a crowded office building on a summer day. The windows were closed and the air was foul and stuffy. Instead of throwing open the windows and letting the fresh air come in, a man went around with a spray, perfuming the air to make it tolerable. It was more tolerable, but not less poisonous. Would it be unkind to say that what India needs most desperately is for the windows to be thrown open, but that

Theosophy instead is spraying perfumed words and misty, occult phrases into a stale atmosphere and making it staler still ? It is a fact nevertheless.

But it is not only Theosophy that preaches the strange as wisdom; this outlook is in the very atmosphere. I asked a Hindu if he had seen a jiwan-mukhta, one who had found salvation, and he replied: "Yes, I think I have. I saw six men on the road one day and I think they had found God, for they looked irrational." And he was serious when he said it! In another place, the proof that a certain man was a jiwan-mukhta was that he could eat huge balls of opium without it affecting him! I asked a sadhu one day why he smoked charas, (the hashish form of cannabis).

"Oh, it makes me see God," he replied.

"Why, it makes you drunk," I said.

"No, it makes ordinary people drunk, but it makes me see God," was the decisive answer.

I asked an intelligent Hindu one day if he had found God. "Why, no," he replied in astonishment at the question. "Do you think I would be doing what I am doing if I had?"

He was the headmaster of a high school! His answer meant that to him God and sane living, education and developing life did not go together. I could think of no place where finding God would be of more real use than there in that high school.

It is a relief to turn from all this to the amazing sanity of Jesus. All his windows are open to God's light and truth. His words have the feel of reality about them. There is nothing psychopathic about Jesus. He goes off into no visions and dreams, he speaks in no ecstatic tongue, and he gets his guidance through prayer and insight. He is not deadly dull. He is blazing with God and spiritual reality and yet how poised and sane. Someone has suggested that the attempt to impose divine qualities on the frame work of ordinary humanity topples over the human and always results in a monstrosity—always, save in the case of Jesus. He moves down through human life, balanced, sane, realistic and poised—yet always approachable. The God-consciousness, instead of making him less fit for life, drives him deeper into the needs and pains and sorrows of men. He seems to be the truly Balanced One in an unbalanced world. He saves religion to the sane, to the balanced, to the truthful, and to the accurate.

Again, I find Jesus saving *creeds and ceremonies and the church to me*. I have watched rigid and unchangeable statements of belief and systems being lost by rigidity and lack of room for expansion. Given to express life, they soon end in throttling that very life. When the expansive pressure is too great, they crack and are lost. But Jesus saves them, for he refused to be rigid. He knew that "life is larger and more dynamic than any theory of it reveals." Life is bigger than our creeds about life. For this reason, we develop discontent with our statements about life. Since our creeds are too small, where can we find something that will hold our life conceptions? Our views of life are only held by a Life. Christ saves creeds for me, for we know that in him we have our life conceptions. He holds them in himself and we can await the adequate words to express them. I can believe in the creeds and use them because I believe in something more than the creeds. When I repeat the words of creeds I have my eye on him and know that he fills in the inadequacy of the words. He, therefore, saves creeds to me.

> **Life is bigger than our creeds about life .... Christ saves creeds for me, for we know that in him we have our life conceptions.**

Christ at the Round Table

He also saves rites and ceremonies by providing for their renewal. The new wine is to be constantly put into new wineskins. The tree saves the leaves by providing for their shedding and renewal. If the old leaves should refuse to be shed, they would kill both the tree and themselves. If there is no feeling of necessity for new wine-skins, if there is contentment with what is, the presumption is that the wine has ceased to be living and expansive—it is dead. It is no longer the gospel.

Jesus saves the church by not founding a rigid ecclesiasticism, blocked off and non-renewable. He founded it upon the simple rock of the corporate confession of the Sonship of Jesus. He gave not formula, but fact. That confession must take wider and wider forms. In recent centuries, men have been content that it be a personal confession of the personal Saviorhood of Jesus, but now we are again discovering that we must confess Christ as Son of God in social, economic, and international relationships as well. The church must embody that larger confession or cease to be the Church of the Living Christ.

So, to me, Christ saves the creeds and the ceremonies and the church by refusing to do other than give life. He knew that life would find its own fitting raiment.

He saves *God* to me. As I have listened at these Round Tables, I have felt that God was slipping away from men. As among the Greeks, the people did not dream of turning to the gods for examples —they turned to Plato and Zeno—so here moral action is not centered in God or in the gods; it is centered in the law of Karma. Tulsi Das said, "A man will be cast into hell for a thousand years if he presumes to imitate the gods." Now, I find Jesus centering morality in God and showing us that the nature of God is bound by the same moral laws as those that bind us. It is a great day for the human soul when it realizes that morality is not an accidental thing, but is centered in the ultimate truth of things, God. We are to be "perfect" as our "Father is perfect." And

Paul gives the astounding statement: "Be ye imitators of God as dear children." I am quite sure that it is impossible to imitate Brahma, Allah, Krishna, Shiva, or any of the others, but we can imitate God, if God is like Christ. We would be good if we did so—yea, the very best that the human mind is capable of conceiving.

But Jesus did not merely trace morality back to the heart of God. He showed that there was service and self-giving in God's heart. Brahma does not serve. In the highest form Brahma is in the Nirguna state, without relationships and without bonds. He is in the non-acting, Passionless Impersonal. Of course, the highest man must be like Brahma; so the highest product of Hindu philosophy is the non-serving man, the man who sits in the jungle, apart from life, with attention concentrated between his eyebrows dreaming himself out into the Impersonal Brahma. It is better to do nothing good or bad; for if you do good, you have to come back into the wheel of existence to get the fruit of that good, and likewise with the bad. The highest is to be action-less. The finished product is the entirely action-less man, for Brahma is the same. Now, in the revelation of Christ, God is the serving God: "My Father worketh hitherto and I work." God enters into service even to a cross. Jesus carried service into the very soul of the universe and laid its basis in God. The highest man is the serving man: "The greatest among you shall be the servant of all."

But as one listened to the statements of the Round Table members, while the word "service" came in again and again, it did not appear to come out of the heart of things—it seemed as if it were something tacked on. For instance, one member quoted a passage from the Gita about service and then went on and said, "Oh, So and So is a really holy man; he cares nothing about money, or his neighbors, or his family." In other words, he was outgrowing the necessity of service and getting closer to the ideal of Brahma—service-less. But Jesus shows the service ideal to be in the heart of the Father, so that when one serves he feels that he is fulfilling the ultimate meaning of things. Jesus is the living expression of that goodness and service.

My heart responded when a Hindu member of our group said: "You do not lower your ideas of God when you think of him as Christ-like." And my heart responded more deeply still when a Christian member said very thoughtfully, "I find that a Christ-like God stands the strain." He does!

> Jesus saves God to us. He did not prove God or argue about him—he brought God. And how beautiful God seems when I see him in the face of Jesus!

I am quite sure I cannot believe in any kind of a God other than a Christ-like one. It is that—or nothing. And a good many of the Hindus not grasping "THAT," take the nothing, for, as we noted, one said: "Of the fourteen ways to find realization, ten are without God. You may or may not meet God on the way." God did not seem to count. God was lost. But Jesus saves God to us. He did not prove God or argue about him—he brought God. And how beautiful God seems when I see him in the face of Jesus!

Is it not worth something—yea everything—that the most beautiful character of history was sure of God?

Jesus saves God to me.

But what hasn't Jesus saved? It seems to me that witnesses rise up from everywhere ready to tell of his saving touch upon them. He saves *peace*—it is the calm of death until he makes it the calm of courage. He saves *humility*—the ancients felt it to be an insult to be called humble, for it meant meanness and cowardice; but in Jesus it is strength and power to strike combined with the restraint that stoops. He saves *forgiveness*—Jesus puts worth and dignity into it by basing it upon the Divine Self-Sacrifice. He saves *love*—for he saves it from being a physical lust on the one side by showing in his own example that it can be entirely free from any touch of it, and, on the other hand, from being a vague, diffused sentiment by directing men and women to love their neighbors as themselves. He saves *joy*—by exhibiting the highest joy as the joy of the shepherd returning with the one lost sheep —it is the joy of redemption through cost. He saves *human personality* by putting infinite worth into it, making it worth more than the whole physical universe, dying to redeem it so that a man is no longer a man—he is "a man for whom Christ died." He saves the *home* by founding it upon one man and one woman living together in partnership in absolute equality and with "the child in the midst," blest and made the type of the kingdom of God. He saves *human society* by providing that the kingdom of God should come on earth by the world-spirit being replaced by the Christ-spirit. He saves *life itself.* He faced life as it is, even though it meant a cross, and there took on himself everything that ever spoke against life and God, and through that very tragedy showed the triumph of life.

He holds my universe together. "In Him all things hold together," says the glowing Paul in Moffatt's translation. He is the Keystone of the arch of life. We rear one side, the arch of our upward craving after God and immortality, and God rears the other side, for his love reaches out of the eternities to us. Jesus is the Keystone, the meeting place of God and man. In him all things hold together. Without him both arches fall and my universe crashes into ruins about me.

He has become "my universe that feels and knows."

Chapter 7

THE TREND TOWARD EXPERIENCE

The basis of our Roundtable Conferences was religious experience. Christianity has followed Plato in his doctrine of ideas and, in following him, emphasis has been thrown upon belief in religion. When this emphasis on ideas was combined with the Roman tendency toward legal and exact phraseology, the stage was set for fierce clashes over doctrine and creed. A Christian was one who could repeat a correctly stated creed. "Isn't it glorious to see our Christians stand right up in the jail before the non-Christians and boldly repeat the creed," said a missionary on his return from a jail meeting. His wife and I burst into laughter, to our friend's bewilderment at our irreligion. It hadn't occurred to him that the creed should have kept them out of jail—to repeat it was the big thing!

The emphasis is shifting to experience. As Buckham says: "The deeper thought of our time is turning from religion as dogma, as sentiment, as theory, as ethics, to religion as experience." Here Christianity will come more deeply into its own, for, as Matthew

Arnold says, "Jesus based himself always on experience and never on theory." The emphasis on experience comes closer to the mind of Jesus: "He that is willing to do the will shall know of the doctrine." You shall know the truth—and with Jesus, to know was deeper than intellectual perception. It meant to know by inward grasp, to realize, to experience— "and the truth shall make you free."

The philosophy of India has broken down under the weight of its own speculations. Christianity would have done the same, had it not had this figure of Jesus who constantly brought it back to his own realism, to his own planting of himself on experience. His call today is to experience life with him. If the Church of Christ will boldly follow him, it will assume the moral and spiritual leadership of the world, for all ways of life are breaking down except the Christ way. The heart of the world through its scientific outlook is being prepared for this emphasis. On this present-day soil of a return to the facts, the gospel of Christ will again become fruitful. It will burst into power if it boldly follows this demand for experience.

> Jesus' call today is to experience life with him. If the Church of Christ will boldly follow him, it will assume the moral and spiritual leadership of the world...

India, too, is more and more turning from wordy disputation to the facts and to experience. In one of our Round Tables, one of the Christians began to narrate the life of Jesus and to semi-preach. A Hindu judge turned to him and said, "We are fairly familiar with the events you are narrating—you tell us what you have found." This Christian, who had been so accustomed to preaching something outside himself, was brought up face to face with the demand that the gospel be not something passed on from a book to another without going through the stream of one's own experience and life, that it must come up out of the soul. "That which is to reach the soul must come from the soul." If it is to be effective, the gospel must partake of a sharing of experience with people, instead of a preaching at people. Mr. Natarajan, an eminent Hindu, pleaded before a Christian audience that evangelism grow out of experience. He was right.

A Hindu medical student of very keen observation and deep spiritual sensibilities asked me one day how he could find God. I took my New Testament to point out certain passages to him as guideposts. I had scarcely begun to read these passages when he leaned over and politely, but positively, closed the New Testament in my hand and said, "Now tell me from your own experience how to find God." It made me think. All of my work with him had to fall back upon my own experience of God. Was it clear and real enough to be adequate? Of course, we cannot close the New Testament, as he suggested. It would be disastrous if we did so, for in the New Testament we are held by the historical Christ from drifting. But he was deeply right in insisting that I had no business preaching Christ as a Savior and the Bringer of God unless I could share that experience with him.

In Luke 8:1, it is said that Jesus and his disciples went throughout cities and villages "preaching and bringing the gospel of the kingdom of God." The kingdom of God was not a kind of fold into which men ran and were safe; it was "the Reign of God" (Moffatt), God reigning in life, God intimate and real as experience. Note they came "preaching and bringing" this fact. They not only preached it, they brought it as well. Where was it? Look in the face of Jesus and you can see the gospel—the joy, the radiant sense of God, the mastery over life. The gospel was not an idea—it was a fact. Men not only heard it, they saw it.

The Trend Toward Experience

No wonder men were astonished at his teaching, for he taught as with authority —the authority of his own experience. Others quoted authorities, he spoke with the authority of immediate perception and realization.

We have preached the gospel, but have we brought it? India does not want preachers of the gospel so much as she wants bringers of it. "If you have found God, I will listen to anything you have to say, but if you have not, I do not care to discuss the matter with you," said a Hindu to a friend of mine. And the Hindu was right.

A lady missionary was giving a Bible lesson in a zenana. In the midst of the most interesting portion, one of the Hindu ladies deliberately got up and went out. After a while she came back and listened more intently than ever. At the close the missionary asked her why she went out—wasn't she interested?

"Oh, yes, I was so interested in the wonderful things that you were saying that I went out to ask your carriage driver whether you really meant it and whether you lived it at home. He said you did, so I came back to listen again."

"Do you experience what you say?" interrupted another zenana woman while another missionary was giving a lesson. And she had a right to interrupt.

An Arya Samajist schoolmaster was addressing his pupils: "You students saw that I was worrying the Christian speaker in the public meetings with all sorts of troublesome, insulting questions. I really wasn't seeking for information. I was seeking to see if I could upset him and disturb his joyous attitude, and show that he hadn't found God; but I did not succeed, for he was the incarnation of the victorious life. I have asked him to come here, and I want you to listen to every word he has to say." Our friend, the speaker, could then speak with the authority of his Master, for he had struck the note the world wants to hear, the note of experience.

But some of us feel that experience does not matter as long as we have "the form of sound words." We are very like the Sikh driver of a missionary's car in North India. He became very interested in the missionary's preaching in the villages and suggested that he be allowed to preach. The missionary was surprised and asked,

"But what will you preach about?"

"Oh," said the Sikh, "I will preach against liquor and tobacco."

"But," said the missionary, "you use both."

"Yes," he promptly replied, "but, sahib, they don't know that."

But don't they? We are all much better known than we think we are.

A Hindu student recently returned from England said to me: "I stayed in the house of a minister while attending the University. His sermons were very interesting, and while he was speaking I felt perhaps there was sound reality in it, but as soon as he stepped out of the pulpit, he was a different man and I could see no difference between him and the rest of us. So, I lost interest." And I found it almost impossible to rouse interest in him again.

The greatest Hindu leader of modern times, Swami Shraddanand, whose murder by a Muslim has sent a shock through the soul of India and has stiffened the whole of Hinduism into greater resistance to inroads from without, was at one time on the verge of accepting Christianity. In fact, he had made up his mind after a long struggle to be baptized and went to the home of the Christian priest for that purpose, saw something there that made him revolt, turned back, gave himself to the propagation of Hinduism with all his soul and succeeded in arousing it from within as no other person of modern times has done. The experience of the Christian was not sufficient to sustain the weight resting on it.

But more impressive still is the fact that Gandhiji at the moment of his greatest religious restlessness, when he was on the verge of accepting Christ, tells how he came in contact with a Christian family in South Africa. "At their suggestion, I attended the Wesleyan church every Sunday. The church did not make a favorable impression on me. The sermons seemed to me to be uninspiring. The congregation did not strike me as being particularly religious. They were not an assembly of devout souls; they appeared to be rather worldly-minded people going to church for recreation or in conformity to custom. Here, at times, I would involuntarily doze. I was ashamed, but some of my neighbors who were in no better case lightened the shame. I could not go on long like this and soon gave up attending the service" (*Young India*, Oct. 14, 1926). This came at a most decisive moment of his life. Shades of John Wesley! "It was a national epoch when John Wesley's heart was warmed in the meetinghouse," said Lecky, the historian. It would have been a national epoch for India if this Wesleyan minister and his people had been in the line of succession of the warmed heart. But they were worldly, dull, and drowsy at the moment when one of the greatest men of modern days was making his life decision. The whole situation rested on their experience of God. It was not sufficient to sustain it.

The leader in the anti-Christian movement in China at the present time, the man who is the brains back of it all, told us that he had decided to become a Christian one night while studying in America. He went to hear a minister speak, found shallowness, turned away from it and became as hard as steel. Our appeals fell upon a flinty soul. China is now in the throes of his anti-Christian movement. A shallow minister shakes China with anti-Christianity!

A great deal of the irreligion and lack of interest in things spiritual can be laid down to the smugness, the complacency, the lack of a radiant God-consciousness and the dying out in the churches of the spirit of adventure in following Jesus. "They practice fastidiousness in Oxford and call it holiness," said Solomon Schechter. And many of us practice being comfortable and call it Christianity —the religion of the thorn-crowned Man.

I am persuaded that we can go as far into the soul of India and of the world as our God-consciousness will allow, and no further. Christian missions are determined in their limits by Christian experience.

> I am persuaded that we can go as far into the soul of India and of the world as our God-consciousness will allow, and no further.

"As examples of worldly prosperity and of business acumen and success, I could turn to the Christian leaders for guidance, but scarcely as imparting the spirit of that gentle heart that broke upon the cross," said a Hindu. There is enough truth in this comment to make it sting.

We were having a series of meetings in a great city. The interest was intense. The large college hall was filled with Hindus, Muslims, and Christians. The last night I suggested that I would ask the Christians to share with their Hindu and Muslim friends what Christ was to them in experience. I suggested that no one exhort or preach, but that we simply share. The first man, a British major, arose, gave a simple, straightforward and moving statement of how Christ had kept alive and glowing his Christian life in one of the most difficult places in the world, the British army. These students, unused to finding spirituality flowering out of such unlikely soil, were so deeply moved that when he sat down they applauded. The next man also spoke out of reality, and when he sat down again there was applause. The messages were going home with power. The third man who arose was a locally well-known teacher. He was very fluent, but in a few moments, we soon saw that his words were mere words. The crowd began to get restless, then began to whisper, some to laugh. The whole situation collapsed. There wasn't enough underlying reality to sustain it. That is what is happening on a widespread scale. Our life must be deepened in Christ before we can go further in sharing Christ. The only way to kill a Christian worker is to kill his experience of God.

No man contributed more to our Round Table Conferences than an American professor of comparative religion. He was well prepared, a fine Christian, sympathetic toward India and her aspirations, and he loved her people. But he had not gone far into the situation before he found that his message was not adequate. It fell short of this overwhelming need. He could teach comparative religions, but this he could not do.

We were in a conference of Christian leaders on the banks of the Beas River. After an address by a Christian sanyasi, Mr. Winslow, a splendid and radiant type of Christian, Professor Winston said he would not be present for breakfast. He went out to the river bank to fight the thing through. "I went out to get my petrol tank filled," he said, "but I came back with a new engine." God had turned him into another man. Now when he spoke, his message was adequate, for he, through Christ, was adequate. And that same sense of victorious adequacy continues upon his return to the Seminary in America. He writes: "Before I went to India, no students ever came to my study with their life problems. They came merely to talk over their preparation for missionary service. But now, they come evening after evening, man after man, and I meet them in groups, to talk about the deep needs of their souls . . ." Both in India and in America, he could go as far into the situation as his experience of God allowed him. The church at home must go deeper in order to send us further into the soul of the East.

India, that yearns for identity with God, cannot be satisfied with an absent God, or a correct statement about God. She wants God in glowing, intimate realization. We must bring that, or fail.

Mr. C. F. Andrews, who has gone very deeply into the soul of India, tells how Tagore, India's great poet, prized the fact of Christian experience in him. "Tagore would urge me again and again to cling fast to my Christian devotional life as a priceless heritage. When he saw me at one time slipping into vagueness, he warned me. He loved me for the very distinction which a deep Christian faith had given me" (*Vishvabarti Quarterly*, October 1925). That phrase "slipping into vagueness" is significant. It is one of the chief dangers to the spiritual life. But the more significant thing is that Tagore expressed what India feels about experience.

At the close of one of the Round Tables, a Hindu nobleman came up to one of the Christians and said: "You have evidently seen Christ and his personality is real to you. You are the first Christian who has impressed me that he knows Christ as real. The early Christians had this, but the church has lost it. India must give this to the world again, for we can never be satisfied until we have seen him." In the inmost depths of my soul I prayed that India might.

"I have a hankering in my heart about God," said a Hindu to me naively one day. It is that "hankering" in the heart about God that will not let us rest until we see him, know him.

"Why did you start out on your long pilgrimage in search for God?" a Hindu pilgrim was asked.

"Oh, there came the ripple in the mind," he replied. And I think we all know what he meant.

THE TREND TOWARD EXPERIENCE

A writer in the *Atlantic Monthly* tells of a dream he had in which a friend, well known to the world, was standing on a knoll with a crowd around the base of it. He was addressing the crowd and his lips were trying to frame a word. But though he tried to utter it, he could not. The crowd knew the word and they tried to help him speak it, but they too could not. The word that they were all trying to say was "God." It is the word that men everywhere are trying to speak, for they know if they can say it from the depths of their being, they will be healed. And they who can speak that word "God" from experience hold the future. The church must say it or perish. And we can say it if we know Christ.

But the church is largely sub-Christian. Paul came down to Ephesus and came across a group of twelve disciples. He saw that their spiritual temperature was low. They were huddled together for protective purposes. They had no power of moral and spiritual attack. They had made terms with their environment and were content to be allowed to live. On the other hand, another twelve disciples were turning the world upside down. They were content with nothing save that men should know Christ and live according to him. They did not settle down to the environment into which they came, for they brought their own. They had found the soul's native air—it was Pentecost, for Pentecost is normal Christianity.

Here the church was born and, in this atmosphere, it lives—lives

> India, that yearns for identity with God, cannot be satisfied with an absent God, or a correct statement about God. She wants God in glowing, intimate realization.

radiantly and victoriously. Take it out of this atmosphere and it withers into a religious sect.

Paul put his finger upon the spiritual pulse of the Christians at Ephesus and found them anemic. He asked them the most direct and pertinent question that can be asked of a Christian— "Have you received the Holy Spirit?" They answered that they had "not heard whether there be any Holy Spirit." The next question revealed that they had been baptized unto John's baptism and were living under its meaning. Now John's Gospel was the Gospel of a Demand: thou shalt do this, and thou shalt not do that. It can bring no more than what Herrmann calls "a troubled piety," a straining to fulfill overhanging demands. Its type is that of the set jaw, of the clenched fist, and the strained soul, and its motto: We will fight it out along this line if it takes until death.

The gospel of Jesus is not the Gospel of a Demand, but the Gospel of an Offer. Christ offers life to men: "He that drinks of the waters that *I shall give him* shall never thirst," for "they shall become in him a well." Here is not an agonizing to live, but an acceptance of life—abundant and full. Just here is the essential difference between other systems and the gospel of Christ. The one struggles upward in order that it may issue in self-salvation; the other accepts an offer and it issues in self-sacrifice. It will not do to counter this by saying, "But we must go out and do something; this other is not active enough." Do something? Active enough? Weren't these twelve under the Gospel of an Offer doing something? They were changing the face and the soul of a world, while those under the Gospel of a Demand were clinging desperately to what they had. One was ending in a conquest, and the other in a collapse. No wonder Jesus said, "He that is least in the kingdom of heaven"—under the Gospel of an Offer— "is greater than John"—under the Gospel of a Demand. This is the kingdom of a realized God, a redeeming Christ and a regenerating Spirit. It is

Pentecost, for Pentecost is not an event in the past. It is a continuing principle in the present, wherever men accept the Offer. And when we find this, we find normal spiritual living. The Ephesian twelve accepted this offer, were filled with abundant life, and began a moral and spiritual offensive; so that men seeing a real and radiant spirituality came and burned their books of magic arts— "so mightily grew the word of the Lord and prevailed."

The church, like a human being, is prey to various ailments when it becomes below par. Raise the temperature to normal and it will throw off the disease germs that threaten its life. "The parasite sin is killed by strengthening the organism upon which it preyed," says Peabody. The church need not spend its time fighting evils and heresies that threaten it. Let it maintain the radiant health and temperature of Pentecost and nothing can harm it. But as "no virtue is safe that is not enthusiastic, no heart is pure that is not passionate," so no church is safe that is sub-Christian. Our greatest danger is not from anti-Christianity, but from sub-Christianity. "Heal me at the heart and let the world come on."

> Oh, spirit of mine, you were made to live by the Spirit of Christ! Experience of him is the expression of yourself — your real self.

But the subnormal church answers as did the Ephesians, "We have not heard whether there be any Holy Spirit." I see a flower pale and anemic trying pathetically to bloom down in the dark. I say to it, "Little flower, I know something that can make you blush with health and bloom in profusion —it is sunlight." And the pathetic little flower answers, "I have not heard whether there be any such thing as sunlight."

I reply, "But, little flower, you were made for sunlight, you were not made for the dark; when you find sunlight, you find life."

Oh, spirit of mine, you were made to live by the Spirit of Christ! Experience of him is the expression of yourself—your real self. His law coincides with your life. Take him. It is an offer.

Of course, at the center of that offer is a demand for repentance, for self-surrender, for following, but once the offer is accepted, the demand dances its way into a delight and is gone.

Does this Gospel of an Offer seem airy and impossible? No, it is the most substantial thing on earth. The other day, a friend pointed to a line of white far above the horizon. "It is a bank of clouds," I said. "No," my friend replied, "it is the mighty Himalayas covered with the eternal snows." And he was right. If what I have said seems as unreal and unsubstantial as a cloud upon the horizon, try it, accept the offer, and you will find it more substantial than the mighty Himalayas.

As Isaiah says, "The mirage shall become a pool" (Isa. 37: 7 Marg.); that which has shimmered on the horizon of your life as a mirage will become the pool of realized fact. The unreal shall become the real. It is an offer. Anyone can accept an offer.

Chapter 8

ALMOST

WE WERE SITTING with one of the most important groups we ever had together. The principal of an Orthodox Hindu college was speaking. His statements about what religion was to him in experience were fascinating. You felt that he came in sight of the promised land, but only in sight of it, for after he had finished, a very able Muslim barrister said in his turn: "I was expecting the principal to say the word, and he almost said it, but just as he was about to say it, he failed and switched off on something else."

As I pondered this statement, I felt that the principal epitomized the spirit of India—it is a land of "Almost." It is written all through her history, all through her soul and all through her quest. You feel that she is trembling on the verge of something big and yet never quite reaches it. So many things come up to the point of giving us what we want and then turn aside. The word that we want to hear is almost spoken, but never quite. The vision that we want to see is almost revealed, and then it fades out. "Have you found satisfaction in your soul?" I asked a Brahmo Samaj preacher, a man of fine spirit. He thought a long time and then replied, "I cannot say that I have found, but I believe satisfaction is in sight." It is that spirit of almost-ness that throbs like a pain through India.

A commission had been appointed from India to go into the question of an institution which had been founded for the benefit of Indians in Britain. As they were making up their report, the Christian member of the Commission suggested that the basis of management be broadened so that non-Christians might be included. One of the non-Christians spoke up and said: "You Christians founded this institution, did you not? Well, let it alone as it is. What you touch succeeds, you have such persistent courage and hope that you carry things through. We begin with a flare, but we do not carry things to completion. What we touch wanes. The explanation is easy. It is not inherent in Indian character, as unfriendly critics would suppose, for India has a persistence in her spiritual search unequaled by any other people. Persistence is there when she believes in a thing, but the lack of it comes from the underlying view of life—she doesn't quite believe in life. Change India's underlying philosophical outlook on life and you change her whole outward life. We are merely tinkering until we touch this. The state of almost-ness comes out of these depths of hidden thinking.

Very often you see buildings in India left incomplete and you ask the reason and the reply comes that this world is an incomplete world, so our houses should express that fact.

Asoka was counted by H. G. Wells as one of the seven great men of history, for while other rulers were planning conquests, Asoka was planning good will and harmony. He believed in peace. We are ready to hear that word come out of the soul of India against the war system. Asoka has prepared us for it and almost utters it, but instead India's last and highest word is Krishna on the battlefield of Kurushetra urging the hesitating Urjuna, who catches the same vision that Asoka did, to fight, and the Gita is the philosophic discourse proving to him why he must fight. Almost, but not quite.

India catches the vision that the ultimate Reality is Spirit, and in this she is deeply right. We are expecting her to break forth into the music of the realization of communion with God, but instead her greatest philosophy passes by communion and strives for identity, misses both and the end is spiritual fumbling. She almost gives us that word of spiritual experience that we so greatly crave, but just misses it.

She recognized that life must have its division of labor and so gave forth the four divisions: the spiritual teachers, the Brahmans; the protectors, the Kshatriyas; the traders, the Vaisiyas; and the laborers, the Shudras—a division into which occupations naturally fall. Instead of its being a great word on economic and social fairness and justice, it became the most cruel caste system ever forged about the soul and body of a great people. Almost, but not quite.

> **India catches the vision that the ultimate Reality is Spirit, and in this she is deeply right. We are expecting her to break forth into the music of the realization of communion with God...**

Buddha almost saw the light. A ray as from the cross struck his soul. He saw that desire was the root of our misery, and so far, it is deeply true; but he did not see that desire can be quenched in a higher desire—the will of God—and that this opens the gate of life. He saw only the negative side, tried to snuff out desire, and opened the gates to Nirvana —annihilation. The light within him turned to darkness and how great was that darkness! Almost.

The Gita is a noble endeavor to find a theistic belief and to provide the Incarnate. These are the two things the world desperately needs. But when the form of the Most High is uncovered and we see him, we find ourselves facing a picture of a Huge Being with men hurrying down his throat, some caught between his teeth and being crushed—and we turn away asking, "Is this the Father?" And when we look for the Incarnate, we find the Krishna of the Gita not historical, and hence, not incarnate. "Almost" gave us the two things needed, but only almost.

There is an underlying unity in India. An Indian is an Indian wherever found. There is a subtle something binding India together. Hinduism has brought men under its aegis in an amazing way and has succeeded in incorporating diverse peoples and types within its hospitable bosom. We would expect this underlying spiritual unity to bind India together into a nation, but India has not yet achieved nationhood. The unity seemed in sight a few years ago during Non-Cooperation days, but it has fallen apart and now a fatalistic hopelessness about it has seized the souls of many. Almost unified, but not quite.

Keshab Chandar Sen stood at a formative period of modern India. The eyes of all Bengal, the intellectual center of India, were fastened on this eloquent son of the new day. Though a Hindu, he caught sight of Jesus as the incarnation of what India craved and needed. He shook the soul of Bengal with his throbbing clarion call to follow Jesus out of darkness to light and out of chaos to freedom. He became a prophet—almost. He almost says the word, but he inwardly hesitated. Who is Jesus? He calls him "the God-consciousness" instead of God, calls him "subjective Divinity" and not "objective Divinity," but *the word* never came out. The shoulders of a Christ less than incarnate Deity were not strong enough to stand the strain put on them to bear India into the new day. The movement inaugurated by Keshab passed into religious respectability and high-minded gentility, but the Spark— the Divine

Spark? The Living Flame? It did not come. Keshab was the prophet of the Almost Divine Savior—but only almost.

But the man who sums up and epitomizes, in its noblest form, this spirit of Almost is Gandhiji. With deep insight and with noble passion, he saw that the final type of power lies in self-sacrifice. He caught the meaning of the cross and embodied it on a scale that was stupendous. India's freedom was to be won by self-sacrifice and suffering. There is before me a letter written by one of his Hindu followers which unfolds the spirit of the Movement: "M. was wholly right when he told you that I am a revolutionary. Revolution is not a bad thing. Revolution is a thing which has come from Europe and the originator of revolution or the first and greatest of the revolutionaries was Jesus Christ. It is he who has taught the whole world to revolt against custom, against orthodoxy, superstition, tyranny and tyrant kings. His revolution was not blood-taking but blood-giving; or, in other words, a revolution of love, which might be called the might of sacrificial love." Put that spirit into human society as a working force and you have approached somewhere near ultimate power. When we saw Gandhiji apply this method, we held our breath—the universe did. Would he show us the way out? He did—almost.

Just after he was released from jail, and when he was about to take up the threads of his work again, I went to see him in the hospital at Poona. He graciously gave me an appointment very early in the morning so I could meet my engagements. I slowly paced the platform of the station waiting for the dawn. I was in prayer asking God to give me some message to give to Gandhiji as he was about to take up his work again. I felt that it was a critical moment for him and for us. I opened my New Testament with a prayer to find some word that would illuminate and give clear guidance. As I threw it open, the first words that my eyes fell on were the account in the first chapter of Acts, where the disciples asked Jesus if the kingdom were to be restored to Israel at this time, and he answered, "It is not for you to know times or seasons... But you shall receive power, when the Holy Ghost is come upon you; you shall be my witnesses both in Jerusalem, and in all Judaea and Samaria, and unto the uttermost part of the earth." I saw the rough parallel: the Hebrews were under Rome as India was under Britain and both wanted their freedom. The disciples asked if the kingdom were to be restored immediately, and Gandhiji had expected it within the promised year. But Jesus offered the disciples something bigger. They wanted the restoration of a temporal kingdom and Jesus offered them a spiritual kingdom that would extend from Jerusalem to the ends of the earth. If they would be his witnesses and witness to his way of life, this kingdom was theirs. They asked for the little and he offered them the big. I saw my message. It was "given in that hour." I told Gandhiji that I was going to the Western world and asked him to give me a message to the West, to tell us how we should live this Christ-life. He thought a moment and then said, "It is impossible to give a message like that by word of lip—it has to be lived. All I can do is to live it." I replied that I thought he was right and we would await with eagerness that message lived out. I then said that if he hadn't a message for me, I thought I had one for him. I quoted my passage and drew the parallels, and told of the offer of the larger spiritual world kingdom which Jesus made to his disciples and which they had, in fact, found through their witness to him. I suggested to him that he stood in the very place where the disciples stood. I told him that I thought the kingdom would sooner or later be restored to India, that the fact of its coming was settled, though the time was not. The coming of that kingdom would take care of itself, but that here before him was a larger kingdom if he would take it. I suggested that we of the West were sick of the methods of militarism, that it was a vicious circle and we wanted a way out; that he stood as the apostle of the non-violent and of the power of self-sacrifice, and that if he came out and gave his clear witness to Christ, a world spiritual kingdom awaited him. He could lead us. I suggested that I did not say this as a mere Christian propagandist, but that we of the West particularly needed him and the leadership he could give to us in this crisis of the world's history. I also suggested that the movement would have to have a spiritual basis sufficient to sustain it and that Christ could form that basis, for these ideals were embodied in him. Would he come out and give his clear witness to Christ? Would he take this larger kingdom? The answer was not given one way or the other, but our eyes were moist as we bowed in prayer together. I cannot get rid of the thought that Gandhiji there met one of the most serious moments of his life.

He did not answer then, but he has in many ways answered since: Rama and the Bhagawad Gita would be the bases of his spiritual life; Christ would be one of the admired along with the rest. The movement then rests down upon Rama and the Bhagawad Gita for support. Is it a sufficient spiritual basis? Whoever Rama was, he is hardly a character who could be a center of a world movement, for, outside of India, his appeal is limited, and even here he is a colorless figure. And the Gita—does it witness against war, or is it founded on it? Does it give a basis for human equality? Is it able to sustain Gandhiji's ideas for the outcastes? Gandhi says that it does. In *Young India,* January 13, 1927, he writes: "For us Hindus, the Gita enjoins on us the lessons of human equality. We are to cherish the same feelings toward a learned Brahman as toward a Chandala [outcaste], a dog, a cow, and an elephant." But in his very quotation of the passage, he rises above it and judges it, for he changes the order. In its proper order, the passage teaches anything but human equality: "The wise looks with equal eye on a learned Brahman, a cow, an elephant, and even a dog, and an outcaste." "Even a dog and an outcaste" is significant. The outcaste is coupled with the dog, and even then, comes last. The passage teaches the reverse of equality. Gandhi is now settling down to being a good man, a great servant of the people, and a Sanatana Dharmist. It is a tragic case of Almost.

India is the land of Almost because she only almost believes in life. Change her there and she will burst into achievement of every type and kind. Galvanize her soul with a radiant belief in life and the possibilities are untold. Some of us have the secret hope that she will, when touched by Christ into life, assume the spiritual leadership of the world.

"I know a Name, a Name

That will set that land aflame, aflame."

But in thinking about the Almosts, the Christian Church will not go from my mind. We have mentioned elsewhere the amazing interest on the part of the Hindus in Christ as a Person. "There are none of us now among the thoughtful Hindus who have not a reverence for Jesus Christ," said a chairman one night, and to my surprise the audience applauded. But this interest in Christ is centered outside the Christian Church and not in it. One can see why this is, for Christ can be separated from Westernism, but the church cannot be so easily separated. India is making a case for Swaraj, and she feels that any confession of a need is a giving away of that case. Any dependence on the West is a confession of unfitness. I am sure the church will not have a fair chance before the soul of India until the political issues are settled and India can stand as an equal to exchange mutual benefits.

But this is not the only reason for the church in India being in a state of Almost. She has come to the birth and cannot bring forth. Why? Because she is not spiritually fit for this hour. She is weak and her temperature is low. We have taught India reverence for Christ, but we are not able to teach her realization of him, for our own realization is dim. Were it clear and victorious, it would be a flame that would race through the tinder soul of India.

"My spiritual experience has always lacked a vital spark," said a thoughtful and noble Y.M.C.A. secretary in one of our Round Tables. "I came near saying 'Hallelujah' once, but it never quite came out." If the Christian Church could ever really say "Hallelujah," and say it from the depths, say it with its whole being, we could set India aflame. When India burns with God, the world burns. But we are not saying it.

India, divided into a thousand cleavages, asks for unity, and we offer a church sundered by denominational divisions. India, tired of the petty roads that lead to blankness, asks for the high road to an open vista, and we trace before her little bypaths of denominational differences. India asks for a love that binds and cements and turns to the church for that love and often finds instead petty squabbles for position and power. India asks for God and we hand her a correct statement about God—a creed.

> India, divided into a thousand cleavages, asks for unity, and we offer a church sundered by denominational divisions .... India asks for God and we hand her a correct statement about God – a creed.

We Christians are in a state of Almost. And when we turn to the mother church in the West and ask for that word, that unity, that sense of bigness and relevancy, that flame, we do not get it. Never would spiritual backing count so much as now in this our hour when we are trying to bring forth a nation for Christ, but we wonder at times if that backing isn't weakening.

At the close of World War I, the church of the West saw the vision of world need, felt the throb and pull of it, determined to follow the Christ into the adventure of healing a world, felt that she could speak the healing word that the world needed so desperately. We bent over to listen to it, her lips framed the word we wanted to hear: "Christ," but other words fell: "Larger and more comfortable churches," "Fundamentalism," "Modernism," "Menace of papacy." We expected the church to ask for a cross, and instead she asked for comfort; we yearned for Christ and they gave us a controversy; we asked for fullness of power and they gave us the fear of the Pope.

The church has spent much time debating the animal ancestry of men. If it had spent a good deal of this time in doing what the Muslim director of public instruction said the Christians had done in Central India for aborigines, "by turning them into men," the controversy would have been lost in a crusade. Our greatest danger is not from a bowing down to the Pope, but from a bowing down to Mammon; not from transubstantiation, but from materialism. We Protestants have swept crucifixes from our churches and put in cushions.

At the time of the most amazing prosperity that the world has ever seen, the American churches are spending more and more on themselves and less and less to sustain that thin line of representatives standing on the frontiers of human need. The fact is that the line is actually being starved. A process of de-Christianization has set in while the world demands Christ.

As Doctor Knudson says: "In Rome Christianity degenerated into an ecclesiasticism, in Greece it became a philosophy, in Germany it became a system of doctrine, in England it became the religious side of Imperialism, in America it is being reduced to Rotarianism." However good Rotarianism is in its place, it is deadly as a substitute for the gospel.

Our savage pagan ancestors roaming across Europe worshiped the mistletoe, a parasite. They felt there was some strange divine vitality in it, for it remained green in the winter when the tree upon whose life it lived seemed dead. We, their descendants, are worshiping many parasites upon the Tree of Life. Things that are sapping the very spiritual life of us are gaining an attention which is amounting to an adoration. Oh, for a cleansing down to relevancy, to worthwhileness, to the real, to Christ!

The church here and at home is in a state of Almost. We are fumbling at a time when a spiritual crisis has seized the soul of the whole of the East. Dynasties are cracking and crumbling, social customs are being challenged and changed, economic systems are breaking under the new strain, religious concepts are proving inadequate to provide a basis for life, men are striking their tents to go on a quest for *life*. We have Life to offer them, but we are only *almost* offering it and showing it.

This crisis may come and go and life may harden again. It has happened before. There was a time when all central Asia trembled in the balance. Would it go toward Christ or toward Mohammed? In Marco Polo's time, Kublai Khan sent a request to the Western world "for a hundred teachers and learned men, intelligent men, acquainted with the seven arts, able to enter into controversy and able to prove to idolaters and other kinds of folks that the law of Christ is best." But the Christian world was divided and filled with squabbles. After a delay of two years, two priests instead of a hundred were sent. When they arrived at the court of Kublai Khan, they asked the Mongols to become politically and ecclesiastically attached to Rome. The Mongols soon saw that they were using the great teachings of Jesus to further the claims of the Pope to world dominion. "Christianity so vitiated was not good enough for the Mongol mind," says H. G. Wells.

They took Islam instead, and then swept across Asia with the sword of Islam spreading destruction and Islam wherever they went. In India, we inherit 70,000,000 Muslims as the result of Mongol invasions, and all central Asia is solidly Islam. The church failed. It was more interested in political power than in people, in controversy than in Christ. It is a most decisive case of Almost.

I wonder what future historians will record of the church of this age. Almost?

Chapter 9

WHERE IS THE PLACE OF CERTAINTY AND AUTHORITY?

WE HEARD AGAIN and again in the conferences the note of religious certainty. Men in contact with Christ seemed sure because they seemed to have hold of reality. Others seemed tentative and uncertain.

"All the old infallibilities are dead," says a recent writer. Are they? If so, I find some of them undergoing a resurrection and coming back to me again.

Man wants certainty. A good deal of loud protesting religion is not certain. Confident assertions are often used to cover a doubt. A Hindu wrote to me: "Come over to the Vedic religion, the religion of great Aryan Rishis of yore. There the sun of truth is always shining with all its splendor. I am always for a dying cause." We are not as naive as this, but a great deal of dogmatically asserting religion, both among Hindus and Christians, is very uncertain. A great many religious men with the more cautious scientific attitude are just as uncertain. A question mark is a poor resting place for a tired spirit. Many modern religious attitudes are expressed in the limerick:

> "Forasmuch, as without Thee
> We are not able to doubt Thee,
> O grant us Thy grace
> To inform the whole race
> That we know nothing whatever about Thee."

We can hardly be satisfied with this. Rather does Saint Augustine voice our feelings when he says: "I wished to be as certain of things unseen as that seven and three make ten." But can he be? Perhaps not. And yet perhaps more so. For "seven and three make ten" appeals with certainty to our reason, but not to our affection and will; it may be that there is a certainty that will take possession of our whole being. Have we felt any rock beneath our feet in the storm and clash of things in India and particularly in these conferences?

In searching for a place of certainty, there have been three great historic answers: 1. An Infallible Church; 2. An Infallible Bible; 3. An Infallible Christian Consciousness.

Men have fled to these three places for security and certainty. The first need not detain us long. There has been only one branch of the Christian Church that has claimed infallibility, and it would not be unkind, but merely stating the facts, to say that "there has been nothing infallible about this church except that it has been infallibly fallible"—just as the rest of us have been. While we cannot accept this dogma of the infallibility of the church, nevertheless I am quite sure that there is a truth lying embedded here, and that truth will contribute to the final certainty. Later we shall see what that truth is.

The second is the place where the conflict is keenest. If a verbal infallibility is insisted upon, then the certainty is very precarious, for of the twelve hundred manuscripts at our disposal no two are verbally alike, and differing translations add to the insecurity. But we may find certainty, if the infallibility is vital, instead of verbal—of the spirit, not of the letter. This, too, will contribute to the final certainty, as we shall see.

The third is the place to which those have gone who feel that they cannot find complete certainty in the first two. They base everything upon the Christian consciousness, upon experience. Here, they say, they are on solid ground, for "he who says consciousness says science, and that which is found in consciousness cannot be controverted." I am not quite sure that, taken by itself, this can bring the certainty we crave. There is a danger of cutting the experimental from the historical. If the connection is cut, or held too loosely, there is invariably a withering of the experimental. As one has illustrated: It is like the kite that tugs at its string to get loose in order to find greater freedom to fly higher, breaks the string, and instead of flying higher comes down with a thud. I think experience will show that the experiential must keep in close touch with the historical Christ in order to reflect experience. Nevertheless, there is a great truth here, and it also will contribute to the final certainty. Where is that place of authority and certainty?

Someone has said that there are two kinds of reality: Objective Reality and the Reality of Experience. Objective reality can be proved to a high degree of certainty. We are certain that Plato lived and that Waterloo happened. Historical research makes these certain. Not absolutely certain, for we cannot look into our consciousness and find them corroborated there, but the certainty is of high degree. On the other hand, some things verify themselves to us in our own consciousness. This also brings a very high degree of certainty, but not the highest. The highest degree of certainty would be found where these two kinds of reality would come together and corroborate each other, where the historical and the experiential witness to the same fact. This is the highest kind of certainty we are capable of knowing.

Now, in the gospel we have these two sides: there are the Christ of history and the Christ of experience. If these two are real, then we have the two kinds of reality mentioned above. The historicity of Jesus I need not pause to discuss. Heaven and earth have been scoured to find evidence for or against the historicity of Jesus, theory after theory has been brought forth to account for him apart from his historicity. They have all collapsed by their own sheer weight or have broken themselves upon the fact of Christ. After a hundred years of terrific battle, the smoke has cleared, and there stands upon the horizon of our thinking a character essentially as the New Testament depicts him.

But we are met with the deeper objection of Gotthold Ephraim Lessing that no event in time could prove eternal truth. The Christian gospel is in time, hence, limited and local; not universal and, hence, not true. And Swami Vivekananda, the great Vedantist, said that "Christianity must go to pieces upon the rock of its historicity."

But one cannot be too deeply grateful that in Christ we have ideas become historical. As someone has suggested, "In any battle of ideas, the victory must go to that side where the ideas are guaranteed by the facts." In Christ, the ideas of the gospel are guaranteed by the fact of Christ. Here are not unrealized ideas floating upon the horizon of men's thinking, but ideas become personalized, looking at us with loving eyes and touching us with warm redemptive touch. A correct code of morals leaves us absolutely cold. Only when that code becomes a character does it shake us. The abstract and the impersonal soon pall on us. "The Impersonal laid no hold upon my heart," says Tulsi Das. We cannot commune with a sunbeam, or say our prayers to the force of gravity, or bow down to the multiplication table, however true they may be. Abstract beauty is tiresome, but a beautiful face never is. Love read about and extolled may disgust, but when love meets us in a person, it is different. Religion may seem the driest thing in the world, but when Religion comes to us bending in lowly services, healing our wounds of body and soul, speaking to our drooping spirits and making them live again, and showing us the Father, then we bow at the feet of Religion, forever captivated.

Moreover, how can we tell whether a thing is true or not "except as we see it to be operative"? It must be put under life to see what speaks from it there. These ideas of the gospel have become operative and they blossom forth in the most beautiful character of history.

Again, what really touches us vitally must touch us where we are, namely, in the stream of history. We are not ideas, we are living facts, and what redemptively touches us, must be historical, must stand where we stand, and then step out beyond us and show us the Way. Does not Christ do this for us? We have seen our ideas realized, and they hold us like a magnet.

Even Swami Vivekananda forgot himself long enough to say that "the soul can receive impulses from another soul and from nothing else. We may study books all our lives and become very intellectual, but in the end, be not developed at all in spirituality. To quicken the spirit the impulse must come from another soul."

And Gandhiji, after saying that he "decided that salvation lay for him within Hinduism," expressed that same craving for an incarnate perfect guru when, after speaking of a certain guru, he says, "Although I admired him, I could not give him my heart. The throne is still vacant and my search continues." Here he confesses that the Hindu ideas he had chosen could not occupy the throne of his heart. He wanted the Personal.

Christ at the Round Table

It is Christ—the Christ of historical realized Fact—that holds us steady. In the Round Tables you felt that, outside of Christ, men had no anchorage for their thinking. There was "a series of dissolving views." Even Krishna in the Gita does not provide it, for men are semiconscious that here is philosophy, but not realized fact. As I talked to a Hindu about the Gita one day, I pointed out that I thought that Arjuna took much higher moral ground in regard to war than Krishna, his teacher, did. He promptly replied, "Then why can't we make Arjuna the incarnation?" He was ready to shift on amoment's notice, provided, of course, that it was within Hinduism. But fancy a Christian confronted with difficulties in Christ saying, "Then why can't we make John the Baptist the Savior?" The Christian bhakta is conscious that it is Christ or nothing. If we can't believe in him, we can't believe in anything. If we are loosed from this historical Christ, we are adrift. He provides the touchstone to which we constantly bring our motives, our thinking, our actions, our social programs, and our very souls, to be corrected and made after the Pattern. If we allow this historical to grow dim and to fade out in favor of what men carelessly and glibly call the "universal Christ," we drift into sentiment, into "sloppy thinking," and into religious "cock-and-bull stories." If we do this, we could be ready to take to Krishnamurtism, the latest bubble that has arisen to the surface of religion from heated imaginations, the imaginations that find it much easier and less demanding to rhapsodize over some future coming one, than to obey and embody the One who has come and who stands in human history vital and unspent, life's Norm and life's Savior.

This fact of the historical Christ brings a high degree of certainty and authority, but not full certainty and authority. For, after all, if Jesus is only historical, it would be authority outside ourselves standing in history. No authority from without can be complete authority for us, unless it can become identified with our very selves, and can speak from within. The Christ of history must become the Christ within.

We cannot live upon a remembrance, however beautiful. We can only live upon a realization. But Jesus becomes that. He told his disciples that it was expedient for him to go away, so he went, but "he changed his presence for his omnipresence." He came back more vital than before. Timid believers became irresistible apostles, for Christ had moved into their inmost souls. Life became merged: "I am crucified with Christ: nevertheless, I live; and yet not I, but Christ liveth in me," cries the transformed Paul. Archimedes, after pondering a mathematical problem, suddenly finds the solution, and in his excitement rushes up the street crying, "Eureka, I've got it!" These men, pondering deeper problems, find a deeper solution, and cry from deeper depths: "We've got it." Christ becomes self-evidencing. The historical passes into the experiential. They become witnesses.

It is often pointed out to us, as a defect, that the New Testament does not teach meditation, and it is claimed that Hinduism supplies this deficiency. It may be true that present day Christianity lacks those depths that come out of meditation and quiet, but it is quite easy to see why there was little meditation in the New Testament. These men had found and realized. They were so filled with that finding and that realization that they had little time or disposition to spend in solitary, self-centered meditation. They hurried to put this cup of joy to the parched lips of the nations. They prayed, sometimes in prolonged seasons, not for their personal realization, but for courage to witness and for the people to whom they were witnessing. Later, when the church lost this radiance, men attempted to re-gain it through the method of prolonged meditation and isolation. Meditation belongs to the period of striving to gain or regain spiritual certainty and realization. In the New Testament, their meditation had turned into a mediation they were joyously sharing.

How do we know that there is redemption in this history? Redemption comes out of it. The only test of light is that it shines, of a

Revelation that it reveals, of a Redeemer that he redeems. How am I to know that God has gone into this Historical Fact? By the test of whether he comes out of it. He does come out of it. He meets me here—meets me redemptively.

> "Whoso has felt the Spirit of the Highest,
> Cannot confound nor doubt Him nor deny:
> Yea, with one voice, O world, though thou deniest,
> Stand thou on that side, for on this am I."

I challenge anyone to get into fellowship with this Christ of experience by repentance and self-surrender and obedience and then say, "This does not touch my soul's inmost need, this is not life." As Coleridge says: "Do not talk to me about the evidences of Christianity. Try it. It has been eighteen hundred years in existence and has any one individual left a record like the following: 'I have given Christianity a fair trial. I was aware that its promises were made conditionally, but both outwardly and in my inward acts and affections I have performed the duties which it enjoins, yet my assurances of its truth have received no increase. Its promises have not been fulfilled. I repent me of my delusion.'"

These are not the words of those who come into touch with Christ. Rather, do the lines of Fannie Heaslip Lea express the aching truth:

"She made a little shadow-hidden grave
The day Faith died,
Therein she laid it, heard the clod's sick fall,
And smiled aside—
'If less I ask,' tear-blind she mocked,
'I may Be less denied.'

"She set a rose to blossom in her hair,
The day Faith died—
'Now glad,' she said, 'and free, at last, I go
And life is wide!'
But through long nights she stared into the dark,
And knew she lied."[1]

Romanes the scientist, entering the world of scientific fact, felt his faith slip from him. At last it was gone. He then confesses: "I am not ashamed to confess that with the virtual negation of God, the universe to me has lost its soul of loveliness. Although from henceforth the precept, work, while it is called today, will doubtless gain intensified force from the terribly intensified meaning of the words that the night cometh when no man can work, yet when at times I think, as think I must, of the appalling contrast between the hallowed glory of that creed, which once was mine, and the lonely mystery of existence as now I find it. At such times, I shall ever feel it impossible to avoid the sharpest pang of which my nature is capable." This loneliness of soul sent him back over the facts again, this time with his plowshare set deeper. Christ verified himself to him, and we hear him now say: "Do not think—try—make the only experiment available, the experiment of

---

[1] Reprinted by permission of the author.

faith. Do the doctrine, and if Christianity is true, the verification will come." It does come. I have watched it being verified around the world. Christ steals into the crannies of the soul with the healing sense of certainty.

Matthew Arnold was right when he said, "Jesus Christ and his precepts are found to hit the moral experience of mankind, to hit it in the critical points, and to hit it lastingly. When doubts are thrown upon their really hitting it, then to come out stronger than ever." Jesus therefore needs no protection. He needs proclamation. He himself is his own witness.

We were in a motor car on our way from Jerusalem to the ruins of Jerash, a Roman city 25 miles from Amman, Jordan. At the junction of the roads, we came upon a signpost on which was written, "To Jerash, Great Aniquities." Laughing over the "Great Aniquities" we continued on our way. But in a little while it dawned on us that in spite of the missing "t" that sign did point us to the place where we wanted to go, to Jerash. We had to turn around, come back and obey the sign post, and it got us there. In our thinking, the whole emphasis had been thrown upon the wrong phrase of the signboard. "To Jerash" was the important thing.

Suppose scholars should find a "t" missing in the accounts of Jesus. The decisive thing is that he points the way to life. Where does the infallibility of the gospel lie? In this: that if a man will take the way that Christ points, he will infallibly find God. This is an infallibility not to be argued about, but to be tried. I did not say that if he takes the way of Christ, he will get to heaven, for that could not be verified now, but this can be verified here and now. I am more certain of this than I am of seven and three making ten, for Einstein with his doctrine of relativity casts doubt upon the latter; but here we are dealing, not with a relative physical world, but with an unchanging God and with an unchanging Christ who is the same yesterday, today, and forever, and with human souls that rest as they rest in Christ.

Rudolph C. Eucken says there are four stages in religious belief: (1) Faith, (2) Criticism, (3) Experience, (4) A final livable creed. The first stage is when we take what has been handed down to us without question; the second is that stage when we turn on our beliefs and question them; in the third, we pass from this negative questioning to positive experience, and the final creed is that which you cannot help believing; it has gripped the inmost depths of life, has become a part of one and fits in with the facts of life. If this be true, then Christ will be the final creed.

During the war, a boy was brought into the hospital badly wounded. Word was sent to the mother that the boy was dying. She came to the hospital and begged to see him, but the doctors said that he was just hovering between life and death and that the slightest excitement might kill him. Besides, he was unconscious and would not know her. She promised that she would not speak to him or make the slightest noise, but begged to sit by the side of his bed and be with him. The doctor relented and gave permission for her to sit there without a word. She sat by her boy with her heart bursting. His eyes were closed. She gently put her hand upon his brow. Without opening his eyes, the boy whispered, "Mother, you have come." The touch of that mother's hand was self-verifying to the boy. He knew it. When Christ puts his hand upon the fevered brow of our souls, we know the meaning of that touch and say from the inmost depths, "My Savior, you have come."

This self-verifying of Christ in experience brings a very high degree of certainty, but not the highest degree, for, after all, there is the possibility that I, as an individual, might be mistaken, self-deceived. It would be a glorious self-deception, issuing in peace and harmony and life, but still there is the possibility that one might be deceived and that his experience could not be verified on a widespread scale. Gandhiji seemed to me to try to break the force of my own witness to him when he suggested this possibility.

On the contrary, it is being verified on an amazingly widespread scale, on a scale as widespread as it is seriously being tried. The Christian Church is terribly divided. The number and narrowness of our sects is a scandal. But if we only realized it, we are the most united people on earth. And united in the deepest essentials of life. Our Round Table Conferences revealed this. At the center, at the place of Christian experience, we are one. We do not have to strive for unity, or ask for it; we have it. No matter who was speaking, whether it was an Easterner or a Westerner, a brown man or a white man, a High Church Anglican bishop or a Salvation Army officer, a Mennonite or a Methodist, a Protestant or a Roman Catholic—wherever men experienced Christ, in reality we felt they were one. Outward differences fell away as irrelevant. When we experience Christ, we realize that the same Life throbs through us all, the same Christ of experience holds us together in the deepest unity that life can find. All other unities are superficial compared to this. The Christian Church is the most united body on earth when it is really Christian. One of the finest moments of our Round Tables was when a Roman Catholic magistrate was telling of what Christ meant to him in experience. As he talked, I found the cords of my heart vibrating in involuntary unison. I knew we were sharing the same Life.

We might be gathered from the ends of the earth at our Round Tables, from many nations and denominations, with no previous intimation of what we were going to be called on to do, so there could be no possibility of fitting in statement with statement, yet the moment we dropped to the level of Christian experience, we were talking the same language. It was akin to the miracle at Pentecost; "we do hear them speak in our tongues the wonderful works of God." It is possible that each denomination may have had the underlying thought that Christian experience is "our tongue," but soon the discovery is made that we all speak the same language when we speak as followers of the Christ of experience.

The truth is there that the individual experience is certified and corrected by collective Christian experience. This is the meaning of the Christian Church. The church is not mechanical; it is vital. It does not depend on mere physical successions— that would be the religious materialism often found in Hinduism—but upon the spiritual succession of a common sharing of life in Christ—that is spiritual and Christian.

Here we find, then, the two kinds of reality, the *historical* and the *experiential*, each bringing a high degree of certainty, coming together and dovetailing, speaking the same thing and bringing the highest kind of certainty and authority that is possible for the human to have. The two realities come together and make *reality*. "Where the flint and the iron come together, there are the stars." Moreover, this is corroborated on a world scale wherever the church becomes Christian.

Where, then, do we find the place of authority? In which one of these three—the Infallible Church, the Infallible Bible, the Infallible Christian Experience—does it lie? It lies in all three. Each contributes. *That place of final certainty and authority is at the junction where the Jesus of history becomes the Christ of experience, and where the resultant individual experience is corroborated and corrected by the collective experience.* The place of authority, then, is Christ revealed in the past, experienced in the present and corroborated by collective Christian experience.

> That place of final certainty and authority is at the junction where the Jesus of history becomes the Christ of experience...

The Historical speaks and says, "Come unto me and I will give you rest;" the Experiential cries, "I've tried it and experienced it. It is true;" and the Collective witnesses and says, "Through all times and climes, we have verified it. It is so."

There is no higher certainty possible.

Chapter 10

INTERPRETERS OF CHRIST

CHRIST MUST BE interpreted. Often in our conferences we felt that the interpretation of him was adequate and compelling, but once or twice it seemed inadequate and confused.

The Gospel is an interpretation. It is the translation of the language of eternity into the speech of time. It is God's redemptive purpose become intimate, actual, available, understandable. It is said that when Dante spoke, the silence of ten centuries was broken. In Jesus, "the silence of eternity" was broken and we have the gospel.

Now we are called on to interpret this redemptive fact. Jesus entrusted it to us to make it plain and meaningful and vital to other men. We are interpreters. Very often that message is emasculated, turned into the trite, its power and meaning taken away when it goes through us. A chairman one night introduced me as follows: "Some years ago the speaker was studying law, and he heard a minister preach, and he was so deeply impressed that he gave up law and became a missionary." Was that all? Here was all the meaning of these years put into these bald meaningless words. I winced under it. I have often thought that Jesus must often wince under our turning the wonder of the gospel into a dead commonplace.

I have learned a great many lessons from the interpreters I am compelled to use as I travel about in the different language areas of India. Our meetings for the educated classes are usually in English, but in the meetings for Christians and in many for non-Christians we use interpreters. They speak many messages to me as they give my message to others.

> The Gospel is an interpretation. It is the translation of the language of eternity into the speech of time.

This began some years ago when I saw myself very vividly in one of my interpreters. I have been gathering lessons ever since. I suggested to him that we go over the message beforehand, but he replied, "Oh, no, I can do it without that." He was cocksure. He stood for a great many of us who take it for granted that we know all about the gospel, we have caught certain ideas and phrases and we say we have it. But the gospel is an adventure —an opening adventure. It should find us standing before it in a state of constant surprise at its opening wonders. The Pharisee and the child in the Gospels stand for opposite types. One had attained, had closed up, was impervious to anything outside of his closed system and his closed soul, while the child was open, eager, full of questions, explorative. Jesus could do nothing with the one and everything with the other. My interpreter stood for those interpreters of the gospel who have the closed mind, the closed soul and the closed system. And Jesus can do nothing with them.

When we stood up before the audience, my interpreter stepped out in front of me, and then began, not an interpretation of my message, but a demonstration of his cleverness, in fact, of himself. I gave short, simple sentences and he turned them into the most amazing language. He dressed up my simplicities beyond recognition, and, of course, killed the message. And all the time a Voice was saying: "Do you see yourself? That's you. That is what you often do with my gospel." And I knew it was true.

In Protestantism, we have rightly emphasized the preaching function of the ministry, but it often turns from being a gospel into a display of the "gospeler" and his cleverness. The gospel dies, strangled by self-interested display.

Another interpreter represented the opposite of this. I soon saw that his words were correct, but were commonplace and dead. One felt that he had spoken into a phonograph and his message came back correct, but metallic and ineffective. In China, a pastor arose during a conference on evangelism and seriously advocated that they procure the best preachers to preach into phonographs and then that these records should be sent throughout China to grind out their message and so evangelize China! Easy, but deadly. Interpreters who are metallic!

In one place, we were having meetings for non-Christians in a most unusual place. A large and deep bathing tank had been dug with the masonry so built that it formed steps leading down to it from all four sides. The tank was dry and it was proposed that a platform be erected down in the center and the audience seated on these steps, the whole forming a perfect amphitheater. It was a splendid place, but my interpreter's first words when he saw it were these: "But suppose the crowd gets out of hand, there is no way of escape for us down there." His first thought was how to escape from the results of our message! But he is not alone! Many of us consider how we can dodge the consequences of our gospel. Interpreters who look for ways of escape!

Christ at the Round Table

Another interpreter was an official Chinese court interpreter, not a Christian. It was gracious of him to do the interpreting for us, but you felt that he wasn't in it. He was still officially interpreting. As I was speaking, I used the word, "Pharisees," and he, not being at home in our religious vocabulary, hurriedly asked, "What seas were they?" This interpreter represents a vast number of us who speak the gospel, but are not really in it. It doesn't come up out of the depths of our souls like a fountain. It is not identified with us. The gospel can never be effective until it becomes so one with us that we cannot think and act and speak apart from it. But our brother interpreting the gospel was still official and his speech betrayed him. It always does.

Akin to this, there was an interpreter who, fortunately or unfortunately, had never been associated with Americans in any close way. He was a bishop's chaplain and rather sedate. I foolishly used some American slang, a thing of which I am not often guilty; in telling a story I said, "She was tickled to death." He paused for a moment, then translated it, "She was scratched until she died!" I am not quite sure how she was resurrected in my story! Word for word he was correct, but the meaning? I am sure when we come to the Gospels, we must enter into them and catch the undertones of idiom and meaning, or else we will end up as far from the mind of Christ as my interpreter ended up from the real meaning of my story. He represents the interpreter of the gospel who seizes the bald literalness in places and does not catch the drift and meaning of the whole.

I had a Chinese interpreter who was not quite sufficiently acquainted with English. I was speaking to a crowd of non-Christian Chinese and I said: "If you do this, you will be a victorious soul." He translated it: "If you do this, you will be one of Queen Victoria's soldiers." He had me out recruiting for the dead queen! But there are many of us recruiting for issues just as dead. I listened in America to professors in a theological institution who were fighting battles that

Interpreters of Christ

were long over and had been for fifty years. The battle had moved on and they were fighting rear-guard actions, but religion was at grips with new living issues. The Jerusalem leaders represent this recruiting for dead issues, while Paul represents the interpreter of the gospel at grips with things that had a life-and-death meaning in them. He was in the battle that mattered.

In one place, they provided me a Hindu as an interpreter—a nationalist. He could not resist the temptation to take my message and give it a political coloring. He used my statements about the gospel for his nationalist ends. He was using my gospel for other purposes. But by doing it, he deeply taught me, for under much of our gospel preaching and work there run other purposes. Men are listening to the overtones, but there is also an undertone that distracts and confuses. Using the gospel for some other ends! How often governments have done it, and how often societies and individuals have done it as well.

I have in mind two interpreters who taught me lessons akin to each other. The one was a Hindu who, while a fine interpreter and very capable, was very self-composed, even stiff. He was in the attitude that he would do what he was called on to do and do it well, but he would not give himself to it. The first night he stood with his hands on his cane and scarcely moved a muscle, but the second night he got so into the spirit of the message that he was waving his arms as much as I was mine. He had let go. He abandoned himself to the message. No great interpretation of the gospel can take place unless the gospel interpreter lets go, unless he abandons himself to the mind of Christ. Some of us have not let go. We are afraid of where it will lead us. We haven't quite got the consent of our minds to be God's fool, if necessary. Only when mind merges with Mind, and will with Will, and being with Being and life-purpose with Life-purpose, can there be the swing of victory and the sense of rhythm with Christ. The religious need of our times is a sane letting go to the mind of Christ.

The other interpreter was a tremendously earnest Christian. He was very anxious that the message go through with effect and power. However, he was tense and very stressed in his role as a spiritual communicator. Although it was cold in the auditorium, within five minutes the perspiration began to roll down his face. It was not that he was nervous about the question of being able to interpret, for he was a graduate of a university, but he was strained because of his inner spiritual anxiety. This sense of strain was spoiling everything. There wasn't the sense of quiet faith in God and the message. I felt like stopping the address, unfolding his clenched fists, and stroking his over-wrought soul into quiet peace and trust and saying, "Now let's trust God. He will see it through." But I could not and the meeting was spoiled. I longed to teach him this lesson, for I had been taught it some years before when my whole work and in particular my preaching was strained. I was so eager that I was overwrought. In a series of evangelistic meetings I was pulling and tugging to get men to decision, but the results were meager. I felt as though I could take a cudgel and beat them into the kingdom of God! After one of the services, I went out and lay down under an apple tree exhausted. The beautiful Virginia apples were hanging on the tree above me. The Master came to me and seemed to say, "My child, you're tired, aren't you?"

"Yes," I replied, "I have a right to be, for I've worked hard."

"And you are out of patience, aren't you?"

> **No great interpretation of the gospel can take place unless the gospel interpreter lets go, unless he abandons himself to the mind of Christ.**

"Yes, I am," I replied, "but I think I have a right to be when they are so dull and unresponsive."

"Do you see this tree?" said the Master. "How is it bringing forth fruit? Is it working itself up into strain and frenzy in order to produce fruit?"

"No," I said. "It seems to be just quietly pouring its life through the branches into the apples and they are becoming beautiful and ripe."

He quietly replied, "You are in Me, as the branch in the Vine. Keep the channels open, let my life flow through you into the fruit, and it will be abundant."

I arose with a new sense of trust and inward poise and calm. I need worry no more about the results.

I would simply keep open the channels for Life to flow. Service was no longer a strain, but a joy. And the fruit was now more abundant, for it was not mine, but his.

The interpreter must be full of calm faith in the One who commissions him and keep everything open to his mind and his will and his life.

But if many of my interpreters have taught me how not to be an interpreter of Christ, many more have taught me how to be an effective interpreter. Among the Syrian Christians of the Malabar Coast, where audiences number thousands, are magnificent interpreters, among them a young priest highly educated and well trained. An Arya Samaj preacher had been through that country preaching that Jesus was a myth and he learnedly tried to prove it. I was answering him and was using the familiar argument that it would take a Shakespeare to forge a Shakespeare, it would take a Christ to forge a Christ. Instead of using the word "Shakespeare," which would have been meaningless to many, he changed it immediately into "it would take a Kalidas to forge a

Kalidas." Now, Kalidas is a great Indian poet. That was familiar, understandable, and it hit home. Shakespeare would not. We who are trying to make Christ clear to men should lay hold of contextual thought forms familiar to the people to whom we preach. Christ must be naturalized in a situation. Paul did this. He says, "I take every project prisoner to make it obey Christ." He took hold of everything to bend it to the service of the Son of God. As educationists have begun in the "project method" to lay hold of every project to make it obey education, we must lay hold of everything to make it obey Christ. We must fling our gospel through it. To do this, we must get into sympathetic touch with the all peoples and we must sit where they sit.

> The interpreter must be full of calm faith in the One who commissions him and keep everything open to his mind and his will and his life.

Another interpreter was a youth who was a born interpreter. I could say anything and as quick as a flash he would run back into Sanskrit, or Arabic or Persian and bring the technical term. But if he were a born interpreter, he was a reborn one. He had a deep experience of Christ, and he heightened and vitalized every expression with the glow of his own soul. He more than pulled half his load. Again, and again I found it necessary to quicken my spiritual pace to keep up with him. One day he was translating so beautifully and so accurately (I knew the language he was using) that I simply stopped, put my arm around his shoulder, turned to the audience and said, "Isn't that beautiful translating?" They applauded—and well they might. Sadly, this interpreter, Calvin Singh, is dead now, cut off in his youth. It may be the Master had some interpreting he needed done in some other world. I lay the tribute of my love at his feet wherever he is. He is interpreting somewhere, I am sure. And the hand of the Master is upon his shoulder in love and admiration. For Calvin is doing it well.

One of the greatest interpreters in India—for he is one of the greatest souls in India—is a priest among the Syrian Christians (Mar Thoma). With his long beard and flowing garments and finely chiseled face, he has the appearance of Moses. And Moses never gave himself more for his people than this Syrian priest has done. For forty years he has poured out his life for his people, his gentle fingers are always unraveling difficulties, his heart is always going out in tenderness toward suffering, and his feet have borne him innumerable miles to address human need in ministry. His experience of Christ is rich and abundant. He has walked with Him these years. When he stands up to interpret, no wonder the great audiences bend to catch every syllable, for his sentences scintillate with a natural eloquence. But it is not eloquence that holds them; it is the fact that forty years of beautiful Christ-like living is speaking. It is not the interpretation of that hour; it is the interpretation of a whole life going into his words. The impact of forty years of unselfish living is falling upon the souls of the people. Christ becomes living and real because the interpreter is unconsciously speaking from the depths of years of intimacy with him. This is interpreting indeed and in truth.

But even the finest of our interpretations are faulty. There has been only one Interpreter-Jesus. He has interpreted God and life and redemption. He has interpreted the Father: "No man hath seen God at any time, but the only begotten Son, who is in the bosom of the Father, He hath *interpreted* Him" (John 1: 18, Moffatt). As I trace the ways and acts of Jesus, God grows beautiful before me. And when I hear him say at last, "He that hath seen me hath seen the Father," I know it is so in very truth. A God like that can have my heart without reservation and without qualification.

We are called on to interpret Christ. And some are doing it so beautifully. As I sat with a Hindu youth, I soon saw that there was a flame in his soul. While still a Hindu, he had organized a dozen Brahman youths into what he called "A Society of the Friends of Jesus." As I sat and talked with him, he told me of his decision to become a baptized follower of Christ. I rejoiced, for I felt it was right and fitting, for Christ was in his heart as reality. He told me how it came about—the flame had been caught from another heart. "Oh, everybody in our city knows Mr. H., and Jesus, and God," he said. I liked that order of the steps upward—Mr. H., and Jesus, and God. If men are going to see Jesus, they must see him through us, and if they are going to see God they must see him through Jesus. We then seem to be the key to the situation.

> We are called on to interpret Christ. And some are doing it so beautifully.

We were having excellent meetings in a Maharaja's theater. The place was crammed. At the close of one of the addresses, I asked, "Would you like me in closing to pray?"

A voice from the gallery called, "No."

It was the first time I had ever had them object, so I replied, "All right, I do not want to force prayer upon you," and sat down.

But a member of the audience got up and said, "Sir, please forgive us. It must have been only a student who objected. We want you to pray."

This statement was so evidently from the spirit of the meeting that I did pray.

The chairman of the meeting, a Hindu prime minister, expressed himself in his public remarks in these words: "I could not help contrasting this meeting tonight with the Christian meetings I attended as a boy fifty years ago. The missionaries preached on the streets and the crowds were there to heckle and jeer and sometimes to throw stones. But tonight, this great audience has sat here listening with breathless and reverent attention to a Christian address, and you could have heard a pin drop. What has made this difference in our attitude toward Christ? Well, it is this: Among us have lived men and women who by their lives have interpreted Christ to us. A few miles away is one of the greatest hospitals in India where Christian doctors serve people night and day regardless of race or creed or color or money. Then nearby is a leper asylum where they attend to the lepers in Christ-like service. Moreover, the speaker has said that in Gandhiji's ashram Brahmans have been doing scavenger work, but these Christians have been doing scavenger work of the highest kind. They have taken hold of the untouchable outcastes and have washed them in soul and body and mind, and have turned them into men and women citizens, respectable and honored. It is this fact of Christ being interpreted to you in Christ-like service that makes possible this meeting tonight."

A Hindu principal of a college, one of the men who in the Round Tables impressed me as having found living reality in religion, said at the close of one of my addresses: "Jesus is lighting up the soul of India as the sunrise first strikes the high peaks of the mountains and then gradually the light sifts down into the valleys. He is lighting the finest among us and the light is gradually permeating down through to the masses. And we are glad to be conquered by that light." Why did he say these things so frankly before this Hindu audience of his own townspeople?

I saw the reason a little later as he talked on. He said, "I once saw Christ, and I have never forgotten the vision. The plague was raging in the city and everybody had fled in terror except the sick and dying.

Whole sections were deserted. I drove down through that plague-stricken section and to my surprise I saw a missionary lady, Mrs. D., coming out of one of the houses where there was plague. She came with her hands extended before her and she said, 'I am sorry, Mr. S., that I cannot shake hands with you, for my hands are plague-stained.' As I looked at her with her plague-stained hands, I saw Christ." No wonder he was glad for India to be conquered by this Light. He saw the interpretation of its meaning in the hands of one of his interpreters. It was Service and Self-sacrifice.

What kind of interpreters of Christ are we?

Chapter 11

MISSIONS AT THE ROUNDTABLE

The missions are at the Round Table. Just what are we trying to accomplish as a result of our work? What is the objective which we have placed before us? Is that objective being fulfilled?

During the last year in India, we have called together leading men from the various missions to study in a three-days' retreat just what we were after, to define our objectives and to judge what is being done in the light of those objectives. In the light of the tremendous amount of criticism to which our whole program is being subjected, and in the light of the mind of our Master, we went over our motives and aims.

We found ourselves eliminating one thing after another in our search for a statement of our objectives. It did not take us long to brush aside such an objective as Westernizing the East. We found ourselves saying, and saying with real sincerity, that we wanted India to keep her own soul and not to be a pale copy of any other country. Only thus can she be creative. We sincerely desire to see India preserve those fine heritages of the past which could not be lost without loss to us all. In that heritage, one of the finest things is India's love of simplicity.

Our civilizations are becoming too complex and put too great a strain on body, mind, and soul. The great things are being lost among the many things. India has a message of simplicity which the world needs. Again, we felt ourselves disclaiming a religious imperialism that tries to impose its views and beliefs in the spirit of dominating the minds and beliefs of other people. We felt that this is a most subtle temptation and must be fought at all costs. Similar to this is the desire to conquer another religious system, satisfying a group superiority complex in doing so. We found ourselves saying that we were not interested, as such, in conquering another religion. That might take place and yet we were very far from the goal before us. Again, we repudiated the idea of an endeavor to build up a communalism over against the Hindu and Muslim communities. Our endeavor is not to build up a political and socially exclusive entity called the Indian Christian community. We also expressed our belief that mere numbers were irrelevant to the purpose in hand. We wanted something deeper. Again, we did not feel disposed to say that we would present to India a blocked-off ecclesiasticism, saying, "Take that or nothing." We felt that India had as much right to experiment along the line of corporate Christian living as we of the West had. We yearned to see an Indian expression of the universal Christ —an expression that would flower forth from the depths of India's genius.

Then just what were we after? We defined our evangelistic objective in this way: *The production of Christ-like character, through faith in and fellowship with Christ the living Savior, and through corporate sharing of life in a divine society.*

We felt that the end in view was nothing less than the production of Christ-like personalities. This sounds high, but Jesus himself raised the standard of perfection saying, "Be you therefore perfect even as your Father in heaven is perfect." Someone has said, "We are inalienably akin to perfection." The most perfect Fact that we know is

Christ and the goal of human character is nothing less than Christlikeness. We know nothing higher. We can be content with nothing less.

We recognize that this creation of Christ-like personality is impossible apart from Christ himself. Through faith in and fellowship with this living Person the inner and outer life take on the moral and spiritual characteristics of Jesus. The beginnings of this may be sudden and decisive, resulting in a new birth, but growth is continuous and will be forever. Christlikeness is the goal.

Moreover, this Christ-like character cannot be created in isolation. Man being what he is, "a divine society" is a necessity. We pray and work that the Christian Church may be coterminous with that "divine society," but often it lags behind, for the kingdom of God breaks out beyond it. But we cannot do without corporate Christian living if Christ-like character is to be produced.

> Our evangelistic objective: The production of Christ-like character, through faith in and fellowship with Christ the living Savior...

In summing up the end and meaning of the Christian ministry, Paul places before us this same objective: "And he gave some, apostles; and some, prophets; and some, evangelists; and some, pastors and teachers . . . unto the building up of the body of Christ; till we all attain unto the unity of the faith, and of the knowledge of the Son of God; unto *a perfect man, unto the measure of the stature of the fullness of Christ*" (Eph. 4:11-13).

Now if this production of Christ-like character is the objective, it brings with it a severe standard of judgment for our work. In the light of this, what are we producing? This brought on deep heart-searching.

Christ at the Round Table

The fact is that while we as a group repudiated some of the above mentioned things as false objectives, nevertheless, some of these very things had been and were actually still taking place.

Westernizing has taken place through Christian missions to a very great extent. I asked a Christian college student whether the students of the college liked a certain Christian nationalist who was lecturing in the college. His reply was, "The Hindu students like him, but the Christian students do not like him, for he discards our costume." Our costume was European clothes! One would not mind the slightest what kind of clothes they wear if it were not the sign of an inward mentality—a mentality that has been often weaned from India to a very great extent.

There is no doubt that a communalism has been built up around the Christian Church in India. Many of the objections made against the church should have been directed against this communalism. We deplore it. But the fault is not all our own. If Christian converts had been allowed to stay in their homes as frank, open baptized members of the Christian Church, this communalism would not have been built up. But they were thrust out and thrown with us and denationalization has taken place. I suggested to Gandhiji that as far as I was concerned, I was willing to see the Indian Christian community, as a community, fade out if the Hindus would allow converts to stay in their homes as frank, open baptized members of the Christian Church. He wasn't quite ready to commit himself to that proposal. There is no Christian community in China; there are Christians, members of the Christian Church, but a communalism has not been built up. In America, we have not built up a Christian community in addition to the Christian Church. Members of church and non-members live together in the same community and often work for the same purposes. We trust the time is not far distant when this fading out of Christian communalism in India will take place. The Hindus and Muslims can accelerate it, if they will, but as long as converts are thrust out of their homes this process will go on.

It will also go on as long as we missionaries are not more deeply identified with India. Some of us are here geographically, but we are not really in India. We have never yet got to the soul of India in deep identification. "How long have you been in India?" someone asked a missionary.

"I sailed for India ten years ago, but I haven't arrived yet," was the reply.

Everybody knew what he meant.

The question of how long a person has been in a country may have little to do with what he knows about that country. People who have been, say, thirty years in a country are often taken as authorities and true interpreters of that country from the mere fact of long residence. However, they may never have been near that country during the thirty years. I saw an English lady, in three months, break through and get to the soul of India far more deeply than many who have been here for years. A deep sympathy, a khaddar (home-spun) sari, and a sincerely Christian soul accomplished it. We can go along the lines marked out by sahibhood and never get near real India. This English lady broke over these lines and India clasped her to her heart.

We must listen to the words of Gandhiji as he spoke at a missionary conference: "It is much better to have the receptive mood. As a true friend, I would tell you that I miss that receptiveness, that humility, and that willingness on your part to identify yourselves with the masses of India, and my message to my missionary friends is that you should identify yourselves with the people as Christ did in his time." These are words worth pondering.

We often speak of "these people" and "this country" instead of "our people" and "our country." Unless there is that deep identification, our gospel will fall on deaf ears. A Christian nationalist has said, "No nation can afford to be proselytized by its conquerors." In doing so it loses its soul. If the gospel, then, comes with power to India, it will come from those who speak from within. One of the finest compliments I have ever heard given to a Christian worker was when a Hindu said to him, "We feel at home when you speak." He was speaking from within.

If the missionaries of the gospel are to have a real hearing in the East in the future, they must become disassociated from imperialism of every type and kind and come in the form of servants. The pedestals of imperialism of every description are tottering and falling all about us, but there will always be place for servants of the East. The day of the pedestal is drawing to a close—the day of the servant is just beginning. In a conversation with a Muslim nationalist, he remarked, "In our national life Tagore is a luxury, but C. F. Andrews is a necessity." Tagore is the poet and Andrews is the servant—the one a luxury and the other a necessity.

> If the missionaries of the gospel are to have a real hearing in the East in the future, they must become disassociated from imperialism of every type...

The deep necessity in the East for the servant type will always be present. And this fits in with what Jesus presents as the Christian attitude. In the twenty-third chapter of Matthew, Jesus suggests three attitudes of mind against which he warned his disciples. In Moffatt's translation, He says, "Be ye not called 'Rabbi,' for one is your teacher" (verse 8). This attitude of teacher predisposes you to the outlook of superiority—the teacher knows, the taught do not—and this tends to become unchristian. The day of the teacher will always be here, but the day of the schoolmaster attitude has passed. Be ye not called "teachers." The second against which he warned is: Be ye not called "father" (verse 9). The "fathers" were the elderly statesmen in religion, the experienced, the type that assumes superior attitudes because of their years. The world is being managed politically and religiously by "fathers," men of static minds and set souls and superior attitudes. Again, he said, "Be ye not called 'leaders'" (verse 10). This also tends toward the attitude of "I lead and you follow," and, of course, easily degenerates into fussy managing of other people's souls. Jesus warned against being called "leaders," yet when we overhear the present-day religious vocabulary, we hear such phrases and sentences as: "Training for leadership," "You are to go to the mission field to be leaders." All of this brings on clash and jostling for place and power. Jesus warns against this attitude, for it is essentially un-Christian.

There is only one attitude with which he could trust his followers: "Be ye called servants" (verse 11). That attitude is the Christian attitude, for it is the one Jesus took: "The Son of man came not to be ministered unto, but to minister, and to give his life a ransom for many."

A Hindu nationalist said: "There are two great words gripping the soul of India at the present time, and those words are 'service' and 'self-sacrifice.' No man is being considered great any more unless he embodies these two ideals." These ideals are embedded in the heart of our gospel and must be embedded in the heart of our attitudes and programs if we are to have any moral authority in the East.

"Have this mind in you which was also in Christ Jesus: who, being in the form of God, counted it not a prize to be on an equality with God, but emptied himself, taking the form of a servant, being made in the likeness of men; and being found in fashion as a man, he humbled himself, becoming obedient even unto death, yea, the death of the cross" (Phil. 2: 5-8). Suppose we read it this way: "He who being in the form of a white man, counts it not a thing to be grasped at to be on an equality with the dominant race, but empties himself, taking the form of a servant, being made in the likeness of the men to whom he goes; and being found in fashion as an Indian, he humbles himself, becoming obedient unto death, yea, the death of the cross for the sake of those among whom he labors." Suppose we could read our names into that, what would happen? Just what happened to Jesus, namely, that "God hath highly exalted him and given him a name above every name," so that the servant of the East would become the greatest of all in the East.

As servants, we would then be loosed from many of the fetters that now bind us, among them the necessity of keeping up prestige and of living up to sahibhood. "Are you going on this train?" I asked an Indian gentleman one day.

"No," he said, "I cannot go, for there are only third-class carriages on it."

"I am going," I said.

"Yes," he slowly said, "you can go, for you are a religious man. If you go first class, it does not exalt you; and if you go third-class it does not degrade you. You are above these distinctions. But I have to keep up my prestige."

The road of prestige and sahibhood is getting more and more difficult in the East, but the way of the servant is absolutely open and will be open more and more. Christian missions, then, must disassociate themselves from imperialism of every type and kind and assume the form of a servant and take up and share the brown man's burden. If they do, their future is assured.

Imperialism is not only without in governmental and economic policies, but it can be in spirit on the inside of mission policies and outlook.

"Why aren't you a Christian?" asked an Indian Christian while in England of an ex-president of the Indian National Congress.

"I am a Christian," was the reply.

"But I do not understand," replied the Indian Christian, rather surprised. "You are not a member of the church, are you?"

"No," was the reply, "but I am a Christian. The reason I am not a member of the Christian Church is that I do not want to put myself under further bondage to the West. You are under double bondage— both governmentally and ecclesiastically— while I am only in single bondage, governmentally." This should make us "furiously to think." How is it that Christ can be separated from the dominant influences of the West and the Christian Church cannot be? Christ is striking root more deeply than the Christian Church. Why? India is more and more feeling that Christ belongs to her, but as yet she does not feel that the Christian Church is truly indigenous.

It still seems to be foreign-managed. We were discussing this fact of Christ being taken into the soul of India far beyond the borders of the Christian Church and our attitude toward it. A missionary arose and said, "If these unauthorized Christians will do so and so, we might let them carry on." I gasped. Who are we to say whether they should or should not carry on? We have no right of eminent domain over the gospel. It is this managerial spirit that makes men still feel that the church is foreign. "Please open the door and then get out of the doorway," said an Indian in regard to this foreign overshadowing.

We stand too much in the doorway after having opened the door.

It is possible to propagate religion with the desire, perhaps unconscious, to dominate the minds and souls of other people. This is subtle and deadly. This is the reason that Jesus says that the only name and attitude he can trust his followers with is that of "servant." Anything else easily passes over into religious imperialism and becomes un-Christian.

A good deal of this spirit grows out of the consciousness of the superiority of the faith one holds, but the superiority of a faith can easily pass over into the superiority of the person holding that faith. We then become patronizing in bringing the gospel of love and humility and self-sacrifice. "I think I would have been a Christian while in England," said a returned student, "if they had loved me a little bit more and my soul a little bit less." Religion often degenerates into a fussy desire to manage the souls of others. It becomes imperialistic. It then becomes unattractive and un-Christ-like.

> **Jesus says that the only name and attitude he can trust his followers with is that of "servant." Anything else easily passes over into religious imperialism and becomes un-Christian.**

Our business is not so much to do a job, but to create men who can do it. When a Y.M.C.A. secretary received word in Europe that his Indian colleague had been appointed as general secretary for all India in his place, he sank back in a chair and said, "Now, thank God, I've succeeded." That was true success. An ounce of Christian service that comes out of the soul of the people is worth a pound of that which is imposed from without. But there are many who are still "benevolent tyrants," overshadowing souls, around whom no one can grow. Very often we create a system which only we can run, for it expresses our genius, and then call other people inefficient who cannot run it because it does not express their genius. Villagers who manage panchiyats (village councils) of their own and do it well, are often at sea with the complicated machinery of our ecclesiasticism, and we call them inefficient. Rather we should question the efficiency of our methods that very often do not seem to run according to the grain of the people.

Our organization should not only be more indigenous, but the very spirit of missions should be the same. I asked a leading Arya Samajist about naturalizing Christ in India. He replied: "It all depends upon the Christian Church. Will it truly express our national spirit and genius?" I asked him what he meant by that, and his reply was: "Will you stand in the stream of India's life and past and interpret Christ or will you stand in the stream of the West and interpret Christ? Will the Christians love Sanskrit as they love English?" We can see his meaning and sympathize with it. We also see the difficulties. After all, the English language has been in touch with Christ and has to an extent been Christianized. A Hindu wrote, "It is now impossible to argue a man into slavery in the English language." Too many ideas of freedom are current in the language. Sanskrit has been Hinduized; it is soaked in Hindu thought and terminology, and therefore, the Christian Church has been afraid of it. The Christian Church was afraid of Plato and his philosophy in the beginning. Then an expurgated edition of him was allowed in the church, and by the third century it was heresy to disagree with him! Sanskrit will become Christianized. Christian meanings are more and more being read into it. "Jesus is one of the names of Bhagwan. It is in the book," said a priest of a temple one day. I asked him to let me see it. He went into the temple, brought out a book in Sanskrit entitled *The Thousand Names of God*. The four hundred and thirty-seventh name was, "Jesus, the beloved, the perfect One, the Son of God." I turned to my friend and said, "He is on the inside—now watch what happens!" As Sanskrit becomes more and more Christianized and the religiously unusable portions of it drop away, we will be more and more able to use it to express our Christian faith and will consequently be more and more in touch with the fine things of India's history.

Moreover, the virtues that appeal to India must be fostered in the Christian Church and in the Christian missionary. The active, aggressive virtues appeal to us of the West, while the passive virtues appeal to India. Both are important, and the Christian expression is unbalanced that embodies only the one side. This demand for an emphasis upon the passive virtues was vividly brought home to me in one of our Round Table Conferences. I had been invited to attend a Theosophical Society meeting. I came to listen. As we sat there before the meeting began, all eyes were turned to me as if I were expected to do something. I felt the pause providential, so I suggested that we turn the meeting into a Round Table Conference and that we share what religion is meaning to us in experience. At the close, we felt that Christ was at the center and all eyes were on him and what he did for life. The Hindus were deeply touched. One of them spoke up and said: "We are moved by what you say about finding jiwan mukti—living salvation. Now, we Hindus feel that if a man has jiwan mukti, he will be delivered from five sins: Kam [low desire], Krodh [anger], Mob [avarice], Lobh [craving for things], Ahankar [self-assertion]. Have you been saved from these five sins?" There I sat, and my judgment day was on! There was no escape. But I felt that it was more than a personal thing. It was Hinduism asking of the Christian Church if it would embody in reality those virtues that touch the soul of India very deeply. How deeply inward these five things are! Robert Owen unfolded to Emerson an elaborate plan of analyzing the world's mistakes and evils. Owen said the five fundamental evils were: "religious perplexities, money difficulties, disappointment in love, intemperance, and anxiety for offspring."

"You are very external in your evils, Mr. Owen," said Emerson. "Let me give you some real mischiefs: living for show, losing the whole in particulars, indulgence of vital powers in trivialities."

Splendid, but I am not sure but that the five Indian sins are more profound, not as profound as the Christian definition of sin—all un-Christlikeness is sin—but more profound than Owen's or Emerson's. And we must embody those virtues of Ahimsa, of harmlessness, of equanimity, of inward calm, of victory over the world, of renunciation. They are all in Christ and more, but we have not put our stress upon these virtues that appeal so deeply to the Indian heart.

> We must embody those virtues of Ahimsa, of harmlessness, of equanimity, of inward calm, of victory over the world, of renunciation. They are all in Christ and more...

As the missions sit at the Round Table a more meaningful example of how to approach the people of another race and civilization could not come before them than that of the centurion in the Gospels. His fellow Romans did not veil their contempt for the subject people, the Jews over whom they ruled. But of this centurion the Jews said that "he loveth our nation," and that his "servant was dear unto him." He was humble enough to love an individual servant and great enough, in spite of the fact that his nation ruled over the Jews, to love a nation. He loved both. Very often we have loved individuals among whom we go, but we do not love the nation—we do not rejoice in the beauties of the ancient culture, in the growth of national awakening, in the signs of a people coming of age, and in the growing ability to take over what we have handled. If we are to have a real place in India and the East, we must love "nations" into being and rejoice as they stand upon their own feet. But this centurion also loved the individual servant—some of us love the nation in the abstract, but not individuals. As one man said, "I love humanity, but I don't like people." It was said of Rousseau that he combined love of all mankind in general with hatred of all mankind in particular. This centurion loved both. No wonder in his hour of distress, "elders of the Jews" and "friends" were there to help him. He formed friendships with the very people who probably were leading the national movement for freedom. He created an atmosphere of friendly good feeling.

Some of us are afraid that if there is this close identification, our prestige and authority will be weakened. But this centurion had authority: "I say to this man, 'Come,' and he comes; and to this one, 'Go,' and he goes; and to my servant, 'Do this,' and he does it." In addition to the authority that the Roman government had given to him, he had gained an authority over the hearts of the people who surrounded him—had gained it by the sincerity and depth of his love for them. This is the authority that really matters. All other authority is a dwindling factor. In the East, this kind is the growing factor.

Moreover, when the time of crisis came, he stepped up from his faith in people to a beautiful faith in Christ. So much so that Jesus exclaimed, "I have not found so great faith, no, not in Israel." He cultivated faith in people and it was then easy for him to believe in Christ. The way for us to gain a great faith in Christ is not by arguing about his glory, but by believing in people for whom he died. We must believe mightily in people, in their possibilities, in their future, in their nation. "Jesus is the great believer in man." He believes in us when we cannot believe in ourselves and his faith in us nurses our souls into health.

At this time, when India is losing faith in herself, we must believe so profoundly in her, in her genius, in her possibilities, that she will be bound to respond to our faith. The fact is that since we believe in life, we are the ones who should believe most profoundly in India's life and in her national possibilities. A leading Hindu nationalist, sensing this, surprised me by saying, "It is you Christians who got Gandhi out of jail and who now believe in him." Another said: "You are the ones who will finally win our freedom. You are not discouraged." These may be overstatements, but they contain a truth. That undiscouraged dynamic that underlies the gospel is one of the greatest national contributions we can give to India at the present time.

But one thing more before we turn from this centurion. His humbleness of mind toward a person of another race over whom he was ruling was remarkable. "I am not worthy that you should come under my roof." This humility of mind is lacking among us. It is the poor in spirit who shall have the kingdom of Heaven, and the meek who shall inherit the earth. We conquer not by haughtiness and pride, but by humility and self-sacrifice. "The love of Christ is more dangerous than the sword of Islam," said a Hindu. We must embody its humble gentleness, if we are to go far into the soul of the East.

> **We must believe mightily in people, in their possibilities, in their future, in their nation. "Jesus is the great believer in man."**

As the missions sit at the Round Table, let them fearlessly go over their motives and aims and spirit and let them courageously eliminate everything that does not fit in with the mind of Christ. In that direction lies the future. Some time ago, I awakened to the fact that I had a very large bunch of keys with very small possessions. These keys had been accumulating for years. So, I decided to take up each key and ask it a question, "Do you unlock anything?" I asked them one by one, and often the reply was: "Why, no, that lock has worn out," "This one has been lost," "This one broken." But for just six of them the answer was, "Yes, this one unlocks something." They stayed. The rest were eliminated. Now every key unlocks something.

> As a result of the work of Christian missions, the greatest movements for human betterment are going through the soul of the East that the world has ever seen.

We must fearlessly go over our faith, our methods, our organizations, our programs, and our spirit, and ask concerning each one the question: "Does it unlock anything? Does it unlock reality, does it fit into the soul of India, does it bring me to God and to people, is it really redemptive, is it according to the mind of Christ?" And we must be willing to lay aside rusted keys that no longer fit into things and no longer bring us to vital touch with Christ and life.

As a result of the work of Christian missions, the greatest movements for human betterment are going through the soul of the East that the world has ever seen. We believe so profoundly in what we are doing, so profoundly in the gospel of Christ and the Christian Church, so profoundly that in Christ is the key to the future, that we dare subject everything, including ourselves, to the most rigid scrutiny and criticism, knowing that if what we are doing is founded on reality, the more searching that scrutiny and criticism the more it will shine.

It is the tendency of all institutions and organizations to become set and rigid. Founded to express life, they often end by throttling that life. They must undergo constant criticism, perpetual readjustment, and recurrent renewing if they are to remain vital. Christian missions are no exception. One of the most hopeful things of the future is that we are subjecting ourselves to a self-criticism that is relentless and perhaps unparalleled in any other body in the world.

We are in a situation that searches us to the core and that demands reality. We must have reality or perish. So, we turn to the Mind of Christ as that ultimate reality, to be subjected to its criticism and to its inspiration and to its healing.

And the best minds of India know that everything depends upon our catching anew that mind and living it out. It was not strange that when a Christian congregation decided to call a meeting for prayer and for self-searching in order that they might catch anew the mind of Christ and experience a revival, a non-Christian lawyer turned up to help pray for that revival. That Hindu kneeling in prayer for a revival in the Christian Church is India, dimly but growingly realizing that in a revival of the mind of Christ in the Christian Church lies her salvation —and ours.

Chapter 12

NATIONS AT THE ROUNDTABLE

SUPPOSE THE NATIONS should sit at a Round Table Conference and through their representatives lay before each other what religion is doing for them in experience. Suppose they should tell of what it is meaning to them as a working program, of what it is bringing to them of inward righteousness, of a dynamic for the cleansing of the social and economic life, of the curbing of the spirit of selfishness toward others and of the creation of the spirit of brotherhood and good will toward all. Suppose they should try honestly to see how religion is working in the national life, and, on the basis of the facts produced, would try to arrive at a common mind in regard to which is the best moral and spiritual dynamic for national living. What would that national witness be? What would the nations that profess the Christian faith say to the non-Christian nations and vice versa?

The above is not a mere supposition, for the fact is that the nations are unconsciously at conference, and we are all listening in to what they are saying as to the meaning of religion as expressed in national life, and we are coming to our conclusions.

The first impression we gather is that each nation considers itself superior and takes itself very seriously indeed. The ancient Jews had a prayer like this: "O God, thou hast made us for thyself; as for the rest of the nations, they are but spittle"; and each day the pious Jew thanked God he was not born "a leper, a woman, or a Gentile." The Greeks had no word in their expressive language for "mankind," for everyone who was not a Greek was of a different species— "a barbarian," and Aristotle thought that some people were "naturally" slaves and some "naturally" rulers, as a dog is naturally a dog and a cat naturally a cat. The Romans despised the nations over which they ruled, and Servius said that "the stupidest and the ugliest slaves in the market are those from Britain," and no Roman lady would ever stain her face lest she be like "the wood-stained Britons." They felt that they were permanently superior and the Britons permanently inferior. The Shah of Persia (now Iran) has a title which he still retains— "The Center of the Universe." I stood with a Burman in the palace of the last ruler of Mandalay, and when we came under the Throne Tower he said, "Now you are at the center of the world." The Chinese call their country "The Middle Kingdom"—they are at the center and we are all upon the margin, and their usual name for foreigner is "foreign devil"; I have heard the name affectionately called after me as I have gone along the streets in China: "There goes Mr. Foreign Devil." The Japanese believe that they have descended from Heaven and are a Heavenly Race. The Mikado signs himself as "Manifest Deity," and the Crown Prince as "the August Child of the Sun." When someone suggested that the Japanese had no moral codes in their ancient literature, the reply was: "But we were by nature moral and needed no moral codes. The Chinese were not by nature moral, so Confucius had to come to them as a lawgiver." The Hottentots of Africa call themselves "the complete people," and the Eskimos call themselves "the men of men." The people on the island of Haiti believe that their island was the first of all created things—the sun came out of one cave and the moon out of another, but they were first.

The people of the United States of America call their country "God's own country." A great newspaper in America carries the legend at the top of its front page, "My country, may she never be in the wrong; but my country right or wrong." A lady from "God's own country" was visiting Japan and telling me of it as she naively said, "The thing that struck me was to see so many foreigners together in one place." They were foreigners—she was not! An American in Scotland on a visit was asked by a Scotchman where he came from, and he proudly replied, "I come from God's own country." The Scotchman looked at him in surprise and replied, "Then you have lost your accent." An Englishman talking to me one day said, very seriously, "You know we never think of comparing ourselves with anyone, for we don't think there is anyone else in the same class." The Irish say, "Sinn Fein," and it means "Ourselves Alone." The Germans say, "The Fatherland over all." The Russians call their country "Holy Russia." A Swedish lady was listening to two British people speaking English in a train in Sweden. She listened very carefully and then turned to a neighbor and said, "Well, thank God, I talk a human language." While speaking upon this subject, I saw some Danish people in the audience and I tried to think of something that showed their feelings about themselves. The only thing I could think of was that Gandhiji had said that the Danish government was the only government he would take from the West. I could not tell them that! So, I asked them at the close what they thought of themselves, and the reply was, "Oh, we are a humble people; we are proud of our humility." After hearing me give this list one day, an Australian lady came up to me and said, rather excitedly, "But you left out Australia." She was unwilling to be left out in the race for absurdity; she would be absurd along with the rest. But I have left out India, the land of my adoption. India too has a name for foreigner,

NATIONS ...

"Mlecha," and it may be translated, "Dirty Devil." When an Indian goes across the seas and returns he has to purify himself by taking a pill made up of the five products of the cow and has to go through other purification ceremonies before he can get back upon the holy soil of India. I asked a Santal, a member of one of the aboriginal tribes of India, what they called the Santals in their language, and his reply was, "Men." And the non-Santals? And the reply was, "Enemies." Their world was divided into "Men" and "Enemies."

And they are not alone, for most of the members of the Round Table of the Nations would have to confess to much the same attitude toward themselves and toward other nations. It would be a good thing if at the Round Table of the Nations each would frankly tell what they thought of themselves. There might be a good general laugh. It would clear the atmosphere, let down the tension, and they could see that they have all been fools together. And then they might talk and act toward each other as normal human beings. Each nation has taken itself far too seriously. It is this megalomania that is back of the world tension and clash to-day. And it is this megalomaniac self-assertiveness that is the most un-Christian element in the nations today.

> **Each nation has taken itself far too seriously. It is this megalomania that is back of the world tension and clash to-day.**

If the "Christian" nations were to speak of what the Christian faith is doing for them, they could recount a great deal. Has it not brought them to civilization? Has it not produced institutions for human betterment unsurpassed in the world? Has not William Lecky, the historian of European morals, said that "the three short years of the life of Jesus has done more to soften and moralize mankind than all the disquisitions of philosophers"? Softening and moralization has taken place. Has this faith not put a corrective at the heart of the nations which, in spite of partial acceptance of it, makes for better living and human progress? Is there not a capacity for human helpfulness there that is not found elsewhere? Where do we turn for famine relief, for the education of the backward races? Where have the great reforms come from? Under what auspices has the League of Nations been formed? Where has human life the largest possible chance for development?

There is something redemptively at work at the heart of "Christian" nations in spite of only partial acceptance. That "something" is Christ. But what is it that negates a great deal of fine work for the world? It is this undertone of self-assertiveness, of imperialism of many types and kinds. As long as this self-assertiveness is there, other nations will not believe that the philanthropic work for the world is disinterested. "First religion, then trade, then empire—is not this the order?" asked a Hindu. I saw a wonderfully equipped, modern, government-endowed Japanese hospital far up into the heart of the Shantung peninsula in China. I could not get rid of the thought that it was there for a purpose other than disinterested healing of the sick—it was the kindly side of a pushing imperialism behind it. That hospital seemed no longer a hospital to me, but a spear-point pointed at the heart of a nation. For the first time, I saw the standpoint of the weaker nations of the East. Concerning everything that is done for them, they ask the question, "Is this because you love us, or because you want to control us?"

When the Non-Cooperation movement was at its height, a brilliant and balanced Indian Christian was seated at luncheon with a group of educationists in Britain when one of them said to him: "But aren't you grateful for what we have done? Haven't we done a lot of good to India? Look at the railroads, telegraphs, posts, new roads, the country organized and kept in peace, a civil service that is the highest in the world—look at all these. Haven't we done a great deal and shouldn't there be gratitude?" The Indian replied: "Yes, what you say is true, and we are grateful, but there is one question that keeps disturbing that gratitude. To illustrate: I have some cows in India and I take good care of them, I feed them well, give them a good home, and were it not for what I do for them they would be roaming in the jungle uncared for. They should be grateful for what I do for them. But why do I do it?" There was a long and painful silence and then an Englishman slowly said, "Do you mean to say that we do these things because we want to milk the situation for our benefit?"

"I do," quietly replied the Indian.

Was the Indian right? Not entirely, for there is a great deal of disinterested, unselfish work going on. Britain has contributed enormously to India. Her officials have been high-minded and above corruption. She has established parliamentary institutions and now says to India, "Arise and we will work together." It is a great record, one of the greatest, if not the greatest, in human history. I do not think any other nation would have done better. I cannot help thanking God for India's sake that there has been this impact of Britain upon her life during these years. I cannot imagine what India would have been without it. Nevertheless, on the whole, I think the Indian was right. Self-interest is back of things. Sir W. Joynson Hicks, home secretary, puts it in these blunt words: "We did not conquer India for the benefit of the Indians. I know it is said in missionary meetings that we conquered India to raise the level of

> **There is something redemptively at work at the heart of "Christian" nations in spite of only partial acceptance. That "something" is Christ.**

Indians. That is cant. We conquered India as the outlet for the goods of Great Britain. I am not such a hypocrite as to say we hold India for the Indians. We hold it as the finest outlet for British goods in general and for Lancashire cotton goods in particular." Disconcerting, isn't it? Is it true?

The American administration has done a great deal for the Philippine Islands. In a few decades, the Filipinos have been prepared for self-government and have been given a large measure of it. We were about to hand over the reins of government to these aspiring people when it was discovered that rubber could be grown in the islands. Now all sorts of reasons are being brought forth, explaining why self-government cannot be given: "Who would protect them from being absorbed by stronger neighbors?" "The Filipino administration is not free from corruption." "We would betray our trust if we took our hands off at this stage." There is truth in some of these statements, but the real reason is self-interest—rubber; and the name for raw rubber is "latex," which is uncomfortably like "milk." All the fine work done there will be negated if the suspicion grows that we are there to "milk" the situation for our own benefit.

The League of Nations was conceived in high idealism and born out of the travail of the war. The mandate system is a noble conception of trusteeship in behalf of the weaker. It would be, if we could get rid of the thought, based on the facts that mandates are, on the whole, taken for "milking" purposes. If not, then why would no nation take a mandate for Armenia? Why was she left to be raped and murdered and destroyed? Why? Because there was no milk there. The breasts of this tortured nation had been drained dry, so the nations passed by on the other side.

As long as this self-interest and imperialistic aggression, however "enlightened" it may be, is there, we take the gospel to the nations with a dreadful handicap. As a statesman of India said, "Your Jesus is hopelessly handicapped with the West." If this underlying self-interest and self-assertion could be given up, if we could become really Christian in our national outlooks, then the other fine things done for the weaker peoples would blossom into beauty and would cover the earth as a garden of the Lord.

An Indian educationist was seated with a group in Britain at the time when Lord Reading had just been appointed viceroy, but had not left for India. One of the group said to the Indian, "Will it not make a difference in India that Britain has appointed a Jew as viceroy?"

"I don't understand," said the Indian.

"Well," replied the Englishman, "the fact that he isn't a Christian should count with non-Christian India."

"Oh," said the Indian, "that wouldn't matter the slightest, for of all the accusations against Britain, we have never yet accused her of being Christian." And yet Britain is probably as Christian a nation as there is in the world today.

The fact is that the East is not afraid of our being Christian, but of our not being Christian. The East knows what Christ stands for and is eager that national life in the West correspond to it. A non-Christian President of the National Congress in India recently said, "I see no hope in India for real self-government, torn as it is with mutual jealousies and personal rivalries, and no hope in the England of today with her love of power. The only hope is in England becoming truly Christian and applying Christ's teaching to the problems of India." That is a challenge that should send a nation to its knees. Suppose it should be decided by people and by Parliament that the challenge would be accepted, that everything un-Christian would be eliminated from national policies and attitudes and everything Christian would be embodied and the Mind of Christ become the determining factor in everything, what would happen? It would thrill the world. A new era of good will and understanding and co-operation would begin in the East, and Britain could lead it.

But the East is fast taking to heart what is happening in China. If China succeeds by violent means in getting from foreign powers what she wants, then the rest of the East will quickly learn the lesson. As an Indian said: "We are watching very closely what is happening. If China succeeds, then we are through with Gandhi and his non-violent methods." A new situation can be created only by a change from being compelled to do something when a pain is felt to the Christian attitude of being impelled by an idea because it is right and Christian.

Our religion should lead us to right attitudes instead of to being compelled by "situations" to adopt them. A Muslim said to me: "Our religion teaches us to fight while yours teaches you to conquer by love. You should, therefore, show us a better example."

And at the Round Table when all eyes are fastened on America, what is the word she has to say? Out of the depths of her spirit speaks a very beautiful word, "Liberty," and that word has been founded in her religious faith and fostered by it. She has been the refuge of the oppressed of the earth and the land of opportunity to the millions. They have come without stint. Only when the life of America was about to be overwhelmed was this flood restricted. She has stood for peace and the non-aggressive attitude toward other nations, and along her Canadian border there is not a fort or a soldier. Cuba, at her doors, was given her freedom. The results of her philanthropy are throughout the world. It would be a wonderful record if other and very embarrassing words were not being heard. One of them is "Financial Imperialism," and recent events in Mexico and Central America make the fear of this imperialism real and justified. We, who have been cradled in liberty, must not now renounce that birthright for the *ignis fatuus* (a will-o'-the-wisp) of the domination of others by whatever means accomplished.

Along with this "financial imperialism" is the undertone of military-mindedness that seems to be growing. Were it not for the strong stand the churches are taking against it, there would be serious concern in our hearts. But until militarism gets religion behind it, it can never sweep a nation. Today the churches stand blocking its progress. But the voice is there and we in the East are hearing it.

One of the things that cause deepest concern to the peoples of the East is the fact that by the immigration law those of a certain color have been branded as inferior. This is the cutting, stinging, blighting thing. A Hindu expressed it to me in these words: "You would get a better hearing for your gospel in the East were it not for your immigration law." And another, stung to fury, sent up this question to me: "After the passage of the immigration law in America, aren't you ashamed to desecrate the platforms of India with your convulsive dancings, falsely called gestures?" I have laughed every time I thought of the "convulsive dancings falsely called gestures," but laughter soon fades away into seriousness when I think of the other side of his question, for concerning this there is a sense of shame for the land of my birth when I stand upon the platforms of India.

Tagore expresses the same resentment when he says that "Jesus could not get into America because, first of all, he would not have the necessary money, and, second, he would be an Asian." It may be that we are doing more than excluding Asian; we may be excluding him. In the last day, he may say, "I was a stranger (literally "foreigner") and you took me not in." It may be that Christ stands in the foreigner, rejected because of the color of his skin, and he may have to go to other lands where he is more welcome. If spiritual dryness begins to pervade our religious life and the presence of Christ seems dim, we must look around for the reasons. One of them will be that in excluding one of the least of these, we excluded him.

The effect of the immigration law has gone through the East. Kagawa of Japan, educated in our American universities, on return to Japan found that he had only one lung functional and that he had but a short time to live. He decided to fling his life away, to go down into the vilest slums of Kobe and share the life of the poor and wretched. He lived among them, took upon his own heart their difficulties, sorrows and sins and soon all the laboring classes were turning to this young Japanese minister. He became the great labor leader of Japan, but all the while he was the evangelist of the Good News. He could charge admission and yet fill any hall in Japan for an evangelistic address. While preaching in Tokyo, three hundred thousand people attended his evangelistic services and six thousand became Christians. He says: "Then suddenly came the Exclusion Act. All this work was undone instantly. For a month after the passage of the bill, I could not preach for fear of attack. The people said, 'Christianity is from America and we have no ears for this doctrine.'"

> **It may be that Christ stands in the foreigner, rejected because of the color of his skin, and he may have to go to other lands where he is more welcome.**

And all this upset was so unnecessary. If Asia had been put on the same quota basis as the rest of the world, only two hundred and fifty people from all Asia would have been admitted. America has a right to exclude, but she has no Christian right to insult.

But for this undertone of resentment, we would not find Gandhiji printing this in his paper, *Young India* (October 14, 1926): "There were Christian clergymen traveling to the Holy Land. An African-American clergyman from the Southern States was to travel with them. His fellow white clergymen refused to allow him to travel with them. The passage was refunded and compensation paid and, thus, he did not join the trip with his fellow clergymen." Ministers of Jesus Christ on the way to view the footprints of the Son of man and to look on those scenes where he bore the cross for us, getting rid of a man and a minister because he was black, and yet it was an African, Simon the Cyrenian, who bore Jesus' cross for him when he was so exhausted he could no longer bear it! I wonder how much those ministers really saw when they got to the Holy Land? They degenerated from pilgrims to tourists.

I am sure they did not see as much as another African-American clergyman, a doctor of philosophy from Harvard, on a pilgrimage to the Holy Land, for at the close of a service in Jerusalem, he came up and said: "I have seen the cross this morning. I have seen too that I must bear it. I have decided to give up my great church in America and go to Africa as a missionary." As he took his cross, he took his place alongside of that other member of his race, Simon the Cyrenian. And that excluded clergyman joined the company of cross-bearers with a very heavy cross of rejection laid upon his shoulders. As Jesus walked in their midst, I think he must have spoken words to them that the others in the crowd who laid the crosses on black shoulders never heard and never knew. Those words were for the inner circle of the cross-bearers. And those words meant life.

There are other pilgrims going to the Holy Land. We were in Vienna when a Zionist Congress was in session. Anti-Jewish demonstrations were being held in the city. Feeling was running high. We asked Rabbi Wise, of America, a leader in the Congress, to address our group. He said: "Zionism would never have arisen if the nations had been Christian and had treated the Jews as Christians should. But the Zionist Jews suffering persecution and intolerable burdens were now saying, 'Farewell, Christ-less world, we are going home!'" As I sat there, I wondered if these Jews, stumbling on to their ancient home with a cross of rejection upon their shoulders, were not nearer, even in their prejudices, to their Jewish Brother than those "Christians" who persecuted them in his name. One of the party requested the rabbi to repeat the twenty-third psalm as we bowed in prayer. Our hearts were well-nigh breaking as he repeated the portion, "Thou hast prepared a table before me in the presence of mine enemies," and we knew that the "enemies" now were those who professed to follow the Nazarene.

> I wonder if there is anything that is such a complete denial of Christ as this spirit of race prejudice, for it denies justice, brotherhood, and humanity.

I wonder if these Jewish pilgrims, when they get back to their Holy Land, will ever see Him? If not, then we must share the blame.

But race prejudice is not confined to geographical areas. It is of recent growth in the West, having sprung up in the last few hundred years. India has had it for centuries, for the word for "caste" is *varna*, meaning "color," a survival of the time when the lighter Aryans coming over the Himalayas constituted themselves high castes and the darker aborigines the low castes. India's caste system was thus founded upon a color prejudice. But this does not excuse us who follow the Son of man.

I wonder if there is anything that is such a complete denial of Christ as this spirit of race prejudice, for it denies justice, brotherhood, and humanity. Jesus taught that mankind is one and that men are brothers: "One is your Father and all ye are brethren."

All sorts of misunderstandings have grown up because we haven't seen this clearly. Our racial relationships have had a mist over them. A man was going through the Welsh mountains in the morning while the mists were over everything. He was thoroughly frightened by seeing a monster moving through the mist toward him. As it got closer, he was immensely relieved to find that it was not a monster but a man, and as it came still closer he found that it wasn't merely a man, it was his own brother. If we could get closer to men and see more clearly, monsters would turn to men and men to our own brothers. Discoveries in human brotherhood will provide a field for the greatest discoveries of the future.

At the Round Table of the Nations, three kinds of imperialism are speaking with un-Christian account: Political Imperialism, Financial Imperialism, Racial Imperialism, and they are throttling the voice of the gospel that would speak out of the heart of these nations. What is to be done?

A speaker was pouring out his heart to a group urging that we cleanse our hearts and civilizations of these racial attitudes. It was a moving appeal. A pompous bishop arose and said, "Yes, I think the speaker is right, we must all be kinder to people." Kinder to people! No, the nations want something infinitely deeper and more fundamental than that. They do not want patronizing kindness. That day has gone by. They want justice. They want to be treated as men and brothers. Something deeper must take place if we are to reach the souls of the nations with the gospel. Imperialistic attitudes of every type and kind must be got rid of. Nothing less than self-renunciation must take place. That self-renunciation must be personal, institutional, national and racial.

If that renunciation should take place, then there would be a personal, institutional, national, and racial self-realization. In those realms, we would lose ourselves in order to find ourselves again.

This is not fanciful preaching. It is the program of Jesus, and his is the only program that life will back, for we must realize that all the old imperialistic attitudes have had their day. Their power has now been exhausted. They are revealing their bankruptcy. They can go no further.

If the white races should renounce imperialistic assertiveness and give themselves to brotherly, unselfish service, they would find themselves again in a new moral and spiritual leadership. A new type of power would be theirs—a type that grows out of the authority of service. The future of the human race belongs to those who will do it.

> People do not want patronizing kindness. That day has gone by. They want justice.

The sociologist Benjamin Kidd, in his book entitled the *Science of Power*, weighs the types of power prevalent through the centuries and says that the final type of power is the power of self-sacrifice. He draws a picture of Christ, standing thorn-crowned and with bound hands before Pilate. Pilate represents the strongest military force of that day—the Roman Empire. He represents self-assertion. Christ standing before him represents self-sacrifice. The two types of power come together. And Kidd says that the center of power shifts from Pilate to Christ, for he represents the final type of power, the power of self-giving.

Let it be burned within our souls that we will have power in the future only as we forget it, only as we turn from Pilate's type to the suffering, self-giving type. For those who embody this hold the future of the world in their hands. Everything else is bankrupt.

If the nations should make the great renunciation, then as they sit at Round Table and speak of the meaning of religion to them, those nations who follow Christ would speak with the voice of a new authority, the undecaying authority of their Master who spoke out of reality, out of service, out of self-renunciation, out of brotherhood.

Will the nations do it? They must or slowly perish.

Chapter 13

THE MOST SACRED ROUND TABLE OF ALL

An earnest Hindu said to me one day, "Sometimes I feel like impeaching Sri Krishna." He felt that Krishna failed him at the vital place of example, at the place where idea is translated into act. It was just here that those at the Round Table who were in fellowship with Jesus felt surest of their ground. Jesus had not failed them. His ideas had been translated into acts. He met life as a man calling on no power for himself that was not available for you and me, and he met it without a break. He was "the Pioneer of life." Men were fellowshipping with Accomplished Fact. They were feeding their inmost souls on Life that had met life.

This comes out clearly at the most sacred Round Table of all. The shadow of the cross had fallen upon the soul of Jesus as he sat with his little company around the table in the upper room. There he did a symbolic act that gathered up the meaning of what he had been and would be doing for them: "He took a cup, and when he had thanked God for it, he gave it to them." He took the wine in the Cup as the thing that would best symbolize what he was giving to them and to the world. Into that Cup that he held in his hand had gone all the experiences of the vine in the past. The soul of the vine, the kind of soil upon which it grew, the prunings, the storms that beat over it, the sunshine and the rain, the crushing of the grapes in the wine-press—all these had gone to make up the quality of the wine he was giving to them. Change that past and you change the wine—everything of the past had gone into the Cup.

He was putting to their lips an Invisible Cup, of which this material Cup was a symbol, into which the experiences of the whole of his past life had gone. All he had said, and thought, and suffered, and prayed, and done, and was, went into the Chalice which he was putting to their lips. They drank of his Life.

In those silent years at Nazareth when he lived in obscurity, working at a carpenter's bench, his hands hard with toil, dealing with the commonplace, with the hardships of poverty, with the dull and narrow life of a country village, with the responsibility of supporting a family after the father had died, and with the Vision all the time in his heart, but unuttered, he conquered the commonplace, so all these things, both the battle and the victory, go into the Cup.

Many of us, most of us, have to live out our lives in that same dull obscurity, battling with the business of making a living, toiling in mine and factory and field and office, dealing with the sordid and the scarring, and all the time there is a vision of something better and nobler held in the heart unexpressed and unfulfilled. He puts the Chalice to our lips, and we drink of his victory over the dull commonplace.

He lays aside the carpenter's tools and goes out to proclaim his message and to enter more deeply into the soul of the race. "He had been baptized into the world's toil, now he would be baptized into its sin." John is calling a nation to repentance. His throbbing words smite the soul of a people, and they come down to his baptism in a repenting stream. Jesus enters that stream, he with conscience unstained and with soul untarnished, he who needed no repentance, he the sinless, enters that line. It may be a harlot ahead of him, a publican behind, and he becomes one of them and is baptized into a baptism of repentance. The identification is complete.

Then comes the reaction in his sensitive soul against this identification. He leaves men and the struggle ensues in the wilderness. Was this the way, absolute identification with people? Was his way to save from within by sharing? For forty days, he faced the issues and then came hunger. He must go back to men and eat. "You need not go back. You are the Son of God—that is enough; stay out here, feed yourself by miracle and live as the miraculous Son of God." It is the voice of the Tempter. The temptation to live apart, to feed oneself on spiritual miracle, to live on mystical communion, to be content with being a son of God is one of the most real temptations of the spiritual life, and into this temptation India's religious life has deeply fallen. But in this, India is not alone. It is the temptation of the mystic. Jesus brushes this aside. He would not be content with being the Son of God. He would be the Son of man. He would live by every word that proceeded out of the mouth of the Father, and that word for him meant identification with men and redemption at deep cost.

Then the Tempter suggested that if he did go back, why stand down with the sordid people? Stand rather on the pinnacle of the temple, sum up the national faith, be looked up to. This, too, is a serious temptation of the religious life, the temptation to stand on pinnacles of ecclesiastical authority, to gain authority by position and display. It is the temptation of the ecclesiastic. Jesus put it aside. His place was not up on pinnacles, but down with the people. He would gain his authority by service.

Then the Tempter suggested: "If you are determined to get to the people, take my way. The method you have chosen is too costly. There are cheaper ways. Advertise yourself. Use the politician's method—bow down to me and my ways and all these kingdoms will be yours." It is the temptation of the politician in religion. Jesus put this way aside, though he knew that the way he had chosen would drive him into an identification that would finally mean a cross. He had been baptized between two sinners, this choice meant that he would be crucified between two thieves, he would belong to men to the utmost limit possible.

It was decided he would be the Son of man. He would bear everything upon his own heart that man bears—and more. He goes straight to the little synagogue at Nazareth and announces his program: "The Spirit of the Lord is upon me because he anointed me to preach good tidings to the poor; he has sent me to proclaim release to the captives and recovering of sight to the blind, to set at liberty them that are bruised." You can feel the throb of deep identification with man sounding through these words. It is the Son of man speaking.

This announcement of his program brought surprise and delighted wonder from his townsmen until he went on and told how wide this message was: it was as wide as the human race, God cares as much for the Gentiles as he does for the Jews, for there were many widows and lepers in Israel, but the prophets were sent to outside Gentiles. When they heard this, then matters changed. People are willing to listen to any amount of truth provided it does not cut across their class or race prejudice. They had no room for this young Dreamer. They arose in anger and led him to the brow of the hill to cast him down headlong: "But he, passing through the midst of them, went his way." The blind home prejudices closed in on him and would have snuffed out his life with the Vision, but the calm courage of the inward sense of commission made him pass through the midst of them to go his way to teach, to heal, and to die for men. All of this went into the Cup.

And when we too are called and commissioned, and the blind, dull, narrow village prejudices close in and would quench the outreaching soul, we can drink of his calm and his courage and pass through the midst of them to go our way to fulfill the heavenly vision at any cost.

Then he became immensely popular. The multitudes hung upon his words that fell like dew upon their thirsty souls, the healed went everywhere telling of the Compassionate, the people found in him a new authority, the authority of reality, and when they found him breaking bread to the multitudes in a wilderness, they came and tried to make him a king by force. "Whereupon Jesus perceived they meant to come and seize him to make a king of him; so, he withdrew by himself to the hill again." He would hold to the high purpose of the Father for him, even though it meant a cross. The dazzling way to power was put away. He would take the long way to his Calvary. All the consecration and decisiveness when he turned down a throne for a cross, went into the Cup.

And when those moments come, when the lower, the easier, the compromised way is offered to us instead of the rugged, demanding way that leads to our crucifixion upon some cross of a chosen pain, then we drink of the Chalice into which this hour has gone, and lo, we are ready for anything—with him.

> "Down through the valley the cry doth ring,
> 'Jesus of Nazareth, King, our King,
> The prophet whose touch means to us bread,
> Hail King!'—was what the multitude said.
>
> "But a thorn-girt path before him lay,
> A torturing cross would end the way.
> Would he take this *way*—for men bleed, die,
> Or would he respond to the multitude's cry?
>
> "Jesus withdrew from low-browed plain
> Silently went to the hill again.
> Here thought was high and the vision clear
> And the Father's will than life more dear.
>
> "The prayer-filled hours wrought like balm
> Forth from his soul came the quiet psalm;
> He would share with men their deepest pain,
> Reject their plan—the plan of the plain.
>
> "O soul of mine, in grief's dark hour,
> Or when lower ways offer place and power,
> If thou wouldst be always strong and sane,
> Come thou apart to the hill again.
>
> "There lay down life at the Master's feet,
> To take it again with strength replete;
> There calmed will be the stress and strain,

> And forward we'll leap to share his pain,
> As we go to the hill again."

They drag a woman taken in adultery into his presence. All the purity of that moment when he stooped down and wrote in the sand, ashamed to look on her shame, all the delicacy and refinement of soul that would not add to the confusion of the guilty victim, all the courage that turned the accusers into the convicted, and all the redemption that says to the woman: "Neither do I condemn thee; go and sin no more"—all of this went into the Cup.

And in those moments when we are tempted to be indelicate, to be impure in glances and inward attitudes, we drink of this Chalice of his untarnished manhood and are strong.

Then came the day when he set his face to go to Jerusalem to meet what was certain to cause his doom. "He set his face to go to Jerusalem." All the spiritual decisiveness that would make men take sides for or against the Father's kingdom; all the tenderness of that moment when, beholding the city before him, he pauses on the side of the Mount of Olives and weeps over the city; all the courage of that hour when, with eyes blazing, he bids them take these things from his Father's House and drives them forth; all the constructiveness of his methods which show him, after the cleansing had taken place and the storm had subsided, seated in the temple "teaching," and "healing" the blind and the lame, and welcoming the children that came to him there—all of this went into the Cup.

There have been those in India who have strongly objected to these storm sides of Jesus' nature, the woes pronounced upon the Pharisees, the doom announced to fall upon the cities, the cleansing of the Temple. It does not fit into spiritual calm and poise, the marks of the perfect man. But no one can question that what he says about the

Pharisees was true to fact; that cleansing storms are necessary to purify physical and spiritual atmospheres, that have grown miasmic; that the force he used to cleanse the temple was not physical, but the force of authoritative personality. Nor can we question that the philosopher was right when he said that no man is strong unless he bears within his character antitheses strongly marked, so that a man is weak who is only passive, and weak when he is only militant; that he is strong only as he is passively militant and militantly passive, and Christ was both. I love the Christ of the blazing eye and the blessing hand, tender, terrible Prophet pronouncing woes over the city and then weeping over it. I love the Christ that let the storm of his redeeming fury loose upon a nation and then let the returning storm beat upon himself on a cross to complete the redemption. I drink of the life of the Christ that loved enough to hate the evil that destroys those whom he loves. I drink of it and am strong.

As he sat with his disciples at this most sacred Round Table, Jesus "knowing that the Father had given all things into his hands and that he was come from God and went to God, he riseth from supper, and laid aside his garments; and took a towel, and girded himself, . . . and began to wash the disciples' feet." He was so conscious of greatness that he dared to be humble. Into the Cup has gone this majesty of soul linked with lowly service. And we, who dare not be humble lest we show our real smallness, drink of the life of him who was so great that he dared stoop, and begin to learn what kingliness really is—the power to bend and serve. It is in the Cup.

Then comes the hour of Gethsemane. All the pain and the agony and the spiritual loneliness of that hour go into the Cup. What brought on this crisis with its bloody drops of sweat and the lonely agony? Was he afraid to die? Hardly, for he came to lay down his life. Was it not this: he came to save men from sin, and now, as he was going on into that next day, he would precipitate the crisis that would arouse men to greater sin, for they would put him to death. No wonder that the Redeemer, who by his determination to go on, seemed to be loosing the worst in men, asked that if it be possible this Cup might pass. And well he might. For this is the hardest thing that any reformer, any bringer of a higher ideal, any redeemer in any realm, has to face. His idea becomes light to those who receive it, darkness to others who blind themselves. But there is no other way. He must take it. This is the tragedy of Gethsemane—and also its triumph, for the wonder of that hour is not in the agony but in the outcome—for, collected and calm, he says: "Arise, let us be going" to meet tomorrow and its Calvary. It all went into the Cup.

> **His idea becomes light to those who receive it, darkness to others who blind themselves.**

And those of us who meet our lesser Gethsemanes drink from that Chalice into which the richness of that hour has gone and we, too, can say, "Arise, my soul, let us be going to meet our cross." And having drunk, we can meet it with calm.

Then they come to take him. His aroused disciple rushes forth and with his sword strikes off the ear of the servant of the high priest. Jesus rebukes him, touches the severed ear and says, "Let me do this at least" (Moffatt) and heals it. That beautiful act of healing an enemy who had come to put him to death goes into the Cup. And when his hands were no longer free to heal, for they were nailed to a cross, he could still pray. He prayed for those same enemies, "Father, forgive them, for they know not what they do." And when even that power was taken away, for he was gasping in death, still he would do the last and supreme thing—he would die for them. All this went into the Cup.

And when our souls are tempted to be resentful toward spite and hate, we drink of this triumph, of the persisting love that would let nothing turn it aside or quench it, and having drunk of that, like Luther, we can say, "My soul is too glad and too great to be the enemy of any man."

There he stood before Pilate arrayed in mock royalty. The Romans had heard that he was "the king of the Jews." Always contemptuous of the Jews, the soldiers felt that this was a supreme opportunity to show their contempt of the race, so they plaited a crown of thorns and put it on his brow, thrust a stick in his hand as a scepter and purple garments around his bleeding shoulders, and bowed the knee and said, "Hail, King of the Jews." And they spat in his face. They had often wanted to do that to the Jews, and now they would do it to their king. The racial contempt directed toward them fell on him and he bore it on behalf of the men who were crying for his blood. All of that went into the Cup.

And we who belong to races or classes who have been despised by those of supposed superior class or color, those of us who have felt the sting of contempt enter our souls, and who have writhed in agony at attitudes more eloquent than spoken words, know that he has shared these contempts and has triumphed over them and that somehow, some way, we too shall share his triumph if we can but share the patience of his unsoured spirit.

There he stood before Pilate accused of many things. He heard his words twisted and tortured to other meanings: "He said, 'I will destroy this temple that is made with hands and in three days I will build another made without hands.'" He was being crucified on misquotation. And he was not nervously anxious to explain, he let it go, for he could wait— he knew that every lie would break itself upon the truth of things. He answered not a word, so that the Governor, used to little men endlessly trying to explain their actions and their words, marveled.

Here was greatness that could wait for final verdicts, consoled by the inward sense of truth. All this went into the Cup.

And those of us who have seen our words misquoted, our finest actions misunderstood, our best motives misinterpreted, and have suffered, can drink of the Cup into which this patient triumph has gone. No one was called to correct the lies about him, but the universe has rendered its verdict against them. He had no witnesses at his trial, but millions would now gladly die to witness for him. And as we drink and share this poise of the heart assured by its own truth, we rest and wait, knowing that the last word shall be God's.

Now lies and hate have prevailed, for he is tortured on a cross. They have nailed those hands, that had blessed little children, to a tree. Those feet that have trod the ways of God in perfect obedience are now fastened on a cross. His good name has been taken away—he is a malefactor—his disciples have fled, he is alone in his agony, and as he hangs there, they beat him back, back into the Dark until it seems that God, too, has gone, for from his lips comes the cry, "My God, my God, why hast Thou forsaken me?" He is forsaken of God and man. Everything is gone. But not quite. Two words remain, "My God"; they could not snatch those from his lips and heart. On the pivot of those words, he comes back from the Dark and in quiet confidence at the last says, "Father, into Thy hands I commend my spirit." Nothing more bitter can go into the Cup, for he has tasted forsakenness by God and by men. None of us can get beyond that and say, I know some bitterness that he does not know—mine is a deeper pain. No, the Cup has everything in it.

And when we have those moments of forsakenness, when it seems that everything is gone, we can drink of the Chalice and find that nothing is gone when one thing remains: My God. With that Fact within our hearts, we can swing back from anything—anything.

Now he is dead, having tasted death for every man. A tomb holds him. But not for long. For the most glorious fact in human history was yet to go into the Cup. Out of that tomb he arose, laid aside his grave clothes, and came forth triumphant and resplendent. He is risen!

If into the Cup has gone everything that life can possibly meet—its commonplaces, its toil, its obscurity, its temptations, its blind home prejudices, its bids for compromise, its lonely determinations, its Gethsemanes, its hours before unjust Judgment seats, its mockeries, and its racial wrongs, its cross and its forsakenness, its death—nevertheless, there has also gone into it the most complete triumph over life that can possibly come: He arose.

Nothing now matters if God's last word is resurrection. Let life do its worst or best, this righting, saving Fact will be at the end. The life of Jesus and especially his cross raises every question about life that can possibly be raised, and raises them in their acutest form. The word "Why?" upon the lips of Jesus as he hangs upon the cross seems to epitomize all the questions that ever trembled upon the lips of perplexed humanity. The resurrection answers them all. God's last word is "resurrection." And it is in the Cup.

The phrase that transformed all from a mere commonplace meeting of life into a sacrament was the phrase: "And when he took the Cup, he thanked God for it." He thanked God for it—for all the pains and the joys, all the companionships and the desertions, for Gethsemane and for Calvary. He took it all as from the Father's hand, thanked him for it, and lo, everything was transformed. All of us have to bear, but only those who have learned triumphantly to thank God for it all can turn life from a senseless suffering to a sacrament.

> **Nothing now matters if God's last word is resurrection. Let life do its worst or best, this righting, saving Fact will be at the end.**

It was this sense of drinking from the Cup of accomplished Fact, of met Life, of the worst overcome, that characterized those in the Round Tables who were in fellowship with Christ. They had put to their lips something that others were not finding.

And they felt they could drink from the Cup of Christ's life without reservation. There are no dregs in it. There is no residuum of failure. Nothing has gone into Jesus' life that we cannot take with absolute safety and spiritual health. He did not fail us.

If he had taken one wrong step, shown one base motive, had slipped into one thing we would have to consider as sin, there would be death in the Cup. But that wrong step was never taken, that base motive never conceived, that sin never committed. The Cup is unmixed and clear.

But something further can and must be said: We can drink of this Cup not only with safety, but also with salvation. In it is not only health, but healing. For into that Cup has gone a dying for sinners. We take into our inmost being the meaning of his life and death for us, and lo, the sense of moral and spiritual healing spreads through our souls.

At the Round Table of Life Jesus passes to us the Chalice of his life, and when our lips have tasted, we know that we are drinking of life itself.

Chapter 14

THE CROSS: THE KEY TO LIFE

AGAIN AND AGAIN when someone at the Round Tables or out of them has said that all religions are the same, my mind would involuntarily run to the cross and its meaning. If what is found here is true and represents the meaning of life, then all religions are not the same. In our conferences, we heard no authentic note of divine self-sacrifice come out of the non-Christian faiths. When Gandhiji desires to inspire self-sacrifice, he points to the example of Prahalada, which is good enough in its way, but lacks those deep meanings we find when self-sacrifice is laid in the Divine. The cross stands out in absolute uniqueness. It towers o'er the wreck of time.

Among the ancient inscriptions and paintings on the tombs of the kings of Egypt, one sees everywhere the symbol of the Key of Life. Strangely enough, it is in the form of a cross. As we sat at our Round Tables, we felt, again and again as in a flash, that the cross is the Key of Life, that here at the cross we saw into the depths of things; we felt that here the Heart of the Universe showed itself, and that if we could catch the Passion that beats here we would catch the meaning of life itself.

THE CROSS ...

It has been suggested that "the answer to the riddles of the universe is God, and the answer to the riddle of God is Christ." Then the answer to the riddle of Christ is to be found in his sacrificial spirit, culminating in his cross. To understand this is to understand Christ, to understand Christ is to understand God, and to understand God is to understand the meaning of the universe and of life. The cross, then, is the key. If I lose this key I fumble. The universe will not open to me. But with the key in my hand and heart, I know I hold its secret.

For weeks and months after I was converted, I wondered why anyone should preach about anything except the cross. The redemptive, glowing mystery of it had taken hold of my inmost being, and I felt that this was life and all else was trifling. I feel that way still.

Not that we can grasp its full meaning. I feel like a child standing upon the borders of a great mystery. But what I do grasp gives me the clue to what lies back in the heart of the Infinite. I find myself using any theory of the atonement that makes

> **As we sat at our Round Tables, we felt, again and again as in a flash, that the cross is the Key of Life, that here at the cross we saw into the depths of things...**

this mystery more vital and clear. No theory seems to be big enough to fit the facts. As Jesus broke the bars of the tomb and stepped out beyond them, so this fact of Jesus dying for men seems to break out beyond our statements. Findlay puts the matter clearly when he says, "His perfect sinlessness left open the avenues of approach from both sides, God-ward and man-ward; for it is sin that bars our way to God and man alike. The death of Jesus was an appeal to man from the side of God, for he was God (moral influence theory); and an act of atonement from the side of man, for he was Man (other theories)." These are all attempts to tell of the "unspeakable gift."

But the most vital method of approach to the cross is not through a theory, but through an attitude. To understand the cross, one must have an attitude of mind and heart responsive to the meaning here. To understand art, one must have art within him; to understand music, one must have something of the musician within him; to understand the meaning of the cross, one must have a moral response to that sacrificial spirit. I have seen many a non-Christian, suffering for a cause, come closer to the meaning of the cross than many professed Christians who, while knowing of the ideas of the cross, live selfishly. The cross is understood, not by an argument, but by an attitude.

We must be reminded that there is in all life a dark, terrible problem—the problem of evil. Spencer defines physical life as an inward correspondence with outward environment. When we take in food and air, we live. When we fail to do so, we die. There must be response to environment. But there is also a spiritual environment to which we must respond, which is made up of our higher self, other human souls and God. When we are in harmony with these three, we live—live spiritually. The facts of life fairly faced proclaim with heartbreaking emphasis that man is, or has been, out of harmony with his spiritual environment. First, there seems to be in man's life a cleavage in his inmost nature. His higher-self stands over against his lower-self. The higher-self craves goodness, nobleness, God. The lower-self craves and conceives evil. As Byron says (and who knew it better than Byron?): "Our life is a false nature. It is not in the harmony of things." There is division and discord in our inward nature. Moreover, we are out of harmony with our brother man. The jealousies, the petty quarrels, the court wranglings, the family feuds, the wars, the social clashes, the despising of man by man because of so-called superior class or caste—

The Cross ...

all these and more tell us that man is out of harmony with man. The brotherhood has not come. But the saddest element, and the most far-reaching in its consequences, is our lack of harmony or correspondence in the highest and most important portion of our environment, namely, God. "The history of man is one long search for God." We stand beside our altars, we breathe our prayers, we make our vows, we crave with unspeakable cravings of the inmost heart and we long for fellowship with God. Something dark, dreadful and often decisive, though, stands between us and God. We realize that he must be pure and because of our conscious impurity, we dare not ask for fellowship with him. We are separated and guilty.

The problem of religion is to make man at one with his highest self, so that his divided soul-forces are fused into one; to bring man into harmony with his brother man, so that brotherhood becomes a reality, and to bring him into harmony with God. The task of religion is an "at-one-ment"—atonement. If it fails to do this, it fails at the vital point. Its ritual may be beautiful, its sanctions may be ancient, its precepts may be good, but if it fails here, it fails vitally and irretrievably. All else is useless, for if this problem of evil is ignored or slurred over, we are like one who dreams and plans about next year's happiness while a cancer is eating at his vitals.

> The task of religion is an "at-one-ment" — atonement. If it fails to do this, it fails at the vital point.

If Jesus Christ has done anything fundamental in the history of mankind, he must have solved this problem of the threefold harmony. If he has failed here, he takes his place as one of the beautiful characters of history, but utterly impotent and powerless to be a Redeemer.

Here is a task worthy of God. If Jesus is other than God, he cannot do it. If he is not God, if he is not that "Personal Approach from the Unseen" meeting us in our environment, he will not be able. Horace warns the tragedian not to bring a god on the stage unless there is an entanglement worthy of a god. Evil presents an entanglement worthy of God. But it is no mere stage affair. It is a tragic fact. To deliver men from evil is a problem that challenges God's power and certainly would have the deepest claim on his love.

What, then, is the real meaning of the death of Christ?

He hung upon the cross in shame. How deep and bitter that shame and degradation we may gather from these words of Cicero: "Far be the very name of a cross, not only from the bodies of Roman citizens, but from their imaginations, eyes, and ears." But he, innocent and stainless, was on a cross. Although blood was flowing from the mock-crown of thorns on his brow, from the back that had been lacerated by cruel Roman blows, from his palms where the flesh was tearing from the weight of his body, and from the pierced feet, yet he refused the deadening drug offered him on a sponge. He underwent the ordeal with brain unclouded and with nerves unsoothed. In their hatred, the crowd watched him suffer. "And they watched him there," is one of the cruelest verses in literature. Then they mocked him, and wagged their heads in scorn, crying, "He saved others, himself he cannot save." Strange as it may seem, the mocking phrase of those hatred-crazed enemies became the central truth of the gospel. He was saving others and, therefore, himself he could not save. That is the deep truth of life. If one is to save others, himself he cannot save. It is an appalling mystery, yet an "everlasting fact that goodness in all moral natures has a doom of bleeding upon it, allowing it to conquer only as it bleeds. All goodness conquers by a cross." Those who save themselves cannot save others, and those who save others cannot save themselves.

The Cross ...

This law of saving by self-giving runs through life, from the very lowest to the very highest life. In any realm, those who save others cannot save themselves trouble, sorrow, yea sometimes, even death. Suppose that a seed has a will. It might decide to save not itself but others. It would be buried—die. Itself it does not save. But the result? A golden harvest! Take the mother; she goes down to the valley of the shadow of death to bring a child into the world. When that child becomes ill, forgetful of herself, she spends her strength, her time, and if need be, her very life. She is saving another; herself she cannot save.

A missionary doctor goes to China. The people all about him are dying of a strange plague. He segregates the germ, tries to take some to America to get the help of specialists in discovering an antidote, but finds it impossible. He goes back to his station with a heavy heart. The people are still dying. He can stand it no longer. While the rest are at church, he deliberately goes into his laboratory, swallows some of the germs, and then takes the first boat to America. He keeps a perfect record of his case and the reactions of the disease germs upon him. He goes to the hospital in Baltimore, turns over the record of his case to the doctors, is soon in a state of coma. But his plea was that even if he died, they should find the remedy and send it back to save his people in China. He was saving others—himself he could not save.

> **Jesus was saving others and, therefore, himself he could not save. That is the deep truth of life. If one is to save others, himself he cannot save.**

This spirit of self-giving is the most beautiful thing in life. Than the spirit of self-sacrifice, there is no nobler spirit. In it life rises to its highest level. This is so true that we can determine the elevation or depression of a life in the scale of being by this important law: *The extent of the elevation of an animal, and, of course, any free moral agent, can be infallibly measured by the degree to which sacrificial love for others controls that being.* Here is a law by which life may be judged. Where the sacrificial spirit is absent from life, that life is lowest; where it is partially developed, that life is higher; and where it is perfectly embodied, that life is highest in the scale of being.

The lowest life is the most selfish. Among the lower creatures, the parent will often feed upon its own young. Rising in the scale, we find the parent animal sacrificing itself for the sake of its young. Then higher still, the parent will not only do this for the sake of its young, but for the sake of the young of the group. When we come to man we find a being who will give himself not merely for his own young and the young of the group, but in the higher reaches will sacrifice himself even for an enemy. Here, life rises to its highest. The highest man is the man of noblest character who is willing to sacrifice most for others.

Now, if this is a universal law—and it seems to be—then, when we come to God, who must represent the highest stage of being, we would expect to find that he embodies and represents the sacrificial spirit most highly developed. If he does not, then at the lowest form of life and at the highest form of life, there is selfishness; but in the middle — at man — there is the sacrificial spirit. If this infallible law holds true on up through the scale of being, even when it gets to man, but reverses itself when it gets to God, then laws are meaningless and the universe is without a Head. But on the other hand, if this law holds good from the very lowest to the very highest, as the sacrificial idea of the cross implies that it does, then the universe is a whole, laws are not enigmas, God is not a disappointment, and the universe has a sacrificial Head.

Otherwise, the highest man would be better than God, and, in that case, the highest man should obtain our interest and our worship.

> "A loving worm beneath its clod
> Were diviner than a loveless God."

Bacon was right when he said that "it is better to have no conception of God than an unworthy one." To think of God, with the sacrificial spirit absent, is an unworthy conception, for man would rise higher than his God. As certainly as God is love, the burdens of lover must fall upon him. For, as Bushnell says, it is "the nature of love universally to insert itself into the miseries, and take upon its feelings the burdens of others." Such a God in love must be a Savior in suffering.

Many men *do* help others at cost to themselves. We ask, "Is man nobler and better than God?" Browning asks this pertinent question and answers it: "Would I suffer for one I love? So wouldst Thou, so wilt Thou." Would I, as a father, would you as a father, suffer for a child you love? Then "O God, our Father, so wouldst thou, so wilt thou."

I cannot believe that God would write a law of saving by sacrifice through the universe and evade it himself. I cannot believe God would put an impulse to sacrifice within our hearts and draw back from it himself. The psalmist asks: "He that created the eye shall he not see?" And Browning adds: "He that created love shall he not love?" And we may ask, "He that created sacrificial love, shall he not sacrifice?"

If there is not a loving sacrificial God in the universe, then there ought to be! The highest in man and the universe calls for it. The old Chinese scholar was right, who, after having listened for the first time to the story of the loving, sacrificing God, exclaimed to his neighbor, "Didn't I tell you there *ought* to be a God like that?"

With Sir Oliver Lodge, we can say, "I will not believe it is given to man to have thoughts higher and nobler than the truth of things." We have thought of a sacrificial God, and common sense would say that we have not thought higher and nobler than the truth of things. If any anxious questionings remain, God assures us: "O heart I made, a heart beats here."

> The cross is the culmination of the identification. If there is incarnation, there is identification; and if there is identification, there is suffering—there is a cross.

Again, if we believe in incarnation or even in immanence, we cannot but be brought to this same thought and conclusion. "Immanence is costly to God. God cannot keep himself so near to sin without suffering the perpetual cross on account of that sin." Our joy becomes his joy and our pain becomes his pain. He is not a mere spectator. An immanent God is a suffering God; and an incarnate God, by reason of the deeper identification with man, passes into a deeper sympathy, and consequently into a deeper suffering, than a merely immanent God. The cross is the culmination of the identification. If there is incarnation, there is identification; and if there is identification, there is suffering—there is a cross.

Jesus was the Elder Brother of a guilty family and he bore the family guilt.

A highly intelligent man told me how he saw the cross and was redeemed. He had a beautiful, intelligent and innocent-minded wife. He

THE CROSS ...

was true to her until he went to Europe, but there he took his first misstep. He continued the secret unfaithfulness after he came back to India. The innocence and the trust of his wife often stabbed him like a knife. Then came the crisis when he knew he would have to tell her. He dreaded it. He was afraid that her anger would wither him, and that she would leave him. He told her the whole shameful story. He said, "I can never forget the look of anguish that came over her face as the meaning of what I had done dawned upon her. She turned pale and clutching at the pain in her heart she sank upon the bed. I could see my sin torturing her. Then she arose and I expected the storm to break on me, but instead she said, 'I love you still, and I will not leave you.' Then I saw in the anguished love of my wife the meaning of the cross. From her love, I stepped up in thought to the cross. I was a redeemed man from that hour." And his subsequent life has shown it.

There is another consideration that brings an impressive lesson, namely, that the higher in the scale of being we go, the greater do we find the obligation of parenthood toward the offspring. In lower life, parenthood involves little responsibility and little consequent suffering on behalf of the offspring. But when we come to man, we find that the lengthened period of infancy involves parenthood in a degree of care and suffering to which lower life is a stranger. When we come to God, we would expect parenthood in him to involve an infinite degree of care and vicarious suffering on behalf of his children. God should not ask the human parent to undergo suffering on behalf of his children, and not be willing himself to undergo the larger responsibility and suffering on behalf of his own.

One of the recent discoveries of science is the fact of the unity or solidarity of all life. We are not isolated particles, without relationship, floating in the ether of time. All life is bound up with all other life. You cannot touch life anywhere without affecting all other life. Jesus Christ stood at the center of life. God and man met in him. As *Son of man*, mankind suffered in him; and as Son of God, God suffered in him. In this synthesis of suffering, the lower life is raised by the higher life, taking on itself the burdens and sufferings and sins of the lower.

But the Hindu and the Muslim find here a difficulty. A leading Muslim college principal put it this way: "A God who would stoop and suffer is not perfect." And a Hindu put it this way: "If Brahma would suffer, he would be unhappy; and if he were unhappy, he would be imperfect; and if he were imperfect, he would not be God." This is the crux of the non-Christian difficulty. Is it not based on a superficial view of life? For the most miserable people are those who are self-centered and who refuse to do anything for others at cost to themselves. The most joyous people on earth are those who are helping others through self-sacrifice. "There is nothing so absolutely blessed as to suffer well." A God who would sit apart from the tragedy of life and would refuse to bear the pains of his children upon his own heart would be a God miserable and unhappy. He would know nothing of the joy of redemption at cost.

But the Hindu, believing in the law of Karma, feels another difficulty: It is unjust for the innocent to suffer for the guilty. If the cross means injustice, would we want it? We do not want a kind universe at the expense of a righteous universe. But there is a justice higher than legal justice in which it is right for the strong to save the weak, the holy to save the unholy. Go to a mother, whose son, in whom she had placed her hopes, is breaking her heart by his wayward living, and say: "It is unjust for you to suffer in this way on account of your son. He is guilty, you are innocent. It is unjust." Surprised and pained, the mother would answer: "Suffer for my son—unjust? It is the very thing that motherhood within me demands I should do. My heart will not let me do otherwise." In the name of a legal justice, would we deny to that mother the privilege of being a mother and of suffering for her son and, by that very act, of being noble? Suppose we should apply legal justice to the home and say to the mother: "You can give to your boy only what he gives to you—nothing more and nothing less." The deepest thing in the home, the thing that makes the home, namely, love, would die and the home would turn to a mart where we bargain for good deeds and pay back in exact coin.

Shall we tie the hands of our Father with the cords of a legal justice and say, "You may give to me only as I give to you"? If so, God becomes a huge Slot Machine into which we put in a good deed and get back its exact equivalent. He becomes as mechanical as his laws and the deepest thing of the universe, divine sacrificial love, dies. Religion is no longer a fellowship, but a bargain.

> You cannot touch life anywhere without affecting all other life. Jesus Christ stood at the center of life. God and man met in him.

It is not enough for God to warn men of the consequences of evil and leave it at that. An inward instinct makes us feel that God must go further. Professor Cairns gives this story: A theological student by the name of Maclean, a quiet, unassuming, but promising young man, had gone out one morning to read in a quiet spot on the links (coastal sand dunes) by the sea, when he saw a boy, a stranger to the place, going out into waters that he knew to be dangerous. He cried out to him and warned him, but the boy took no heed. After a while, Maclean heard a cry far out at sea and, looking up from his books, he saw that the boy was struggling with the current. He made straight for the water and swam out to him with a plank he had snatched up by the way. He reached the lad in time and, as the current swept them both outward, tried in vain to hold him on the plank. But the lad was exhausted, and again and again slipped off. He felt his own strength giving out, but up to the very end persisted. At last he succeeded, but his own powers were exhausted. He sank and was drowned, but he had saved the lad.

But suppose the story had been told in this way: When the student heard the cry he deliberately walked to the shore, watched the boy hopelessly struggling with the waves and said, "I warned you—that was quite sufficient." We all feel that there is something wrong with that. What is it? This: within us there is an instinct of a higher justice, a justice in which we feel it is right to save even at cost to oneself. That instinct is a witness to the fact that the universe is centered in love. And love must bear if it is to remain love.

There is something more just than legal justice; it is to forgive and recover and save. But the forgiveness that God offers in Christ is not a cheap forgiveness. In a certain war, two children whose parents had been killed in a bombardment of the town where they lived, were in the charge of a rough soldier. The little boy in an argument with another lad used an ugly word which was forbidden in the careful home where he had been brought up. He looked fearfully at the soldier to see if he had been overheard. The soldier laughed carelessly and said: "It doesn't matter. Say all of that sort of thing you like." In a sudden revulsion of feeling, the boy burst into tears and said: "If you were my father, you would not say that," and he walked away to play with the other children and to try to forget the sudden thrust of pain. We want to live in a kind universe, but we do not want to live in a universe which is too kind. If forgiveness were cheap, our souls would revolt against it. Gandhiji was brokenhearted that immorality had come into his ashram. Out of sheer pain of heart, he began to fast and kept it up for a week. At the end of the week, when the guilty youths stood before him and begged for forgiveness, could he offer it to them? Yes, for the forgiveness he now offered was no longer cheap, it had the moral dignity of the protest of his own suffering upon it. He had taken it himself and now the forgiveness was at deep cost and was worth something. The cross is the price that God pays that the forgiveness may not be cheap.

But someone asks: "Can there be forgiveness in a world of cosmic law? Is not the law of sowing and reaping more scientifically intelligible than the doctrine of forgiveness?" There is a truth in the law of sowing and reaping which is the truth underlying the law of Karma. Paul teaches this very definitely when he says, "Whatsoever a man soweth that shall he also reap." Can it be reconciled with forgiveness? There are two facts in this physical law of sowing and reaping. First, we reap in kind: wheat brings forth wheat, not thistles. Second, we reap more than we sow: we sow a single grain and we reap the many. The reason for this larger harvest is the outside addition to the grain: the sunshine and the rain and the richness of the earth. Were it not for this outside contribution, the larger harvest would never come. Now apply this law to the moral realm. We sow repentance and rectification of life, which is a changed attitude toward evil, and we reap forgiveness which is a changed attitude toward ourselves. We sow a changed attitude on our part— repentance—and we reap a changed attitude on God's part-forgiveness. We sow in kind and we reap in kind. But the harvest is greater than the sowing! Yes, for God adds to our sowing of repentance, the richness of his redeeming grace, the sunshine of his love; and like the falling drops of rain, the very tears of the suffering Son of God upon it, and, lo, forgiveness is ours. We do not break the law of sowing and reaping—we fulfill it. Here is its highest manifestation. It bursts into full meaning at the cross.

But the Hindu asks, "Is the evildoer to get off scot-free through forgiveness? Is he not punished at all?" Yes, and very severely. In the cross, the punishment is inwardly transferred, "the pain of penitence takes the place of the pain of outward punishment, so that the outward punishment can be lifted from the soul without loss or degradation to the soul." Were those boys for whom Gandhiji fasted, punished?

Outwardly, no; but inwardly, yes. And very deeply. For long after any pain from physical punishment would have died away, this inward pain of penitence persisted and punished them.

Neesima of Japan, a devoted schoolmaster, commanded his boys to lay the rod upon his hand when they were guilty of an evil deed. Were those boys punished? True, there were no stripes across their hands, but there were stripes across their hearts. The broken cane hanging upon the wall of Neesima's university, with an inscription under it in memory of the teacher who loved them enough to suffer for them, is a sign of that inward pain of penitence that punished long after the physical pain would have died away. The cross punishes, but it punishes by a pain that purifies while it punishes. Paul calls it "this pain divine" (2 Cor. 7: 9-11, Moffatt).

Forgiveness in the hands of Jesus does not become "a concession to human frailty or an encouragement to evil, but an injunction against further sinning." Instead of forgiveness doing away with law, it binds the forgiven to obey law as the unforgiven never are. Those who truly find forgiveness at the hands of Jesus hate sin as the unforgiven never do. The law of love becomes the love of law. The "expulsive power of a new affection" casts out the love of the lower. A leading psychologist tells us "that an impulse can be replaced only by a higher impulse." No negative suppression will suffice. That higher impulse is an inward passion for Christ.

It is this inward passion, lighted by the cross, that sends men and women to the remote corners of the earth and into the slums of the great cities to save and heal. Nothing can quench it. It never knows when it is defeated. A doctor goes to the Sudan to heal the sick. He is infected by the disease of his patient and loses his eyesight. But he is still inwardly radiant, and, even in his blindness wants to go back again to serve the people by whom he was infected. A missionary and his wife were murdered in Africa, and today five of their children are working among the murderers of their parents. Bishop Hannington was murdered in Africa. His son, going to that place later, won the murderer of his father as his first convert. Some outcaste converts went to Mesopotamia during the war. A theological student asked that government to send him as their chaplain in order that he might help keep them from falling into evil. It could not be arranged. He went to the missionary and said: "I cannot stand it. I must go. If they will not send me as their chaplain, I will go as one of them." So, he enlisted as a sweeper, shared their life, and the contempts that fell on them fell on him. He wrote their letters, kept them from evil and brought them back to India clean and true. He had caught the passion of the cross—the passion to share.

> At the cross is loosed the power of the redemptive God. No man need live in sin unless he wants to. Power is available to live victoriously.

It has been said that Christian missions are founded on American dollars and British pounds and Continental currencies. True, men fling fortunes at the feet of the Son of God, but the underlying passion cannot be bought with money. It is kindled at the cross.

At the cross is loosed the power of the redemptive God. No man need live in sin unless he wants to. Power is available to live victoriously. Someone has said that "the inner strength of another life is directly transmissible. "If this be true, then the inner strength, the purity, the holy sacrificial love of Christ's life is directly transmissible—transmissible to our tempted, sin-defeated, habit-ridden lives. During the late war, a soldier was brought into the hospital frightfully wounded. He had lost so much blood that life was almost gone. The doctor looked at him and shook his head, "Nothing can be done for him. He is too far gone." Then he added, "We might save him by transfusion of blood." An orderly standing by came round in front, saluted the doctor and said: "Sir, did I hear you say that you needed blood for this man? If so, I am ready."

The doctor replied, "You do not understand; if you give this man as much blood as he needs to bring him back to life, you will probably be ill for some time and there is a chance that you may die."

Again, the orderly saluted and said, "Sir, I am ready."

But the doctor said: "What is this man to you? Is he a friend or a relative?"

"No, sir," replied the orderly, "I have never seen him before. But please, sir, I would like to do it."

The doctor opened the veins and transfused the life-giving blood of the orderly into the withered veins of the dying man. He lived. In a richer, deeper way Jesus did that for us. At the cross, he was riven for us. He pours his rich, full, holy life into the withered moral and spiritual veins of a sin-wounded race. That inner strength of his life—so pure, so holy, so divine—is now available for you and me.

This, then, is not the message of a sect. We can build no fences around it. It belongs to India and to the world as much as it belongs to me. I proclaim it, but have no sovereign rights over it. It is the uncovering of the heart of God, the God for whom all men have dimly searched.

The cross is not an accident in the universe, something read into things by loving hearts; it is inherent there; it is the revelation of the heart of the Father. It is founded upon the facts of the universe, and the need for it is written in the constitution of our souls. In a previous chapter, I said that "the kingdom of heaven was like unto Dohnavur." But even here was one girl who would not respond to the wonderful spirit found there. She closed herself to it and lived against it. The missionary did all she could, but the girl was unresponsive. Finally, when all other things failed, she called the girl into her room, bared her arm and said, "I am going to thrust this needle into my arm."

The girl was shocked and protested saying, "But that will hurt you."

"Yes," said the missionary, "it will, but it will not hurt me nearly so much as what you are doing is hurting me."

She thrust the needle into her arm, and as the blood trickled down, the girl looked at it for a moment and then threw her arms around the neck of the missionary. "I didn't know you loved me like that," she sobbed. "Forgive me for what I've been and done." She was changed from that hour. That outward blood was the sign of an inward wounded love—wounded on account of sin—and. showed the girl what she had not seen before. She was redeemed by that blood.

> **The cross is not an accident in the universe, something read into things by loving hearts; it is inherent there; it is the revelation of the heart of the Father.**

How could we who are limited by our senses know of that inward cross that is upon the heart of God on account of our sin, unless—unless, he showed it to us by the outward cross? Now we know what God is like. The cross has lighted up the nature of God. He is self-giving Love and bears upon his heart our sins. That is the meaning of the cross. It is the meaning of the universe. And it must be the meaning of our lives, too.

A student deeply perplexed said to a friend of mine, "I do not understand the meaning of the atonement." My friend illustrated as follows: Suppose there were a plague-stricken district and here was a doctor with medical skill; if love should be at the heart of his skill, would he not carry that skill down into the heart of the plague-stricken district to cure it? Here is an appallingly ignorant people and here is a wise man; if love should be at the heart of his wisdom, would he not carry that wisdom down into the heart of that ignorance and bear with its limitations to cure it? Here is a famine-stricken people and here is a man with wealth; if love should be at the heart of his wealth, would he not go down into that famine-stricken section to share it? Here is a section where impurity and sin have spread their pall and here is a good man; if love should be at the heart of his goodness, would he not carry his goodness into the heart of the evil, bear with it, take on himself the shame of it, let it break his heart if necessary to save men from that evil? Here are we with the appalling plague of sin upon us and here is God, whose very nature is love. What will He do about it? To get into it to cure it will mean bearing it, and bearing it will mean atonement. "Oh," replied the student, "if you put it that way, I do not see how God could keep out of it. And moreover, I do not see how I can keep out of it."

That is the meaning of the cross: We, being what we are, and God being what He is, He could not keep out of it. And since God has gone into life as deeply as a cross, we too must catch the Divine Passion— we must know the cross by sharing it.

Chapter 15

THE WAY

We come now to face the central and the most important question raised by these Round Table Conferences: Which is the Way?

Gandhiji says in *Young India* (Aug. 4, 1927): "I have not found him, neither do I know him, but I have made the world's faith in God my own."

"Why doesn't Gandhi find God?" asked an English captain, sympathetic toward the great Indian and toward the non-Christian faiths. "Doesn't God love him? Then why doesn't he reveal himself clearly to him, for no one seeks more earnestly and sincerely?"

I replied that I was sure God did love him, and if there were degrees in the divine love, he probably loved him more than he loved some of the rest of us, but that he probably loved him too much to reveal himself to him under the circumstances. And why? Gandhiji is seeking God through Rama and through Krishna. In the worship at the Ashram, the center seems to be Rama, for "Jai, jai Rama" runs like a refrain through all the worship. Now and again, I hear the name of Krishna invoked and the Gita is the most used book in the Ashram. It is true that Gandhiji says that by "Rama" he means "God"; others in the Ashram say that Rama and Sita stand for a national history, summing up national feeling and ideals. In either case, the center of the worship is Rama and the approach is through him. Now, suppose God should give himself clearly through that Rama-approach, it would then fix in the mind of the seeker, through that realization of God in experience, that God in character is like Rama. But may it not be that he cannot commit himself to this because he is not Rama-like? So, he, in love, withholds, giving the seeker just enough of the sense of the intimation of the Divine to let him know that he is there. May this not be the explanation why Gandhiji does not "find" in clearness?

Would not the same thing hold true when the approach is through Krishna? For he would, thereby, back the idea that he is Krishna-like. Does not the thoughtful human heart sincerely hope that he is not?

When the Vedantist posits the Impersonal and says that God is like that, and strives to merge himself into this Impersonal It, though he strives with the patience that Shankara, the great exponent of this philosophy, says one must have, yet the universe remains stolid, life does not break through to release and realization, there seem to be no witnesses; but the soul, still hopeful, puts off realization to another birth and makes of its patience a virtue. And why does God not answer? If he did, he would be backing the idea that he is the Impersonal. Would that not be backing the untrue?

Others strive to find God in themselves, but here, too, is the same difficulty: the absence of a character norm that truly represents the moral and spiritual facts of the universe. If he gave himself through this approach, he would be committing himself to the position of being in character you-like and me-like. Those who seek this way argue that it can be done, but as far as observation goes, life does not break forth into a witness that it has been done.

There are others who would seek him through this physical universe, but those who look up to God through this physical universe come to one conclusion: God is law. He is, but not that only. God is love. But concerning this, nature's voice is uncertain. So those who seek here must be content with seeing the fringe of the garment of God instead of standing face to face.

The same problem faces us when we seek God through a sacred book. All literature gets its meaning from the life that surrounds the literature. A word in one place will mean one thing and in another place another thing. We use the word "home" before an audience. To one, it means a place akin to heaven, and to another, a place akin to hell, according to the experience that has gone into the word. Literature does not rise higher than life. If it were possible to give a book that would be supposed to contain the revelation of God, it would be largely the revelation of us. We would read into it our highest thinking, but it would still reveal us. A book, by itself, cannot be the final revelation. The final revelation must be through a Person who will lift up these words which we have dragged to the level of our own lives and will put the content of his own life into them, so that we may see them, not in the light of what we are, but in the light of their divine illustration. Only a person who is like God in character can reveal the character of God—can reveal God himself. The Scripture is the inspired record of the revelation—that revelation is Christ, the Person. But a book, apart from this divine illustration, would largely be a revelation of us and, hence, God cannot give himself fully through a mere book approach, for would he not, thereby, commit himself to

> Only a person who is like God in character can reveal the character of God — can reveal God himself.

something other than the truth about himself? Hence, those who come through a book approach, as the Muslims and the Arya Samajists do, usually become strong on the letter disputations about truth, but hardly glowing with the sense of God and realization.

Why is it that men, when they come through Christ, find? Is it arbitrary on the part of God that he has ordained and fixed this way—a way, that if one does not take, he is damned for disobedience? No, it is not that. Is it not because God can give himself through Christ, for he is Christ-like in character? Does he not want to fix in the soul of the seeker that he is that? Does he not back the thought that Christlikeness is the very revelation of his nature? We believe with all our hearts that it is so. God is Christ-like. Hence, Christ is the Way.

When Jesus stands and says, "I am the way, the truth, and the life: no man cometh unto the Father, but by me," are we to suppose that it is arbitrary presumption that speaks? No. He is saying what all human experience will sooner or later corroborate. Through the Vedanta, you may come to Brahma and get from it all that the Impersonal can reveal and give. You may come to Allah through Mohammed and the Koran and get from it all that this conception can give and reveal. You may come to Nirvana through Buddha and get from it all that Nirvana can give and reveal. But if you come to the Father—the Ultimate Reality, the Truth about God, the Heart of the universe—if you come to the Father, then you must come through Christ. It is not that God would not appoint another way; there is no other way, for there is no other Christ.

"But," said a Hindu at the close of one of the Round Tables, "you Christians seem to find God too easily. We Hindus have to struggle through many ages and births, but your way is too easy. You find God too cheaply." I reminded our brother that this self-giving on the part of God called for the same on our part. He withheld nothing and we could not do less. It costs our all. That what seemed too easy meant simply that the way was open and that God in Christ is available to human need.

And men in Christ do find God. A Hindu, not seeing this, said to me one day: "You Christians start out to find God, stop at Christ, and become hero-worshipers. You are content with someone who comes between you and God—a Mediator." But we know that Jesus is a Mediator only in the sense that he mediates God to us. When we take hold of him, we take hold of the very self of God. He is not someone standing between us and God—he is God become available. He is not the verandah of the Temple of Reality which we pass by on the way to the Inner Shrine. He is the heart of the Shrine. Jesus will not, therefore, be left aside after he has introduced us to the Father, for we shall be forever exploring God along the lines of Jesus. And we shall be forever seeing that the very nature of God is Christ-like.

If this statement that God in character is Christ-like seems strange in that the universal God could scarcely be revealed in a local Person, however divine he may seem to be, we are reminded that a ray of the sun reveals the very content of the sun. Scientists analyze the ray and, finding barium, calcium, sodium, radium, and helium there, they know that they are also in the sun itself. Analyze the character of Jesus and you will find what the Eternal God is like. I can say nothing higher of him.

"What is the unique thing in Christianity?" I asked of Harnack.

"It is the doctrine of the Father," he replied.

"Is it not Christ?" I asked.

"Yes," said he, "for Christ is the mirror of the heart of the Father."

But is he not more? Is he not the very Heart of the Father? "He that hath seen me hath seen the Father."

Christ at the Round Table

This statement that Jesus is the Way is not a claim, but a corroboration. We subject this to the scrutiny of life and await its verdict. Will not the final verdict be that "the soul is naturally Christian," as Tertullian has said? We will find that it is unnaturally evil, or agnostic, or atheistic, or anything else, no matter what that may be. This is not a cheap fling; it is the very verdict that life is now rendering. The soul finds itself only as it finds itself in Christ. Here it lives. A great fly wheel in a factory revolves with tremendous speed and power, and yet with perfect silence. Why? It is adjusted; it has found its center. But take it off its center and make it eccentric, it then shakes itself and the building to pieces. It has become a thing of destruction instead of construction. Life in Christ has found its center, and it silently sings to the music of its found rhythm. But take life out of Christ and it becomes eccentric, inwardly full of friction and outwardly full of clash. Out of Christ and in Christ is the difference between the fish gasping on the shore and that same fish back in the water swimming its way to freedom and harmony and life. Life out of Christ is out of its element. It is gasping on the shores of life—gasping for *life*. Christ is its true element. Here it *lives*.

> This statement that Jesus is the Way is not a claim, but a corroboration.

I climbed a great tower to get a view across the Holy Land. As I trudged up the stairs, little slits in the walls gave me just enough light to encourage me to believe that at the end there would be an open vista. When I got to the very top, though, there was nothing but a roof above me—a roof shutting the world out and shutting me in. The promise of freedom ended in futility. In England, I read on a sign-post, "Road with a Dead End." How many roads to promised freedom end in dead ends?

The Way

And when examined, those roads have an amazing likeness, whether they are found in East or West. Let us take four of them.

The West has given itself to a vast self-assertion. This has broken out into devastating wars, into exploitation of weaker peoples, into a selfish jostling for the markets of the world. Napoleon epitomizes this spirit of selfish power. He stands in history as the absolute opposite of Jesus Christ. But this way of selfish power breaks down and destroys itself. Its symbol is Napoleon banished upon an island, his empire crumbling to pieces. The end of this way is futility—a road with a dead end.

Let us look at another road. An American college graduate walked out into life and with a carefree gesture put aside this Way, said that things were not good and bad, they were only beautiful and ugly, and he would decide his life upon that basis. He walked across the moral laws of the universe, and they flung him back, a quivering, bleeding person. Two years later, he sat in utter misery, his life in ruins about him. Appalled at the desolation, he asked a friend to help him get back upon the way. He had missed the Way of life. The mad search for pleasure in the West, regardless of moral consequences, typified in this youth, ends in futility—a road with a dead end.

Take another: A millionaire, who counted his wealth in hundreds of millions, installed a great pipe organ for his own personal use. He had the greatest musicians of America come and play—it lifted him out of himself and made him forget himself and what he was. After one of these performances, he turned to a friend of mine and said very slowly, "I have learned how to make money, but I have not yet learned how to live." He had missed the way. Hundreds of millions of dollars were no compensation. The West has given itself to materialism and is finding, as typified in this disillusioned millionaire, that its end is futility—a road with a dead end.

Another: Bertrand Russell, who has a great mind and a tender social passion, but holds an agnostic philosophy, feels that the end will be a vast futility and the only attitude to take is what he calls "an unyielding despair." He wrote *Proposed Roads to Freedom*, but seems not to have found the way to it. Agnostic philosophy in the West, as typified in Bertrand Russell, grows weary and cynical, its end is futility—a road with a dead end.

When one turns to India, he finds parallels to these four endeavors for freedom and life. We find India taking this same road to a vast self-assertion. Here it has turned religious and we have two religious communities, the Hindu and the Muslim, jealous, watchful, and breaking out into bloodshed. This is paralyzing the whole of India's national life. Its end is futility—a road with a dead end.

Take the second way. The Hindu believes in the law of Karma, but he is oppressed by its terrible exactions. This law of cause and effect is iron, exacts the last jot and tittle, knows no forgiveness, and is blind in its application. I say the Hindu believes in this law and its corollary, transmigration, but he gets no joy from them. Foreigners who dabble in it may enthuse over its beauty and delicate justice, but the Hindu knows better. He seeks to escape from this iron system through the three ways—the Gyana Marga, the way of knowledge; the Bhakti Marga, the way of devotion; and the Karma Marga, the way of works. The first turns toward the Vedanta and absorption into the impersonal Brahma as the way of escape. The second turns toward Krishna or some other personal god.

They turn toward Krishna. Why? To me it has always been a mystery. Why does this great people turn to Krishna when the vast majority are far better than the character to which they turn? I think I see the reason. Krishna seems to promise relief from this awful law of Karma. He is the incarnation of the irresponsible. He steps outside all

THE WAY

laws and codes. He is a carefree figure, standing with one foot crossing the other as he plays his flute; as a baby, he kicks a cart to pieces, he steals the butter and the curds, plays pranks on everyone, runs away with the clothes of the bathing gopis (milkmaids), and hides in a tree and laughs at their distress. He entrances the wives of the cowherds of Brindaban and gaily dances with sixteen thousand of them at night and marries or consorts with whom he pleases. He walks across all codes and laws and seems to promise freedom from Karma, for he himself seems to be free. He is the incarnation of the happy, the irresponsible, the Karma-free. "To the strong there is no blame," his devotees cry. Caught up in the love of Krishna, they too shall be free from Karma. It is the spirit of the carefree American youth—he would be aesthetic even in breaking free from the shackles of the moral; and India, always incurably religious, would be religious even in following the care-free, the Karma-less Krishna. But have not both missed the way? Law can be escaped only by obedience and making it identical with one's own self. Chaitaniya, Krishna's abandoned devotee, with arms extended, rushes into the ocean at Puri to follow the moonlit path to his divine lover, but instead of finding, he drowns. Tragic symbol, the devoted but drowned life! Has it not missed the way? The end seems to be futility. Is it not a road with a dead end.

Others turn to the Vedanta as the way. Here the idea of life's futility is built into a philosophical system; one's own personality and this universe is maya or illusion. The only reality is Brahma and the hope is to lose oneself into It in some birth present or future. Here men finding life to be futile, posit the doctrine of Illusion, try to leap clear of it and to be lost in the impersonal bliss of Brahma. It reminds one of the American millionaire trying to forget himself and the maya of his millions by the method of music which carried him away on airy wings of harmony to the untroubled and the peaceful. Only here, the attempt is more thoroughgoing. Instead of music, it is withdrawal within the self, and the reiteration over and over, "Aham Brahma," "I am Brahma." In either case it is a hypnotism out of the present into the impersonal. But neither way works. The rich man says, "I have learned how to make money, but I have not learned how to live." The Vedantist silently confesses, "I have learned how to philosophize, but I have not learned how to live." "The Vedanta is not practicable for man circumstanced as I am," said the college principal. It does not seem to fit into life. Swami Rama Tiratha's torch gone out is its symbol. The end seems to be futility. Is it not a road with a dead end?

> If you believe in life, will you not have to follow the way of Christ? If you believe in life's futility, will you not have to follow the way of Buddha?

But all these were mere tyros in believing in futility compared to Buddha. This great soul went deeper than all of them. He said that all this striving, all these desires, even for God and for life, were futile. Life itself is futile, for existence and evil are one. Snuff out desire and then pass into Nirvana, the state of "the snuffed-out candle." Life's futility could not be more deeply expressed. It is Bertrand Russell's "unyielding despair," turned religious, but in both cases calling on man to be compassionate to others. Here futility is named Nirvana. Does it not seem a road with a dead end?

After all, the final issue is between Christ and Buddha—the rest of the ways are compromises between. If you believe in life, will you not have to follow the way of Christ? If you believe in life's futility, will you not have to follow the way of Buddha? "I have come that ye might have life, and that ye might have it more abundantly," says Christ. "I have come that ye might be disillusioned about life and to show you the way of escape," says Buddha. "I am the life," says Jesus. "I am the Buddha, the enlightened one about life's futility," says Buddha. "I give you peace—in life," says Jesus. "I give you peace—apart from life," says Buddha. There you have the issue. There are just two ways, the rest are merely bypaths. Disillusionment could have no nobler representative than Buddha. Life could have no more perfect embodiment than Christ.

On the walls of the great Pagoda at Rangoon is a representation of the Buddhist sage sitting cross-legged in deep meditation upon life and its meaning. Before him pass its different stages: the romping, laughing child; the aspiring youth; serious middle age; decrepit, decaying old age; gasping death; dogs feeding on the entrails of the corpse; and the end is a bleached skeleton lying on the sand. That is life, meditates the sage. As I gazed on it, the picture seemed to fade away and in its place, I saw Jesus and his attitude toward life: he blesses the little children as they climb into his lap and says, "Of such is the kingdom of God;" he looks on the young man and "loved him," and bids him follow him into the adventure of life; calls to the middle aged and says, "Come after me and I will make you;" offers to those who are getting "old"—in hope, in joy, in life —a new birth from above to renew them in their inmost being; speaks to the most forlorn of hopes as it writhes in agony on the cross and says, "Today thou shalt be with me in paradise;" stands by his aged servant Paul so that in the strength of that companionship he cries: "The time of my departure is at hand, I have fought a good fight . . . Henceforth, there is laid up for me a crown of life;" speaks into the tomb of the decaying Lazarus and says, "Come forth," and the dead comes forth to life; He walks from his own tomb, brings an Easter morning into the world's dark night of sorrow and separation; stretches forth his hands and says, "I am the resurrection and the life." Here is Life looking at life unabashed and conquering it.

If you want life, Jesus is inescapable; if you do not, then Buddha is inescapable.

Christ at the Round Table

In my notebook there are five leaves, four of which were plucked from trees—one was taken from a book. All five leaves stand for five great outlooks on life. The first is a leaf from the Koran, whose leaves are supposed to have fluttered down from paradise. The second is from the tree which is the supposed successor of the one which Krishna climbed at Brindaban in his escapade with the gopis; the third is from a tree overhanging a famous Ashram from which the Vedanta philosophy has gone to the ends of the earth; the fourth is from the Bo tree at Bodh Gaya, successor to the one under which Buddha sat and received his "enlightenment"; the fifth is from an olive tree on the Mount of Olives, successor to the ones under which Jesus knelt in prayer.

Which leaf is for the healing of the nations?

These ways must be tested at the touchstone of life. Do they give life—life abundant? Do these ways throw open the door to fuller life?

When I examine the first, I find it is a vast attempt to turn back this tendency toward fuller life by jamming life back into the letter of the Koran, a religion of rules. There it becomes static, unprogressive. In a religion of rules, one of two things happens. Either the people in growing break the rules or the rules are so strong, that they break the people.

I asked a leading Muslim, an educational minister, this question, "You have a way of progress in Islam in the principle of Ijma [agreement]—can you use it? If so, you might make progress."

"No," he thoughtfully replied, "it cannot be done; it is impracticable since the faithful are so scattered. Moreover, whenever it has been tried, it has proved a failure, as in the hijrat to Afghanistan and the fatwa identifying Islam and Non-cooperation."

"What is left then?" I asked.

"There is the letter of the Koran. We must go back to that, for life and civilization have gone astray and we must bring it back."

Back to a sixth-century conception! The Muslims of Persia, Bukhara and Turkistan are still singing, "Religion and life are antagonistic." The newly emancipated Turks are going further and are saying, "The first characteristic of modern civilization is the separation of religion and life" (*Khalk*, Feb. 18, 1926). In trying to make life fit religion by strait-jacketing it in the letter of the Koran, as the minister of education suggests, or in trying to make religion separate from life, as the Turks suggest—in either case, the result is fatal both to life and to religion. They must coincide to live. But Islam is attempting to live against this fuller and developing life. The result is a paralysis to life. The universe does not back it. This leaf is not for the healing of the nations.

> If you want life, Jesus is inescapable; if you do not, then Buddha is inescapable.

The next leaf is that of Krishna representing the Bhakti schools. This leaf at the lowest represents that desire for what James calls "a moral holiday," the deification in India of what America is so madly pursuing—the desire for thrills, "to get a kick out of life"; India chained to the iron system of Karma and the West chained to the machines of an industrial age want freedom; so they both consciously or unconsciously bow at the shrine of Krishna, the Irresponsible. They take this leaf for their healing. This is Bhakti in the lower form. But you cannot get rid of law by defying it; you can get rid of it only by making it identical with your own being; then it is no longer a law—it is a liberty. Take it even in the higher, where it is sublimated in the Bhagawad Gita, and this historical Krishna drops away and the philosophical Krishna takes his place—even here it does not issue in their fuller, victorious, abundant life. I mentioned the most devoted of the bhaktas seated on the path in the dust. His mentality was wasting away, his whole life being reduced to a minimum. "I once knew English," he said, "but it is now gone." If there is calm, it seems to be the calm of a reduced vitality, peace purchased at the price of personality, life nearing that of the vegetable.

I talked to another famous bhakta who had not been out of his ashram for forty years. "Why do you not go out?" I asked.

"If I should, I might be tempted; I might see a woman or money; that is why I have not been out for these forty years," he replied.

"But suppose everyone should take your attitude toward life, how would the world go on?" I asked.

"Well, we try to avoid, but we do not succeed— that is how the world goes on."

Life goes on only as religion fails! He was laying bare the fact that the whole endeavor was to live against life. I could not get rid of the memory of fifteen hundred widows who each day for seven hours continuously chanted the name of "Hari Ram." It would break a heart of stone to see them there, and yet the heavens did not open before this devotion, for their faces were the blankest I have ever beheld in human beings. This fuller life was not coming into being—life was withering away. The universe did not seem to be backing this endeavor. This leaf is hardly for the healing of the nations.

The Vedanta is also an attempt to live against this urge for fuller life. It asks us to consider this universe an illusion — that wipes out that much life; to consider our personalities an illusion—more life goes, and we are asked to take the Impersonal as compensation. But the Impersonal is emptied of all attributes, the Everlasting Not (Neti, Neti, "not that, not that" is the only way it is said to be described).

"Describe to me Brahma," said a pupil to his guru.

The sage was silent for a long time.

"Will you not tell me?" the pupil urged.

"You have received your answer," replied the sage.

Brahma was the Vast Silence. We are to lose ourselves and the universe in order to gain THIS. It is a vast negation of life. In trying to make God everything, it makes him akin to nothing. It cheapens him. "I am Brahma," called out a man from the audience one day while we were discussing God. I replied that I did not feel inclined to worship! At the close he came up to me and said: "I apologize for what I did tonight. I have a very crooked and irresponsible nature." And yet he was God! Here God was all—and nothing; the man was nothing—and all. The exaggeration had ended in prostration, as all exaggeration does. To take another illustration: a Hindu chairman in his opening remarks said, "I think God and religion do not matter," and before he was through, he said, "I think it will finally be found that we are God." He was all, hence, nothing. Suranda Nath Chakravati in Prabhu Harata diagnoses this negation of life as India's real difficulty: "India seems to be gradually awakening from the stupor of age long self-hypnotism..., but we are far from the goal, we are yet under the spell of the Everlasting No, so we have still got the stoop of decrepitude."

In a recent conference, a fine spirited Hindu nationalist said: "Our trouble is not poverty, appalling as that is in India. Our trouble is sloth. That is at the root of our poverty." But I felt the trouble was deeper, for the sloth was the result of a lack of faith in life and its possibilities. If there is an undertone of Maya, why endeavor? The Indian people are naturally no more slothful than other people. The false view of God and life paralyzes the whole.

Christ at the Round Table

My mother gradually lost use of her arms and limbs and then of her whole body. Doctor after doctor tried to diagnose the difficulty, for it was not ordinary paralysis. Finally, one found that a tiny blood clot had formed on the brain due to the rupture of a small blood vessel. It was a tiny thing, no larger than a pin-head, but it paralyzed her whole body. If we could have lifted that, she would have risen to life. A creeping paralysis has come over Mother India. She can no longer stand upright among the nations. Why is she prostrate? The blood clot that is upon her soul, paralyzing the whole, is a false view of God and life. Lift that and Mother India will rise to health and to the service of the nations.

But the Vedanta is an attempt to live against life. The universe does not seem to back it. This leaf is hardly for the healing of the nations.

Here is the leaf of the Bo tree—the place of Buddha's "illumination." Because of this experience, he taught that existence and evil are one and desire even for life must be cut. This is summed up in the doctrine of Sunyavadi, or "the doctrine of Nothingness." This stands as the supreme attempt to live against life. A spiritual dryness invades the souls of those who hold it. In Burma, I lay on the veranda looking up at the starlit heavens. I had come back from addressing a meeting in this Buddhist city—a city of fifteen thousand monks. I was tired, for I had felt the dryness of the soul of the people to whom I had been speaking. The Big Dipper hung in the heavens above me. We call it the Big Dipper, but in the East, it hangs with its face down —it dips no water for thirsty people. That, thought I, is Buddhism. Its symbol is a dipper turned upside down. Men gaze at it, but they do not drink from it. No wonder a Buddhist schoolgirl had said that day, "My heart is so thirsty that I hope these meetings will go on." She had gazed at the inaccessible empty Big Dipper with thirst unquenched, and was grateful for the simple cup of cold water I was offering. The Buddhist endeavor ends in the spirit's lassitude, for the universe does not back nonliving. It backs life—and this is not life. This leaf is hardly for the healing of the nations.

The last leaf is from the olive tree under which Jesus knelt in prayer. There he carried to the heart of the universe, to the Father, the needs, the sorrows, the sins and problems of life, and there in communion came strength, not to escape life, or to drug oneself with mystical devotion ending in itself, but to face life and carry into its heart healing, courage, strength, redemption. As he came down in the morning, "the power of the Lord was present to heal." Here was Goodness going straight into the heart of evil to cure it, Health going to the bedside of sickness to bid it rise and serve, Joy wiping the tears from the face of sorrow, Peace laying its quiet hand of benediction upon the deep unrest of the heart, Life coming to the withered hopes and wasted souls of men and bidding them live, God coming in answer to the craving of the orphaned heart of the world, that cries, "Show us the Father." He is here. The lineaments of his face—how tender! The touch of his hand—how healing! The love of his heart—how full of refuge! His bosom, where we can weep out our sins and follies—how full of compassion!

A Hindu friend, seeing this, bursts into the music of these words: "We have been talking to the dumb silences and Jesus is the Voice that has answered us. We have been reaching up in the dark and Jesus is that Hand-Clasp from God reaching down and lifting us." Jesus takes that Big Dipper from the sky, turns it over, transforms it into a drinking cup and bids men drink. "He that drinketh of these waters"—the waters of material possession, of lower lusts, of philosophical systems—"shall thirst again" —they have the doom of thirst upon them—but "he that drinketh of the water that I shall give unto him shall never thirst." Jesus removes desire, not apart from its satisfaction as Buddha tried, but through its satisfaction. And when anyone drinks, he knows within him that *this is the water of life!*

Jesus stands for life. If you want life, you cannot escape him. In the entrance hall of a great hospital in America, there stands a statue of the Healing Christ. By whichever door people enter, Jesus seems to be facing them. No man can go into life's hospital to serve, to heal, to lift without standing face to face with Christ. He is inevitable.

"I was an atheistic socialist," said a brilliant lover of the people to me, "but I was led to Christ by the very pressures of life and its needs."

As he went into life, he stood face to face with *Life*.

"The more is sacrifice needed in India, and the more it is made, the more will Jesus find a home in the land," said Keshab Chandar Sen, one of the greatest of India's sons.

Yes, the more that sane sacrificial living is needed, the more that life is needed, the more Jesus will find a home in human hearts everywhere. The redemptive God is so desperately needed in our world that Jesus is inevitable. We simply cannot do without him. Can the lungs do without air, the eye without light, the heart without love, life without Life? No more can we do without Christ.

"Now that self-government is beginning, and the demand for self-sacrifice and service is greater, I commend the love and self-sacrifice of Christ to you," said a Parsee principal of a college to his pupils. He looked down the road of the future and could not help seeing a cross.

"Begin with India and her needs and you will come out at the place of Christ," said a thoughtful Hindu.

"Our economics and our nationalism make Jesus inevitable; there is no getting rid of him until we have transcended him," said a discerning Englishman.

As we face life, Jesus is inescapable, for he is the epitome of that upward urge for life. You ask me to define life—I cannot. But I have seen life. There it stands—Christ: I fall in love with life and living as I see him.

He stands, as Frank N. Riale says, "as the race purpose drawn out in living character." He is the living expression of our moral and spiritual universe. In him it has become personalized. If Jesus is the meaning and goal of our universe, then the universe could have no richer meaning or goal. Jesus is no accident, for, as Cairns says, "Here is something that discloses the very nature of the universe itself. The stars themselves move along the lines of Jesus."

And the laws of life in him are the very laws of our own being. Butler in his *Analogy* was right when he said, "Jesus publishes anew the laws of our nature, which men had corrupted, and the very knowledge of which to so large a degree had been lost." I know this to be true when I try it. I find it works: Love is a law of life in Christ. Love, not hate, is the law of my being, for hate eats like acid into my soul, while love makes it glow with radiant health. Purity is a law of life in Christ. It is the law of my being, for impurity withers the inner life, while purity makes it tingle with freshness. Goodness, not evil, is the law of my being, for evil cuts into the soul as sand cuts into the eye, while goodness is akin to gladness. Self-sacrifice is the law of Christ's being. It is the law of my being, for selfishness spreads a pall of unhappiness and misery within, while the heart sings as it bleeds and bears for others. Christ is the law of my nature, for when I have him, know him, live in fellowship with him, share life with him, then my soul rises up to meet him, gladness too deep for words steals through my being and life catches its rhythm and harmony. Christ and the soul were made for one another.

William James, feeling his way to this truth, says, "The universe . . . takes a turn genuinely for the worse or for the better in proportion as each one evades or fulfills God's commands." "God's command" for us is Christ—to live according to him. And we find our universe taking a turn for worse or for better as we evade or live life according to him.

Jesus is not a set of irksome restrictions upon life; He asks that the grave clothes be taken from life and that life be let go into freedom. Religion has too often been expressed according to its etymology —to bind. In Christ, it means to loose. It is the affirmation to life. Paul expresses this when he said, "The divine 'yes' has at last sounded in him" (2 Cor. 1: 20, Moffatt). In all other ways, the No has sounded.

Islam is the way of the will—the will cannot be affirmed, so it must be submitted (Islam). The end is an entire losing of the human will—a negation. The deepest Hinduism is the way of the mind—to recognize one's identity with Brahma. The mind cannot be affirmed, so its end is to realize that it does not exist, that only Brahma exists. The end is a losing of the human mind—a negation. Buddhism is the way of the emotions—suffering and existence are one. The emotions cannot be affirmed or completed, so they must be snuffed out in Nirvana—a negation. The human personality cannot be saved and affirmed in these, so it must be negated. But Jesus is the affirmation. I am the Way—the way of the will; I am the Truth—the way of the mind; I am the Life—the way of the emotions. Here the human personality is not despaired of and negated, but redeemed and affirmed.

Side by side are two great representatives of two great outlooks on life: Marcus Aurelius, the Stoic, and Paul, the Christian. In his *Paul of Tarsus*, Glover finally draws the contrast. The No had sounded in the one, and the Yes had sounded in the other. Paul had found the Way.

Religion needs the sense that the universe is behind it in order to make it unabashed and victorious. In Christ, there is this sense of backing by the universe of moral and spiritual values. Larger Life backs our smaller life.

In a recent issue of a Muslim paper was a front page account of Mohammed's name being written in the sky. Independent groups of observers had seen it at Allahabad and at Saugor, so the report read. The comment on the supposed happening was: "From this we see that the triumph of Islam is closer than we had dared dream." But religion will not conquer because a name is written in the heavens. It will conquer because that name is written in the constitution of our very being.

The name of Christ shall be above every name, not through propaganda, or any trick of fate, nor even through the heavens' proclamations, but because it is inscribed in the constitution of our universe and in the makeup of our own souls. "Lift the rock and thou shalt find me, cleave the wood and I am there," is an early saying attributed to Christ; and we may add, "Look into your nature, not this false nature created by sin, but into your real nature, and you will find his name written there."

In the consciousness of this power to give human life just what it needs, Jesus stands and, stretching forth his hands, cries, "Come unto me and I will give you rest, for my yoke is easy and my burden is light." Why is his yoke easy and his burden light? Is it because he demands little? On the contrary, he makes the deepest demands on us that can possibly be laid on human nature, for he asks that we surrender our inmost being to him. Nothing—absolutely nothing—is to be kept back. And yet, everyone who tries it, cries out that his yoke is easy and his burden is light. Why? Because Christ and the soul were made for one another. His yoke is our yearning. His commands are our cravings, his purposes our persons.

Try all the ways to peace that you know and they will end in heavy yokes and dead ends; try this way in Christ and you will find the light yoke and the open vista.

Chapter 16

CHRIST — THE UNIVERSAL

A THOUGHTFUL HINDU asked, "If God is one and humanity is one, why cannot we be one in religion?" I think he expressed an undertone of craving that is very widespread. We long for the universal. We cannot rest except in the totality of things. "The world cannot remain half pagan and half Christian," remarked an Indian. His friend replied, "No, it cannot remain half anything."

The whole trend of life is toward the universal. Science is giving us a universal language—the language of fact; philosophy, in spite of James, is giving us, not a multiverse, but a universe; sociology is more and more giving us a universal human concept, namely, that mankind is one. We are catching the same diseases, partaking of the same healing by medical science, being subjected to the same ideas. Commerce is giving us a universal intercommunication, through universal trade. "The League of Nations is giving us universal political concepts—international law and international cooperation." Can religion give to all this an international soul? Or will it be local and divisive?

Christ at the Round Table

In the Round Tables this yearning for universality was expressed again and again. I noted three ways by which men hoped to see it come: first, by Command, that is the Muslim way; second, by Comprehension, the Hindu way; third, by Christ, the Christian way. The first need not detain us long, for we have arrived at a stage in the world's thinking when to say, "It is God's will," does not settle it. We must be sure it is God speaking. For that we must get the verdict of life. The other two ways we will examine in this chapter.

We must remember that no universal, either in religion or in other realms, can be arrived at hastily or without a great deal of sifting. Science is giving us a universal language of fact only at tremendous cost in sifting fact from myth and fancy. Slowly the facts emerge. It will not be otherwise with religion. You cannot wave your hand over religions and say, "Now let us have universality." It will come through patient sifting of truth from error, of the relevant from the irrelevant, of the universal from the temporary and the local. It will come through putting religions under the facts of life to see which is the spiritually fit to survive, which corresponds to the facts of the universe, which can satisfy universal human need. That process of sifting and testing is now taking place. The universal will emerge—is emerging.

It is not to be denied that this way to universality in religion is no easy way. It involves clash, and it brings in the beginning not peace, but division. Only when an idea has conquered by its own inherent truth does peace come. The Copernican idea in astronomy fought its way through division to acceptance and then there was peace. The truth made men free. It is much easier to take the Hindu way to universality, namely, the method of comprehension. As Professor Radhakrishna says, "Hinduism developed an attitude of comprehensive charity instead of a fanatic faith in an inflexible creed." Everything is comprehended in its tolerance.

"Who is a Hindu?" I asked a Hindu judge, an authority on Hinduism.

"You can believe anything and be a Hindu," he replied, "anything from pantheism to atheism."

"Yes, I know," I said, "but where does the Hindu end and the Non-Hindu begin?"

"Well, you can believe in anything provided you do not reject the rest," was his final statement.

He put his finger on the genius of Hinduism, for it absorbs everything, good, bad, and indifferent, and rejects nothing. Even concerning those religions outside itself, it says that they, too, are ways to God.

This method of universality by comprehension seems the easiest and most charitable method. But I wonder if it really does lead to universality? Does a mixture of error and truth make for universality in reasoning? Does the putting together of the Ptolemaic and the Copernican views make for universality in astronomy? Do disease and health make for universality in physical living? Do evil and good make for universality in the moral life? Do Kali and Christ make for universality in our ideas of God? To all of them, we must answer, "No." There is only one side of those statements that leads to the universal: truth, Copernican, health, good, Christ. The other side leads to limitation and collapse. Truth, by its very nature, is universal, while error, by its nature, is local and limited. Five plus five make ten around the world; it is universal; but five plus five make eleven is limited, for it is not in touch with the universe of mathematical truth. Spreading out water beyond certain limits does not make for a wider and finer river—it makes for a swamp. As John Oman says, "We do not advance merely by widening our outlook. The new can be won only at the expense of combating the old"[1] As a Hindu said concerning a certain leader, "He is everything in religion and hence nothing." He had become a swamp. Tagore senses the necessity of elimination more than Gandhiji. They were talking together when the latter said that he would let the ignorant people have idols as he would give crutches to a lame man. Tagore arose and said, "Yes, and in doing so, you would further lame them."

India needs nothing so much as she needs a prophet whose fan will be in his hand to cleanse the threshing floor and separate the chaff from the wheat. As physical life depends almost as much upon elimination as it does upon assimilation, so also does the spiritual life depend upon cleansing.

This method of universality by comprehension appeals to three classes: First, those who are world weary and are suffering from loss of nerve in thinking and living; second, those who are indifferent to religion and find this an easy way of solution; third, those who know that truths are embedded in almost every error and are anxious that these truths be not lost.

Concerning the first, we need pause only long enough to say that it needs courage to be seriously religious. For, as Principal Jacks says, every religious perplexity presents itself in the form of a question: Concerning this, will I be a hero or a coward? Will I take the low easy

---

[1] John Oman, *Grace and Personality* (1917), p. 83.

road or the high difficult road? Only the courageous can be religious, for religion is a call to strike tents to higher life. The cowardly sink back and accept the *status quo*. So, no higher truth opens to them, for they are unwilling to act upon it. Only those who do, know. Lack of courage to face things and eliminate rooted evils is back of a good deal of the demand for universality by inclusion.

Concerning the question of preserving the good embedded in the error, we must recognize that any religion that would be universal must take cognizance of these embedded truths and preserve them. It must fulfill them. Christ does this, as we shall note later.

I know what I have written will sound narrow and bigoted to some. They will wave their hands and say: "Do not all rivers finally run into the ocean? Though they may have wandered through devious ways, they all arrive at last." But the illustration is not true, for some rivers do not get into the ocean; one runs into the Dead Sea; another starts toward the ocean and is lost in the desert sands of Africa. Nothing is more patent to a real observer than that life very often runs into Dead Seas. The Round Table Conference of life reveals that.

The fact is that all great truths are narrow. That two and two make four is narrow. Why not be broad and liberal and believe that two and two make five, or even six? That sounds liberal. But put it into mathematical life and test it there—put it into a sum and see how it works. Every statement except two and two make four breaks itself upon the mathematical universe; the sum will not come out right. But two and two make four sings its way into mathematical harmony. The narrow leads to freedom, the supposedly broad leads to confusion and collapse. It is only the truth that can make us free.

When we face the facts, we find that other ways are undergoing feverish modification to save them from breakdown. The non-Christian faiths are undergoing revival, but it is being accomplished by what

Christ at the Round Table

Doctor Farquhar calls "an inner steady decay." A revival is a good thing *if you can stand it*. But a revival may shake a system to pieces if it is not founded upon ultimate realities. A revival may prove very dangerous. It is so now. Systems are in fact being shaken to pieces by the very movement that is taking place.

When Israel was about to appeal to Egypt for help against the Assyrians, Isaiah protested that Egypt could not help. She was so loosely hung together that movement would cause her to fall to pieces. "Their strength is to sit still," he concluded. It is so with these systems: their strength is to sit still and maintain the sanctions of the past, but movement is going through everything and that very movement is causing disintegration. As a Hindu correspondent wrote to Gandhiji, as reported in *Young India* of December 9, 1926: "However much you try to liberalize such religions, you will never truly liberalize them before you have improved them out of existence altogether. To mend them is to end them, and one can only liberalize them *away*."

In our Round Table Conferences, we urge that men feel at home and that they be free to speak of Krishna and Rama and Mohammed, if their faith centers in them. But, however much you urge, one has the feeling that Krishna and Rama and Mohammed are not at home in the atmosphere of scientific education, social advance and spiritual demand. They are brought in apologetically. They do not fit into these surroundings. They are at home in the surroundings and mentality of the temple and the mosque, but not amid the scientifically educated mind of this age. They are dwindling factors.

The stages through which the religions and the philosophies of Greece passed with the impact of the gospel upon them are being paralleled in India today. Among the Greeks the first attitude was that of supercilious contempt. "What will this babbler say?" asked the philosophers of Mars' Hill and they epitomize the whole attitude at first. The gospel in its simplicity and its lack of metaphysical speculation seemed absurd alongside of the highly wrought out philosophical theories of life. It was so in India at first. The proud philosophers scorned the simplicity of the gospel. It did not seem sufficiently learned. "Crude" was the term often used.

This supercilious attitude began to harden into serious opposition. The second stage set in. The gospel could not be laughed out of court, so they would prove it false. "It is not true," they argued —both in Greece and India. But the truths of the gospel began to prove self-evidencing. They began to hit the intellectual and moral consciousness, and to hit it hard.

Then the attitude changed again. "It is not new," they argued. "The same things are found in our sacred books." Then by methods more clever than accurate, new meanings began to be read into the sacred books and then triumphantly read out again. Words were tortured to express gospel meanings.

Then the process of spiritualization set in. Stories concerning the gods, both among the Greeks and the Hindus, which had been accepted literally with no compunction of conscience began to cause uneasiness. The white purity of Jesus shone into the situation. The psychological climate changed. It became necessary to find spiritual meanings in gross stories. The process of spiritualization, one of the first refuges of the skeptical mind, was on. The grossness was refined away.

Among the Greeks, two systems were born out of the impact of the gospel upon the situation, namely, Gnosticism and Neo-Platonism. Both tried to cut the nerve of the gospel, one by amalgamating pagan ideas with it, the other by a strong philosophical defense of a new refined paganism. In India, two parallel movements due to the same influences have been born, namely, Theosophy and Neo-Hinduism. The former is a mixture of ancient Gnosticism, Hinduism and a scattering of Christian ideas. The latter is militant and strongly defends the old, now refined and presented in a rationalized garb.

But as among the Greeks, the content was gradually taken from the old and foundations were dug away. They became floating systems of mystical thought without foundations—they were modified out of existence, so in India. Content after content is being given up, so that what formerly seemed solid and substantial is now becoming airy and without foundation. Rationalization is slowly becoming ruin. Spiritualization, giving comfort for awhile, is exacting its price.

In the process, Christ had been put as one along with the rest of the Greek gods. He found his place in the Pantheon. But as the old lost its content and its authority, Christ became more and more regnant. He more and more provided a solid basis for men's thinking and a resting place for their distracted souls. He rose to supremacy and the old succumbed to him.

In India, Christ is being put in as one along with the rest, but gradually he is gathering moral and spiritual authority to himself. We watch that gathering of authority with bated breath and with the hush of prayer.

Can we find universality in Christianity? If we mean by it the system that has been built up around Christ, then I am not sure that we can. It has gathered up into itself many local, temporary and limiting things. To give two extreme illustrations: A theological professor in the

West wrote learnedly about the danger of allowing India, with the New Testament in her hand, to interpret Christ according to her own genius. He said that no one could be trusted to interpret Christ, neither India nor the West. He forgot, of course, that the New Testament is itself an interpretation and our systems of doctrine are interpretations of that interpretation.

We are all forced to interpret, and I have a secret hope that India may do better in her interpretation than the professor, for when he laid down the principles on which a commission was to judge of the soundness in the Christian faith of a certain institution, the name of Christ was not mentioned! An interpretation of Christianity with the name of Christ left out! Have we built up a system around Christ in the West?

To take another: A lady missionary asked a clergyman of a certain church if he would let Christ preach in his pulpit.

"Certainly," was the reply.

"Would you allow him to administer the communion?"

The clergyman hesitated. "I am afraid I couldn't, for he wasn't ordained."

One excluded Christ by a doctrinal system and the other by an ecclesiastical system, but both eliminated him. These are admittedly extreme cases and not typical, but there is no doubt that "Christianity is a smothered religion." Tagore puts his finger on this when he says, "Christianity appeals to all nations, races and creeds, but you have made it so ecclesiastical that it appeals to nobody."

The Jerusalem leaders came near smothering the gospel in the beginning. It was Paul who loosed it from its Jewish fetters. He dared follow the living Christ into the heart of paganism. He came back and told what God had wrought. The Jerusalem leaders were forced into liberality by the facts produced, but when they drew up some of the things considered essential for the Christians among the Gentiles, we find among essentials: "to abstain from things strangled and from blood." Binding up the gospel of Christ with that! Of course it dropped away, for the gospel was at grips with bigger issues. It may be that to future Christians some of the things that we consider essential in our systems will seem just as absurd as this does to us. Through Paul, Christ broke through the system and found the soul of the people. He must and he will do it again today.

Plagues are said to come upon those who add to or subtract from the book of Revelation. The things that have plagued Christendom in the past and are now plaguing it in the present are the things that we have added to the gospel and the things that we have taken from it. The plagues of controversy and division and weakness will be largely lifted when we get back to the center—Christ.

For there we come to our Universal. Bishop M. S. Hughes has drawn our attention to the fact that in many realms of life we come to an ultimate, and that this ultimate is the starting-point for further progress. In the realm of mathematics, we have discovered that one and one make two. We cannot improve on this. It is fixed. But this does not stop mathematical progress, for on fixed ultimates such as this, the whole vast system of mathematical calculations is built up. "Things equal to the same thing are equal to each other," is an ultimate in geometry. But it does not stop progress, it begins it. In the realm of music, we are adding no new notes to the scale. But this does not prevent musical progress. It begins it. For out of the fixed scale came the symphonies of Beethoven, and others yet to be born will come from it.

In the realm of religion, we believe that Jesus is a moral and spiritual ultimate. Here we feel that we have touched finality. We have come to a fixed point in our moral and spiritual universe. We have something to work on. We know what life ought to be. We have seen someone stand where we wish to stand and we have seen what God is like. We know if we are to be seriously religious, we must be religious after the mind and spirit of Jesus or else fail to be religious. These are the only terms on which we feel religion is worthwhile. Religion as custom, or religion as creed, or religion as national self-assertion, we cannot seriously consider, but religion as Christlikeness gets us and holds us.

"There is no doubt that in India the term 'Christ-like' is becoming synonymous with purity of character," said a Hindu to me one day. This is true, but more, it is becoming synonymous with what life ought to be.

> In the realm of religion, we believe that Jesus is a moral and spiritual ultimate. Here we feel that we have touched finality.

"His emphasis was not in any of the seven kingdoms in which men win their crowns—Art, Literature, Philosophy, Science, Invention, Statesmanship and War—and, yet, we call Jesus great." Wherein was his greatness? It was in the realm of character. Character is supreme in life; hence, Jesus stood supreme in the supreme thing. He did not come to teach science or philosophy, for had he done so, he would have limited himself, since these can be the pursuit of only the few. These are marginal. But character is central in life. Jesus, therefore, came to show God's character, to provide an ideal of character, and to redeem and uplift human character. Jesus was greatest in the greatest realm. In the majesty of pure living, in the breadth of his sympathy, in the balance of his character (no virtue being fostered at the expense of another) in the unselfish, sacrificial outlook of his life, in pure, disinterested love; in fact, in all those qualities that make up real character, Jesus Christ was supreme, so supreme that "when we think of the Ideal we do not add virtue to virtue, but think of Jesus Christ," so that "the standard of human life is no longer a code, but a Character." Philosophy knows nothing of a realized ideal, but here seems to have been realized a *Character-Ideal* unimproved on after centuries of ethical thought and progress.

> And so the Word had breath, and wrought
> With human hands the creed of creeds,
> In loveliness of perfect deeds,
> More strong than all poetic thought.

Sin is becoming more and more to mean un-Christlikeness, and good to mean Christlikeness. The Judgment seat of Christ has been set up among the nations. We find everything being brought more and more to the bar of this Judgment seat to be judged. He is not an arbitrary Judge assuming this role because he has the authority, but he is Judge because we know no other standard. K. T. Paul, the thoughtful secretary of the Y.M.C.A. in India, says: "Down underneath things there is being set up a standard by which non-Christians are judging all their actions and motives. That standard is the character of Christ."

Jesus says, "When I am in the world, I am the light of the world." When Jesus is in any situation, he is the light of that situation. When the sun is in the heavens, it is the light of the heavens—when it arises, the stars fade out. All other methods of living and views of life fade out when Christ appears, for he is light. Others may have caught certain colors of the spectrum. He is light, the sum total of those colors.

There are those who in order to be more universal, tone down the distinctively Christian things. But you cannot be more universal by being less Christian. In the Round Tables, those who struck the deepest

Christ—The Universal

Christian notes made the more universal appeal. For "the soul is naturally Christian."

"Can you give me a definition of religion?" I was asked one day by a Hindu.

"I am not sure that I can define religion," I replied, "but I have seen Religion—Christ."

Here is Religion, not a stiff code of rules, but bending in lowly service over the lost. Here Religion does not sit in state demanding obeisance, but it suffers and bleeds for others and it bids us follow, and soon it has our obeisance and more: It has us. Religion turned Christ-like is Religion turned authoritative and final.

Jesus is Religion. He is not a religion, or the religion, but Religion itself. I cannot be satisfied with a mathematics, but only with Mathematics, the truth about the mathematical world. I do not want an astronomy, but Astronomy, the truth about the stars. I crave not an ethic, but Ethics, the truth about the moral universe. So, I cannot be satisfied with a religion, or even with the religion, but only with Religion, the truth about our moral and spiritual universe. I can be satisfied only with Jesus who is Religion. The whole endeavor in mathematical education is to get the child from a mathematics, which is the child's

> **Jesus is Religion. He is not a religion, or the religion, but Religion itself... The whole endeavor of moral and spiritual progress is to get men from a religion to Religion, in other words, to bring men to Christ.**

view, to Mathematics, which is the truth of the mathematical world. The whole endeavor of moral and spiritual progress is to get men from a religion to Religion, in other words, to bring men and women to Christ. Evangelism is inherent in the nature of things.

Moffatt translates Matt. 12: 18: "He shall proclaim religion to the Gentiles," not a religion but Religion, for he presents himself. Jesus is not the Founder of the Christian religion, Jesus is its Foundation because He is the Foundation of our moral and spiritual universe.

Pilate looking at Jesus saw that he had stepped out of ordinary humanity and cried, "Behold the man!" He saw that he was not a man, just one among the many, he was the Man. He came near the truth, but not quite. Bishop Temple offers the truth when he says: "Christ was not a man, but Man, he was not a God, but God." In him we see what man is and how far we have fallen, in him we see what God is and how far we may rise. He is the universal meeting us personalized. Since I am a person, the universal must meet me personalized.

In Mark 2: 2, it says that "Jesus spake the Word unto them"—not words, or a word, but the Word. This is the Word that gathers up all other true words within itself, the fulfillment of "the sure word" of Plato and the Eternal Shabd or Word of the Hindus that reverberates through all worlds and changes all things.

Jesus changes everything he touches. Call him a man, and you will have to change your ideas of what a man is; call him God, and you will have to change your ideas of what God is. You can transfer every quality of Jesus into God without the slightest sense of loss or blasphemy. And when you set him up as man he appeals to universal man.

He is the one Figure in history that is not local or national. Moses was a Hebrew, Mohammed was an Arab, Buddha was an Indian,

Socrates was a Greek, Confucius was a Chinese, but Jesus is the Son of man. "Isn't Jesus the Oriental Christ?" asked a Christian friend of a Hindu.

"No," he replied, "He is the universal Christ." All nations feel at home with him when they really know him. The West sees in him the Doer, the Bringer of the kingdom of God on earth; the East sees in him the Realization of the Divine in life. Both man and woman see in him their own highest qualities, for he combines the tenderness and gentleness of woman with the oak strength of man. He appeals to both. His heart is as simple and unaffected as a child's, and children gather about his feet and see in him childhood's hero.

> Jesus changes everything he touches. Call him a man, and you will have to change your ideas of what a man is; call him God, and you will have to change your ideas of what God is.

How sifted from the local and the temporary and the trivial his mind was! He was always on the worthwhile, on the thing that mattered. He was never misled by a subordinate issue; not once did he slip away from the primary into the secondary. His finger goes unerringly to the essentials in every matter.

Jesus was universal because sinless. It is sin that narrows; when man sins, he feels orphaned and alone in the universe; when he is good, he feels that the world belongs to him, he feels universalized, for goodness is in touch with the truth of things, the universal; the perfectly good is the universal. All founders of religions went through some experience of restoration from a clouded and broken life to a clear and restored life—all except Jesus. "All of us," says Bushnell, "go on into goodness on the principle of rectification." We judge our past, criticize it, repent of it, rectify it, and thus pass on into goodness. There are no exceptions to this and the better the man, the more thorough the rectification. But Jesus rectifies nothing. He recalls no word that he ever spoke, retraces no step that he ever took, undoes no act that he ever did, no prayer for forgiveness was ever upon his lips and no tear of penitence upon his cheek. He never once said, "I am sorry." He taught his disciples to pray the prayer, "Our Father .... forgive us our trespasses," but he never prayed that prayer. He said, "If ye then being evil," but he left himself out of it. His last word was not a prayer for restoration or acceptance, but, "It is finished." As Willibald Beyschlag, a German theologian says:"He who with incomparable keenness has pursued sin into the inmost recesses of the heart, found no shadow of guilt, even in the most critical hours of his life, arising out of his own heart to transform the countenance of his heavenly Father into the countenance of a Judge— not in the storm which threatened his life, not in the total wreck of his earthly hopes, not even in Gethsemane or Calvary."[2] Jesus is the Sinless Exception to our humanity, therefore the Universal Man.

What would I add to him. to make him more perfect? What would I take from him? Nothing.

But if he is the perfect, he is also the progressive. We have discovered an Ultimate, but this does not stop progress—it begins it. We have a Fixed Point, but the point is not fixed. Jesus is not behind us in the past. He is the great Contemporary. More—he is ahead of us. "He stands on the further side of our twenty centuries," calling us into the new life. He has not been surpassed, not even approximated. He is no spent force. Jesus is God's final but unfolding word. More and more

---

2 Willibald Beyschlag, *New Testament Theology* (1891), p. 76.

light breaks out from him. Since our code is a Character, we can never say we have attained. We are always discovering new meanings in him.

A religion founded upon rules is soon outgrown, for rules are temporary, growing out of temporary conditions; principles are never outgrown, they are the same yesterday, today, and forever; but principles meeting us in a Person are not only eternal, they are eternally concreted, kept close to life, always illustrated. Jesus did not give rules, he did not even give principles alone, he gave principles illustrated by what he was and did. Hence, he is never outgrown.

Everything is undergoing modification, everything except Jesus. He is the Modifier—he stands unmodified. "Higher education is not a good thing for our Hindu girls," said a leader in Hindu education, "for it undermines their faith, and when that is undermined, they go to pieces morally, but it is a good thing for your Christian girls." Why? Because the faith of the Christian is laid in an Ultimate. He has "received a kingdom that cannot be shaken." For as Romanes, the scientist, suggests, "there is an absence from the biography of Christ of any doctrines which the subsequent growth of human knowledge, whether in natural science, ethics, political economy, or elsewhere, has had to discount."

This is true: Jesus will not be outgrown, for we have found in him life's crown and consummation.

Some, as the Brahmo Samajists, have tried to find universality through eclecticism, a putting together of the best truths in all faiths.

But "all eclectics are skeptics"—there is a doubt hidden away under all eclecticism, none seem satisfactory, therefore, combine all. But it would take a divine mind to pick out what was essential from all religions and combine them in a symmetrical whole. When men do it, it becomes a mere patch-work. One cannot give himself to a patchwork with any enthusiasm, so the Brahmo Samaj lacks driving force, and it will be said of it as it was said by Harnack of Neo-Platonism, a similar movement, "It lacked exclusiveness, and of that lack, it died."

The issue regarding universality is between a patchwork and a Personality, the former trying to combine the good points in each and the latter gathering up in himself all that was fine and noble in the past and fulfilling it in himself. Of the two I choose the latter, for, as has been said, "Syncretisms combine, eclecticisms choose, but only life assimilates." Christ, being Life, assimilates, gives old truths new expressions, but adds something entirely lacking in them, namely, himself.

As he gathers up all that was fine in the past of all nations, so he gathers up into himself all virtues that seem to be in conflict. "Virtues seem to live at the expense of each other," but not in Jesus. He combines them in a living whole. For he was the Aggressive and the Submissive, the Idealist and the Realist, the Mystic and the Master, the Realizer and the Regenerator, the Devotee and the Doer, the Terrible and the Tender, the Pure and the Approachable, the Concentrated and the Catholic, the Progressive and the Patient, the Sweet and the Severe, the Judge and the Justifier, the Balanced and the Blazing, the Immaculate and the Imitable, the Sunshiny and the Sad, the Player with children and the Purposer of a cross, the Victim and the Victor, the Son of Man and the Son of God.

Out of the conflict is emerging a Universal— Jesus. Other ways of living and other interpretations of life are gradually being eliminated from the minds of thoughtful men and the Universal is emerging. Everything, as Jacopone says,

> "... Must yet
> Give place, give place
> To that one Face,
> To my dear Lord of Love."[3]

No life, no ideal, no person has ever been subjected to such criticism and even hatred, and yet he quietly emerges through the conflict as resplendent as when he emerged from the dark tomb on Easter morning.

---

3 Fra Jacopone da Todi, O.F.M., was an Italian Franciscan friar and poet from Umbria who wrote in the 13th century.

Chapter 17

THE COSMIC ROUNDTABLE

AT THE COSMIC Round Table, everything witnesses to the Christian way of living. The universe is ours because we have found its secret—Christ.

Professor Radhakrishan, one of the leading Hindu philosophers of India, in his Upton Lectures, says: "The Hindu philosophy of religion starts from and returns to an experimental basis. Only this basis is as wide as human nature itself. Other religious systems start with this or that particular experimental datum. Christian theology, for example, takes its stand on the immediate certitude of Jesus, whose absolute authority over conscience is self-certifying and whose ability and willingness to save the soul is impossible not to trust. Christian theology becomes relevant only for those who share or accept a particular kind of spiritual experience, and these are tempted to dismiss other experiences as illusory and other Scriptures as imperfect. Hinduism was not betrayed into this situation on account of its adherence to fact.[1] The criticism resolves itself into this: that Christian

---

[1] S. Radhakrishan, *The Hindu Way of Life* (1926), p. 19.

experience has reference to the immediate realization of Jesus as self-certifying to the conscience and to the saving of the soul and is valid only in that particular realm and for those who hold it, but it does not provide anything as wide as human nature, as Hinduism does.

It must be admitted that Christian experience has often been presented as confined to this particular saving impact of Christ upon the soul, but the New Testament and subsequent Christian experience amply show that Christian experience is broader than that, and that it provides a life view and is as wide as the facts of life. The center of Christian experience is in personal saving realization of Christ, but its circumference is the universe. Browning puts it in these words:

> I say the acknowledgment of God in Christ
> Accepted by thy reason solves for thee
> All questions in this world and out of it,
> And has, so far, advanced thee to be wise.

But Paul goes further and in an amazing passage shows the sweep of Christian experience when he says: "All things belong to you; Paul, Apollos, Cephas; the world, life, death; present, and the future; all things belong to you; and you belong to Christ and Christ belongs to God." Here the experience of God in Christ brings us into possession of a new universe, all the facts of which belong to us because we belong to Christ. Christian experience is as wide as the facts of life. This passage sums up the philosophy and reach of Christian experience and will sum up the meaning of our Round Tables.

There has been a conflict through the centuries between liberty and law. Sometimes life swings to one side and sometimes to the other. At the present time, we are in the liberty stage. The great demand of life is for self-expression. There is an impatience with anything that savors of authority. The revolt of youth is a symptom of a very widespread undertone of feeling. Both liberty and law have a truth within them, but life is weak if it embodies only one. To be strong the two must be blended and embodied. Paul in this passage puts the two together in a remarkable synthesis.

Here is the liberty: All things belong to you, Paul, Apollos, Cephas, the world, life, death, the present and the future—all things. A universe is thrown open. Was there ever such liberty offered to human beings as this?

Here is the law: You belong to Christ—the most amazing bondage ever insisted on in life. For this ownership and sovereignty goes down to the last thing, the most secret aspiration—to our inmost self, nothing is left out of its sway. Was there ever such a law imposed on human nature as this?

> But this synthesis of freedom and law can be only in one place, namely, at Christ. Christianity is Christocentric.

But this synthesis of freedom and law can be only in one place, namely, at Christ. Christianity is Christocentric. As we center in him, we find we are at the center of the moral and spiritual universe—a place where liberty and law do not conflict, but coincide.

Life depends upon finding its center. All life that is not centered in Jesus is eccentric. It then becomes full of friction and clash. The Corinthians had slipped off the center. One said, "I belong to Paul;" another, "I belong to Apollos;" a third, "I belong to Cephas." There was a centering of life in these great and good men, but since they were off the center, Christ, there was confusion and chaos. They had become denominational-minded, instead of Christian-minded. The result was that they were promoting their class instead of Christ.

Paul, with remarkable insight, puts his finger upon their difficulty: "You are all wrong," he said. "You do not belong to Paul or to Apollos or to Cephas. You are not centered there. You belong to Christ; but Paul, Apollos and Cephas belong to you."

All great religious teachers are yours. Here the gospel offers intellectual and spiritual liberty. Provided we remember whose we are, we are free to take from all religious teachers whatever of light and truth they have discovered and realized. Martin Luther standing for rugged truth; Calvin, reasoning from God down; Wesley, flaming with a mighty evangelism; the churches standing for the solidarity and continuity of the Christian centuries, are all mine. They are all a part of my inheritance. There has been a verse that has seemed peculiarly my own for many years. Just before speaking, as the audience bows in silent prayer, I remind God of my verse: "Ye have not chosen me, but I have chosen you, and ordained you, that ye should go and bring forth fruit, and that your fruit should remain: that whatsoever ye shall ask of the Father in my name, he may give it you." One day I mentioned this as being my verse before a group of ministers, and at the close a Presbyterian minister came up and said, "But that is a Presbyterian verse." I had been living on a Presbyterian verse for years and had not known it! They all belong to me. But I do not belong to them. I remember whose I am.

Some Christians are sincerely afraid of reading and studying sympathetically non-Christian literature and of exposing themselves to its thought and cultures. But they need not be afraid if they remember whose they are and whose bonds are upon them. When I went to Doctor Tagore's Hindu Ashram to stay for some months, it frightened some of my missionary friends: "We do not know what may happen to Stanley Jones; he may become a Hindu," they said. But I believed in my gospel so utterly I was willing to expose it to the finest and highest that Hinduism has. There is only one refuge in life, namely, in reality. If Jesus is not supreme reality, the sooner we find it out the better. But the fear that I should become a follower of Tagore was unfounded, for Tagore belongs to me. I do not belong to him. Remembering whose I am, I can be at perfect liberty to appropriate anything of truth, goodness or beauty wherever found. For they are all finger posts that point to the perfect expression of them—Christ.

When Gandhiji's name was anathema, some of us discovered his moral greatness. We felt that we had something to learn at the feet of this great soul. And we still feel that way. But to anxious friends I could say, "Anything Gandhiji has to contribute is mine. He belongs to me, but I do not belong to him."

> If the Christian Church is sure of her Lord, she is free to take from that great inheritance of India's past. Everything fine in that culture and thought belongs to her.

If the Christian Church is sure of her Lord, she is free to take from that great inheritance of India's past. Everything fine in that culture and thought belongs to her. This does not mean that we build the Christian faith upon Hindu foundations, for "other foundation can no man lay than that is laid, which is Jesus Christ." But life assimilates, and if we are sure we have Life, we can assimilate from India's past or present. We can feel free to study the literature of that past, not with a critical eye to find only the faults, but sympathetically to find the facts. It all belongs to us.

I wonder if this attitude of Paul toward the other great religious teachers would not help us in the situation within the borders of the Christian Church at the present time. Evidently, Paul and Apollos and Cephas differed sufficiently in their interpretations of the gospel to produce groups in Corinth to whom the respective interpretations appealed. They were in danger of being permanently divided because of this fact, when Paul arrested the process of disintegration by showing them that at the center, Christ, they were one; that they were wrong in centering their life in the differing interpretations rather than in the Interpreted Christ.

Has this any message for us today? Many times, I have been asked in the last few years whether I belonged to the Fundamentalists or the Modernists. My answer usually is, "Let us see what our Fundamentalist brother has found, for anything good he has found is mine." He says, "I believe in these outstanding things: the deity of Jesus, the virgin birth, the atonement for sin, the miracles of Jesus, the inspiration of the Scriptures and the new birth." And I find my soul assenting to each one of these. "Then you belong to the Fundamentalists." "Oh, no, the Fundamentalists belong to me." Fundamentalism is an attempt to tell what is fundamental. But Jesus is greater than all our attempts to tell who he is. Paul says he is "the unspeakable gift." All our attempts are approximating truths about the Truth. I cannot commit myself to an attempt to tell who he is. I can commit myself only to the Person who is bigger than all the attempts. I belong to Christ, but the Fundamentalists belong to me.

Then I ask my Modernist brother what he has found, and he replies that he believes in two outstanding things: in the scientific method of asking for the facts in religion, and in the application of the gospel to the social as well as to the personal. To both of these, again I find my soul assenting. I am sure that if the gospel of Christ cannot stand the scrutiny of the facts, it is in a bad way indeed, and it will wither under the touch of the criticism of the future. But if it is founded upon the facts, the more it is scrutinized, the more it will shine. I am convinced the only way to have a faith that is real is to put it under the facts and say, "There it is—break it if it is breakable." Jesus is the Real, hence, we have nothing to fear from real science. Again, when the Modernist says that he believes in applying the gospel socially, we can only agree most wholeheartedly. Those who live in the spiritual succession of John Wesley's revival have the precious inheritance of "entire sanctification." The last people on earth to object to the social application of the gospel are the people who hold this inheritance. If the sanctification is entire, it should be entirely applied. It should begin with the individual and go as far as his relationships extend—to the social, economic, national, and racial.

"Then you belong to the Modernists." Oh, no, the Modernists belong to me. Modernism is a set of modern tendencies. I cannot commit myself to a set of modern tendencies, for these tendencies will run out and a new set of modern tendencies will set in. They are constantly changing. I can commit myself only to a Person, who was here before the tendencies set in and will be here when they are replaced. Jesus is the same yesterday, today, and forever. He is not only modern; he sums up the past, he gathers up the present, and he anticipates the future. However, anything fine the Modernists have discovered is mine. But I remember whose I am.

And that remembrance of possession by Christ is the inward standard by which the chaff can be separated from the wheat. His mind is the final but unfolding standard by which all things must be judged.

I belong neither to the Fundamentalists nor to the Modernists. I trust I belong to Christ and am a Christian holding the fundamentals of the Christian faith and holding them with an open mind, so that they may be under the constant correction of the mind of Christ. The ultimate standard is Christ's living mind, and the ultimate stand must be at the place of that mind—that mind as revealed in the Scriptures and unfolded to us by the Holy Spirit who dwells within us.

Paul in this passage offers amazing intellectual liberty with the most rigorous bondage. All great teachers are ours, conditioned only by possession by Christ.

The apostle goes on and says that the three great facts belong to us: the world, life, death. "The world" belongs to us. One is surprised at this, for religion has been afraid of the world. It was something to pass through as quickly as possible. The Muslims have a tradition that Jesus said, "The world is a bridge; pass over it, but do not build your house on it." But the gospel goes far deeper: the world with its beauty and art and love and music is yours. When you are Christ's every bush becomes aflame with God and every meal a sacrament and every relationship religious. The world is to be the scene of the final redemption and is to share in it.

> I can commit myself only to a Person, who was here before the tendencies set in and will be here when they are replaced. Jesus.... sums up the past, he gathers up the present, and he anticipates the future.

To the Muslim the world of art and painting has been forbidden lest he slip into idolatry. But Jesus cures us of that dread. He takes the place of idols, he is "the express image of God," but an image that is spiritual and the exact reproduction of the moral and spiritual likeness of God. Idolatry misrepresents God, but Jesus represents him. We are now unafraid of the world. So, it is no chance that the best of art, music, and literature has come from the inspiration of his person. He stimulates to life in every realm. He brings the gospel of the healthy-minded.

But there is a true instinct in religion in its being afraid of the world. There is a world with a sting in it. Liberty can turn to license and the license to a lie. It is that empty-hearted worldly world which we must fear. Where do we put in the stop? Is there any rule? Hardly a rule, but this principle of possession by Christ is the determining and limiting element. Whatever does not minister to the deepening of that possession by Christ is a false World. After the General Conference of the Methodist Church, a rather worldly-minded lady eagerly asked me what had been done about the amusement clause. I told her that the law against particular forms of worldly amusements had been replaced by the statement that we are not to take "such diversions as cannot be taken in the name of the Lord Jesus." Her face fell. "Why, that is harder than the other," she said in dismay. Of course, it is. The world is yours, but the world with a sting in it is inhibited by this sovereign law of possession by Christ. Love Christ and do what you like—that is the law and the liberty.

The apostle further says: Life belongs to you. This goes deep. Life, not cloistered, sheltered life with no suffering in it, but life as it is, with its pains and disappointments and separations and joys, belongs to you. This is the most radical offensive ever offered. Here we go to the citadel and capture things at the center—at life itself—and when we have that, we have everything. Jesus is the only one who dared take hold of the nettle of life at its thorniest places and say that even here it is yours.

He promised no escape from troubles to those who became his followers. In fact, he promised an increase of them. There is a passage in Luke 21 that vividly illustrates Jesus' realism. He assured them in this passage that evils and calamities would come upon us from about seven different avenues: wars and rumors of wars, earthquakes, famines, pestilences, dragged before kings and governors, strife in one's own household, hated of all men for his name's sake. What are we to say in regard to these evils that come upon us from without, evils which are not the result of our own choosing?

The Stoics had their answer: Life is such; steel yourself against it. Buddhism gives its answer: It is the result of existence, for existence and evil are one, therefore, escape existence. Hinduism, answers: It is the result of the deeds of your previous birth, therefore, eat the fruit of it. Islam answers: It is the will of Allah, bear it. What is the answer of Jesus? It is to be found in the midst of the description of these calamities: "It shall turn unto you for a testimony." You are to find your finest opportunity for witnessing through these very troubles. In other words, you are not to bear your calamities, you are to use them. You are to turn your trials to a testimony. Life belongs to you at its hardest places. The things that come upon you to break you are to be turned and used to break evil itself. Far beyond steeling yourself against life, or escaping from it, or patiently accepting what comes from previous births, or bending under it—far beyond these attitudes, you are to go on an offensive, not merely to the conquering of life, but to the using of it, even when it is bitterest and hardest. Here is a distinguishing characteristic of the gospel. Watch this method of meeting life at work in Jesus and in those who followed him.

They dragged Stephen before the Sanhedrin and lied about him, but the more they lied, the more he shone. They saw his face as if it was the face of an angel. He used that moment for a testimony. While they were extinguishing his life amid a shower of stones, even here he turned things for a testimony, for he flung back a prayer upon them, smiting the heart of the young man Saul. In that dread moment Stephen accomplished a life's work. Life belonged to him even then.

Paul became the apostle of this throbbing Life. In the midst of his mighty witness, probably through being himself stoned at Lystra, there was given to him "a thorn in the flesh"—"a messenger of Satan to buffet him." Thrice he asked Christ to remove it, but the answer from the Master was: "I will not remove it, I will do something better, I will give you power to use it." "My grace is sufficient for you." Paul caught the meaning, arose and cried, "I take pleasure in infirmities...for when I am weak, then I am strong," He not only bore his thorn; he used it, and the result was that Paul was stronger than before—life at its most difficult places was his. He fed on his frailties. He turned his miseries into ministers.

Watch Paul use this method of facing life. He is giving his very life for the Corinthians. He weeps with those that weep and rejoices with those that rejoice, but they turn upon him in criticism: "he is not a real apostle, his bodily presence is weak and his speech contemptible." This is the result of his work; this is his reward. He dips his pen in the blood of his broken heart and writes: "Love is very patient, very kind, love knows no jealousy . . . never selfish, never irritated, never resentful; love is never glad when others go wrong, love is gladdened by goodness, always slow to expose, always eager to believe the best, always hopeful, always patient." His pain had burst forth into this paean. Such literature can come out of no place save pain. They flung their criticism upon Paul and he turned it into this testimony of love that lives on, immortal. He possessed life even when it was most bitterly cruel.

What triumph of spirit walks through the pages of the New Testament! Peter and John go up to the Temple and a lame beggar asks for an alm. They had none to give. Modern men feel the hell of an empty purse more than anything else. Theirs was empty. But Peter turned to the lame man and said: "Look on us... Silver and gold have I none, but such as I have, give I thee. In the name of Jesus Christ of Nazareth rise up and walk." And he did! They turned their poverty to power.

But the Man in whom this works preeminently is Jesus. He turned everything into an occasion for a testimony. They bitterly criticized him for his association with publicans and sinners. "He is like them. That is the reason for the association," they said. He immediately turned that criticism into the matchless parables of the lost sheep, the lost coin, and the lost son. He flung back the curtain from the heart of God and showed his self-giving, redemptive nature—showed it through a criticism. A lawyer stands up "to tempt him," and Jesus turns the temptation into the parable of the good Samaritan and raises the standard of ethics to their most sublime heights when he teaches men that they must not pass by on the other side when there is human need.

But at his darkest hour—the hour of the cross— this method of using evil shines brightest. They put him upon a cross, place of shame, and he makes it a place of glory; here they showed sin in its most hideous form, and Jesus turns it into a place of healing for sin; here hate is darkest, and here love shines brightest; here man is at his worst, and here Jesus is at his best; here reviling turned into revelation.

The cross is the supreme torture of Life and out of it comes a testimony that heals the world.

What can you do with a religion like that? It sings at midnight in a Philippian jail and before morning the foundations of a church are laid and a letter will be written to that church that will bless the world. This is religion turning its impediments into instruments, its difficulties into doors, its Calvaries into Easter mornings, its troubles into testimonies. It is unconquerable because it has conquered life itself.

Christ at the Round Table

The family of six children of Mr. and Mrs. Lee is wiped out by a landslide in Darjeeling. Mrs. Lee comes to the memorial service radiant. Their home broken up, they set up a home where they are mother and father to three hundred children. On the simple tombstone at Darjeeling in memory of their children are these words: "Thanks be unto God which giveth us the victory through our Lord Jesus Christ."

A missionary repairs a leper's house in South India. While on furlough in Canada, he develops leprosy. He is given a hut in a forest. There he is segregated, isolated—a leper. An old friend from India visits him and shows by his tone his deep sorrow and sympathy. The missionary with leprosy stops him: "You are sorry for me. You must not be. This hut is radiant with His presence and here I live in heaven."

> **The cross is the supreme torture of Life and out of it comes a testimony that heals the world.**

In the midst of writing these pages I was talking to an aged saint. She had spent her life in the service of Christ. She was going blind, but in referring to it she said with a smile: "I am willing to bear it and rejoice in it, if it is God's will, though it would be a little inconvenient!" A little inconvenient!

Pandita Ramabai is left a widow with a little daughter. What could an Indian widow do? Her home broken up by death, she sets up one of the most remarkable homes of modern times—a home where as many as two thousand widows and orphans live and are brought into touch with redemptive influences. Her daughter, now grown to womanhood and showing the same qualities of leadership and spirituality as her mother, was ready to take over the home from the aging Pandita, when she took sick and died. It was a cruel blow. Mrs. Ramabai Ranade, a

Hindu lady, goes to comfort the Pandita in her sorrow. She comes back amazed and says: "Pandita Ramabai is the most wonderful woman I have ever seen. I went to comfort her and she comforted me. She preached the gospel, to me."

Again, I ask, "What can you do with religion like that?" It overcomes life. Life belongs to it. But some of us belong to life. We knuckle under it, we echo it, we descend to its level, we belong to it. But those who belong to Christ, who is Life, find that life belongs to them. They conquer life, for they have been conquered by Christ.

But further, death belongs to us. We do not belong to death; it belongs to us. The gospel is the arresting of the whole process of decay and dissolution and death, within the individual and the social order. Sin wears life away. The life lived out of Christ is under the law of universal decay and death. The new man conquers death in all its forms.

It is this note of victory over death that the gospel strikes. Principal Jacks says: "Religion is being presented today in terms which are inadequate to the problems it has to solve. It should be a challenge to the universal death. It is a tremendous theme, the scope and majesty of which have been missed by orthodox and modernist alike. The subject is waiting for treatment by a thinker who is competent to deal with it." Christ brings life and immortality to life. He has abolished death.

When we are in Christ, who is life, we feel the impossibility of death. As Tennyson puts it, "We are lifted up at times in that fullness of the Spirit, when we feel death is almost laughably impossible." And Shakespeare in his Sonnets preaches the same message in these great lines:

> Within be fed; without be rich no more.
>
> So shalt thou feed on death, that feeds on men;
>
> And Death, once dead, there's no more dying then.

I once stood in the presence of the Victory and saw Death become "almost laughably impossible." The happiest person I have ever seen was a dying woman. The doctors said she could not live another hour, but she lived for several days, radiant with a triumphant spiritual joy. Her intelligent mind was clear as crystal as a stream of people passed through her room to look on her face that shone like an angel. I have never seen such triumph as she would clap her hands in an ecstasy of joy and say: "They tell me this is death. It is not death, it is life." I knelt by the bedside to pray for her, but I could not pray, my lips would not frame a prayer, for there was nothing to pray for, for she had everything, including death. I could only kneel in silent adoration before the miracle. But while I could not pray for her, she could pray for me. She put her hands upon my head as I knelt there and prayed that God would help me to preach this gospel and that he would make me a winner of men and women . As she placed her hands upon my head, I felt anew "the mighty ordination of the Pierced Hands." Death was her servant. She ordered it to throw open the doors and she laughed her way into larger and fuller life. Death belonged to her, for she belonged to Him who had abolished death and left an empty tomb behind.

But those who do not belong to Christ do belong to death. They are under the process of decay and dissolution and death. Jesus says: "He that gathereth not with me, scattereth"—he that lives life in any other way than mine is under the law of collapse, of the scattering and breakdown of the forces of life. Life lives only as it lives in Christ.

In his amazing sanity and balance, Paul brings us straight back from death to the present. Religion is not merely a conquest of death: "The present belongs to you," he said.

As we face life at the Round Table and as we look about us, we find this literally true. Everything else is breaking down, everything is

THE COSMIC ...

showing its moral and spiritual bankruptcy, everything fails to fit into life—everything except Christ and his way of Life.

Upon my return to India from furlough, I wondered how the tides would be running. India is subject to moods, and in answer to prevailing winds, emotional waves sweep across her responsive spirit. Was this interest in the personality of Jesus about which I had written and spoken while absent just a ripple on the surface, or was it a Gulf Stream flowing through the depths of educated India's life? There was deep anxiety to know the answer. It soon came.

In one of the first cities visited, we began our meetings in the Theosophical Hall, but soon outgrew its capacity and moved into the largest hall of the city. One night the Muslim chairman said in his closing remarks, "I am frank to say that I believe it will be the Christ who will finally unite our divided world." In a group meeting, a Brahmo-Samajist preacher had said to the group: "Organized Christianity may not conquer India, but the Christ-spirit will." A Hindu had just said: "If you preach this kind of a Christ to us—just Christ himself—then we Hindus will worship him ten times more than you want us to." (I am afraid he did not know how deeply I wanted them to!) The last night of the series, after my address on "The Cross," the Hindu chairman said: "The speaker has emphasized how Jesus took his cross for us. I would like to lay emphasis on the other side: Now we

> **Everything else is breaking down, everything is showing its moral and spiritual bankruptcy, everything fails to fit into life— everything except Christ and his way of Life.**

must take up our cross for him." The audience applauded. It was significant. The audience was not of the easily applauding type, for they had given my statements no applause except the customary one at the close.

Here was the answer to my question, for here was the gathering of the thought of differing minds, the Brahmo-Samajist, the Muslim, the Hindu, around the personality of Jesus. He was drawing them like a magnet. This interest was something akin to the Gulf Stream and not a ripple on the surface. And my contacts since have confirmed it.

The silent conquest of the mind and heart is going on far beyond the borders of the Christian Church. As the *Indian Social Reformer*, a Hindu paper, says: "There is a widespread and growing interest in the personality of Jesus Christ" (Sep. 11, 1925). And, again, it says: "The influence of Jesus Christ in India is but faintly reflected in the Christian community in India." He has gone beyond it.

For instance: the Rama Krishna Mission is doing noble work in the service of India. It provides the medium of service of Vivekananda Vedantism. When I turn to its genesis, I find *The Morning Star of Patna* (Dec. 1925), the official organ of the movement, giving it as follows: As some of the followers of Rama Krishna Paramahansa and of Swami Vivekananda were seated about a fire, the conversation turned toward Jesus of Nazareth and gradually it centered about the cross and the self-sacrifice it showed. Every heart was stirred and the question arose, "Why cannot we give ourselves in this way for India?" Then and there was founded the monastic order which became the Rama Krishna Mission. The flame was kindled at the cross.

Bishop Tubbs of Tinnevelly, at the close of one of our meetings, remarked: "I had no idea of the vast change that has come over the mind of India in these twenty years. I remember that twenty years ago Sherwood Eddy talked for fifty-five minutes to an audience of Hindus and Muslims at Allahabad before they would allow him to speak the last five minutes on Christ. It was a very hostile audience which he faced, but here you begin at once on Christ, have no other theme, and the best men of this city are asking for more. There is a vast psychological and spiritual change."

Some lawyers were holding a banquet. At the close, a man came out to entertain them. He told humorous stories of the gods and mocked them. This Hindu audience roared with laughter. Then he went on to mock Christ. A silence fell upon the audience. The silence turned to resentment and these non-Christian lawyers hissed him off the stage. They could stand the mockery of the old, but they could not stand the mockery of the white purity of Jesus.

The character of Jesus is becoming the silent Judge of all things. "We must study the Bible," said a non-Christian student in a farewell address at a college closing, "because there are many things in our religion that need correcting and we must correct them by the Bible." This quiet setting up of a new standard in the inmost thinking of men is seen in the Hindu who said to a friend of mine, "He has been doing things behind my back, but I hope I am a good enough Christian not to mind that." My friend had not suspected him of being a Christian at all!

We asked the leading Arya Samajist in India what he felt that he, as a Hindu, had to object to in the Gospels. I expected many criticisms, for the Arya Samajists are our bitterest opponents and their leading book, the *Satyarthprakash*, written by their founder, drips with bitterness against Christianity in every line. He replied that he had just finished reading the four Gospels and the only thing he could find that he could object to was the story of the killing of the fatted calf in the parable of the prodigal son! (Cow-killing is one of the chief sins to the Hindus.) "But," he added, "it is not an integral part of Jesus' teaching and it is only a parable." One realized how the trenches have been pushed up into the mind and soul of educated India when the only objection that could be found was against the reference to the killing of the fatted calf!

I asked another leading Arya Samajist, a political figure, what objection he could find against Christ. He replied, "I can find a great deal of objection against Western civilization."

I answered, "So can I."

He continued, "I can find much that I must object to in the Christian Church."

I again replied, "So can I."

He went on: "I can find a great deal to which I can object to in you."

And I said, "So can I—more than you can! But what objection do you find in Christ?"

"Oh, I have none there," was his final and thoughtful answer. And his answer is the growing conclusion of India and the world.

At the close of an address, a Hindu chairman who is prominent in the central government of India said: "There was a time when none of us in India wanted to claim Christ, but now everybody is trying to claim him. They are trying to prove in South India that he was born in the Tamil country and was a Tamilian, all of which is significant. The fact is that some of us Hindus are much better Christians than a good many of you Christians. Mr. Jones' work is well over half done." I could only wish it were true! But his statement is significant of a trend in thought.

Politically, India is going through a stage called Diarchy. Some subjects are reserved by the British government and some are transferred to the legislative bodies responsible to the Indian people. Gradually everything will be transferred to the control of the Indian people and there will be Diarchy no longer. Educated India is religiously going through the same stage of divided allegiance—a Diarchy. Some of the departments are reserved for the old thinking and some are being transferred to the allegiance of Christ. But gradually he is gathering more and more power and authority over the mind of India by the sheer force of what he is.

> But Christ arises more and more sovereignly. As men search more and more for the facts, he becomes inescapable. The present belongs to us, if we belong to Christ. There is no other way of living.

This gradual putting of Christ deeper and deeper into the soul of India does not seem important to many. They want immediate individual conversions. So, do we. But a greater situation is being prepared, on a widespread scale—a situation in which individual conversions can take place more easily. "It is easy," said a Hindu at the close of one of our Round Tables, "for you to turn to Christ in your spiritual need, for he is in your race consciousness. But Krishna is in our race consciousness." Christ is going down deep into the race consciousness of India, though, and when that is done, India will find it easier to turn to him in her spiritual need. Individual conversions often take place suddenly in Christian countries because there Christ lies back in the race consciousness. A word, a prayer, a memory, and lo! the man turns to Christ and is saved. But this will take place in India only when the conditions are the same. Now conversions are more gradual.

Christ at the Round Table

But Christ arises more and more sovereignly. As men search more and more for the facts, he becomes inescapable. The present belongs to us, if we belong to Christ. There is no other way of living.

Moreover, the apostle says that the future belongs to those who belong to Christ. In the noblest and purest living in our race is the tendency away from the Christ-like type of character or toward it? It is toward it. There is nothing better, or even remotely comparable to it, on the horizon. A thoughtful Hindu said to a friend of mine: "The future is with you. I can't join you, for your Christian Church is not related to India's life. But go on, the future is yours. You are winning all along the line."

Yes, the Christian Church will have to be related to India's life and the political conflict between East and West adjusted and settled into brotherly relations, and then Christ will have a fairer chance before the soul of the East. Then the future will belong to him.

"Yes, there is a widespread turning in thought toward Christ among us, but without open acknowledgment," said a Hindu to me one day. As I slowly repeated the phrase: "without open acknowledgment," he smiled. That smile revealed the hidden clash within, the yearning to save the national soul, the hesitancy to acknowledge a further debt to the West. When this hidden clash is resolved—then!

The Mosque of Saint Sophia in Constantinople (Istanbul) is a transformed Christian church. It was one of the most beautiful churches of the world. All the Christian inscriptions and symbols have been painted out and Muslim inscriptions and symbols put in their places. As we stood under the great dome, we could see that the figure of the ascending Christ with outstretched hands in blessing, which had been painted out, was coming back through the wearing off of the covering paint. I turned to a friend and said: "He is coming back. You cannot blot him out. Through the accretions and daubs of the centuries, he is coming back again. He shall yet reign. The future belongs to him!" It does.

A Hindu, a Muslim and a Christian were seated in the train talking about the Hindu-Muslim clash. The Muslim, who was a highly educated man, said: "No, we cannot expect to get Home Rule. The Hindu and the Muslim will try to get the best of each other, and then finally, after exploring all avenues, they will become followers of Christ, for it is Christ alone who is uniting the world everywhere."

"But," said the Christian, "are there any signs of this now?"

"Well," he replied, "I am thinking of years ahead."

While teaching in a Hindu ashram one day, one of the students requested me to tell my personal religious experience. I did so. They seemed deeply impressed. A few days later, I was talking about the coming victory of light over darkness, and said: "I know when I talk this way about the coming victory, I am like a night bird singing in the night of the dawn, when there is darkness all about me."

But one of the Hindu students spoke up and said, "Yes, but aren't you singing of the dawn because you have felt the dawn?"

He was right. We sing of this coming dawn because we have found Christ, who brings the dawn. But he is more. He is the Dawn. "The Dawn from on high hath visited us." The future belongs to him.

I sat, one morning, out under the open sky in the dark and watched the stars fade out as the dawn began to break and the sun to rise. "This," said me to myself, "is India. Christ, the Dawn, is breaking and the stars that have lighted up India's night through the ages are fading out before him. The future belongs to Him."

But that future will belong to us only as we belong to Christ. An able Hindu editor in discussing this widespread permeation of

Christian thought in India ended his editorial in these prophetic words: "There is no doubt that we are on the eve of great, yea, almost startling religious developments in this country." We are on the eve of the most startling religious developments of modern times, but there must be no light-hearted optimism, for we can bring this day into being only to the degree that we belong to Christ. The future belongs to us only as we belong to him.

> At the Cosmic Round Table, all things.... rise and witness to the Lordship of Christ ... At the Round Table of Life, all life submits to him who is Life.

To be sure that nothing is left out of the amazing recital of the things that belong to those who belong to Christ, the apostle sums up everything and cries, "All things belong to you." The liberty is complete. Nothing of reality is left out. Here is the great affirming of life. Here is salvation in its root idea of wholeness or health. Christ is life's complete affirmation.

At the Cosmic Round Table, all things—all teachers, Paul, Apollos, Cephas; all facts, the world; all realities, life; all changes, death; all time, the present and the future—all things rise and witness to the Lordship of Christ and of their submission to those who submit to him. At the Round Table of Life, all life submits to him who is Life.

Our last word, though, must be in regard to the condition—the inexorable condition upon which all this rests. You belong to Christ. We must not say that glibly. Nothing goes deeper. The last thing must come under His sway. And the last thing we ever give up is just ourselves. We have seen many a missionary leave loved ones, friends, home, business, prospects, and come to other lands and find that he had given up everything except—just himself. Self was still there, assertive and jealous of its place and honor. Jesus asks us to lay down that last thing. For this life of complete liberty cannot be lived apart from the acceptance of a complete law—the law of self-abandonment. Only then are we able to say: I do not want anything, therefore, I am afraid of nothing. Only as we lose ourselves do we find ourselves again. We become utterly poor and yet possess all things. We take the cross and find an Easter morning. Self-surrender is the door to abundant life and there is no other door.

General Booth, the founder of The Salvation Army, lay dying. He had lived a wonderful life. Hundreds of thousands had been rescued by the Salvation Army from broken, cramped lives. As intimate friends and loved ones gathered about his bed, they said, "Tell us, General, before you go, what has been the secret of your wonderful life."

The old veteran thought a moment. "If there is any secret," he slowly said, "it has been in this, that Christ has had everything there is of me."

Simple secret, but it touched the depths.

His long stormy life had left this secret in his heart at the last. If these Round Table Conferences have left anything with us, it has been that same secret. We said that as we entered them we always felt our hearts beat a little faster. What would be the outcome? What would we find that we had when we laid everything bare before other ways of life? A friend wrote to me after I had come from Gandhiji's Ashram: "I was afraid when I saw you go there and get into intimate contact with that great soul. I was afraid you could not come out *a missionary*. But you *have*." The fact is that I was never so deeply committed to the way of Jesus as when I walked out of these eight days. And the same feeling

Christ at the Round Table

lingers in my heart after these conferences, for I can now say with the consent of all my faculties: Christ is the Way.

A new rich meaning is in the words, "All things are yours, if you are Christ's."

About the Author

A Portrait of E. Stanley Jones by Shivraj Mahendra

(Acrylic on canvas [16"x20"]. This portrait was presented by the artist to The E. Stanley Jones School of World Mission and Evangelism at Asbury Theological Seminary, Wilmore, Kentucky on May 17, 2017)

E. STANLEY JONES (1884-1973)

E. Stanley Jones was described by a distinguished Bishop as the "greatest missionary since Saint Paul." This missionary/evangelist spent seventy years traveling throughout the world in the ministry of Jesus Christ. Jones wrote and spoke for the general public and there is little doubt that his words brought hope and refreshment to multitudes all over the world. As a well-known, engaging, and powerful evangelist, Jones delivered tens of thousands of sermons and lectures. He typically traveled fifty weeks a year, often speaking two to six times a day.

Jones worked to revolutionize the whole theory and practice of missions to third world nations by disentangling Christianity from Western political and cultural imperialism. He established hundreds of Christian Ashrams throughout the world, many of which still meet today. E. Stanley Jones was a crusader for Christian unity, a nonstop witness for Christ, and a spokesman for peace, racial brotherhood, and social justice. He foresaw where the great issues would be and spoke to them long before they were recognized… often at great unpopularity and even antagonism and derision to himself. Many consider Jones a prophet and his honors — and he did receive them — were all laid at the feet of Jesus Christ. Jones would readily admit that his quite ordinary life became extraordinary only because he fully surrendered his life to Jesus Christ!

Jones' writing and preaching did not require people to leave their intellect at the door; his presentation of Jesus engaged both the intellect and touched humanity's desire to experience the living Christ in their lives. When Jones wrote or talked about Jesus, it was as if he knew Jesus personally and could reach out and touch him. Jones described himself as an evangelist… the bearer of the Good News of Jesus Christ. The countless illustrations found in his books and sermons speak to a cross section of humanity and demonstrate, in a multitude of ways, the transformative impact of Jesus Christ on human existence. Few readers or listeners could miss identifying with one story or another — virtually all would find stories that touched their lives. All were offered hope that they, too, could experience the transformation available through self-surrender and conversion.

About the Author

In presenting Jesus as the redeemer of all of life Jones used his wide ranging study of the non-Christian religions, medicine, psychology, philosophy, science, history, and literature to make the case that the touch of Christ is upon all creation — that the totality of life was created by Christ and for Christ. We were all created to live upon Christ's Way. Jesus' Sermon on the Mount lays out both the principles and the Way.

Jones wrote twenty-seven books. More than 3.5 million copies of his books have been sold and they have been translated into 30 languages. All proceeds from his books have gone into Christian projects. He gave all of his money away! Now more than 45 years after his death – his books and sermons (many written in the 1930s and 40s) are not out of date and with few exceptions are entirely relevant to today's world.

According to his son in law, United Methodist Bishop James K. Mathews, "the most salient and spiritually significant characteristics of Stanley Jones were the spiritually transparency, clarity and persuasiveness of his personal witness for Christ. For thirty five years I knew him intimately and had occasion to observe him closely for prolonged periods. He rang true! Once when I asked a Hindu how he was, he replied, 'As you see me.' So it was with Brother Stanley, as he was called. He was as you saw him."

Even after a severe stroke at the age of 88 robbed him of his speech, Jones managed to dictate his last book, *The Divine Yes*. He died in India on January 25, 1973.

Jones' monumental accomplishments in life emerged from the quality of his character cultivated through his intimacy with Jesus Christ. As he lived in Christ, he reflected Christ. That experience is to us when we invite Christ to live in us!

Follow E. Stanley Jones

on social media

Other Books by the Author

Christ of the Indian Road
New York, Grosset & Dunlap, 1925.

Christ at the Round Table
New York & Cincinnati, Abingdon, 1928.

The Christ of Every Road: A Study in Pentecost
New York, Cincinnati & Chicago, Abingdon, 1930.

The Christ of the Mount: A Working Philosophy of Life
1st edition: New York & Nashville, Abingdon-Cokesbury, 1931.
New edition: The E. Stanley Jones Foundation, 2017

Christ and Human Suffering
New York, Cincinnati & Chicago, Abingdon, 1933.

Christ's Alternative to Communism
New York, Cincinnati & Chicago, Abingdon, 1935.

Victorious Living
New York & Nashville, Abingdon-Cokesbury, 1936.

The Choice Before Us
New York, Cincinnati & Chicago, Abingdon, 1937.

Along the Indian Road
New York, Cincinnati & Chicago, Abingdon, 1939.

Is the Kingdom of God Realism?
1st edition: New York & Nashville, Abingdon-Cokesbury, 1940.
New edition: The E. Stanley Jones Foundation, 2018

Other Books by the Author

Abundant Living
New York & Nashville, Abingdon-Cokesbury, 1942.

The Christ of the American Road
New York & Nashville, Abingdon-Cokesbury, 1944.

The Way
New York & Nashville, Abingdon-Cokesbury, 1946.

Mahatma Gandhi: An Interpretation
New York & Nashville, Abingdon-Cokesbury, 1948.

The Way to Power and Poise
New York & Nashville, Abingdon-Cokesbury, 1949.

How To Be A Transformed Person
New York, & Nashville, Abingdon-Cokesbury, 1951.

Growing Spiritually
New York & Nashville, Abingdon, 1953.

Mastery: The Art of Mastering Life
New York & Nashville, Abingdon, 1955, 2018

Christian Maturity
New York & Nashville, Abingdon, 1957.

Conversion
New York & Nashville, Abingdon, 1959.

In Christ
1st edition: New York & Nashville, Abingdon, 1961.
New edition: Seedbed, 2017.

The Word Become Flesh
New York & Nashville, Abingdon, 1963.

Victory Through Surrender
1st edition: New York & Nashville, Abingdon, 1966.
New edition: The E. Stanley Jones Foundation, 2018

A Song of Ascents: A Spiritual Autobiography
New York, & Nashville, Abingdon, 1968.

The Reconstruction of the Christian Church
Nashville, Tennessee, Abingdon Press, 1970

The Unshakable Kingdom and the Unchanging Person
1st edition: New York & Nashville, Abingdon, 1972.
New edition: The E. Stanley Jones Foundation, 2017

The Divine Yes
New York, Cincinnati & Chicago, Abingdon, 1975.

About the E. Stanley Jones Foundation

The E. Stanley Jones Foundation is dedicated to bold and fruitful evangelism which shares the life-changing message of Jesus Christ to persons of all ages, backgrounds, life asituations and locations. The Foundation is also dedicated to preserving and extending the legacy of the late E. Stanley Jones who blessed millions of people around the world with his preaching, teaching and prolific written words proclaiming Jesus is Lord! Our vision is to reach every generation with the message of Jesus Christ; enlighten spiritual growth through education and inspiration; prepare both Christian leaders and laity to be followers of Jesus Christ, and make known the Kingdom of God today.

For more information and our current programs, kindly visit us at:

www.estanleyjonesfoundation.com

Follow us on social media

OTHER PUBLICATIONS
FROM THE E. STANLEY JONES FOUNDATION

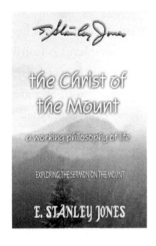

**The Christ of the Mount:
A Working Philosophy of Life**
Authored by E. Stanley Jones
List Price: $15.99
6" x 9" (15.24 x 22.86 cm)
312 pages
ISBN-13: 978-1542896030
(CreateSpace-Assigned)
ISBN-10: 1542896037
BISAC: Religion / Biblical Meditations / New Testament

The Life and Ministry of Mary Webster: A Witness in the Evangelistic Ministry of E. Stanley Jones Authored by Anne Mathews-Younes
List Price: $14.99
6" x 9" (15.24 x 22.86 cm)
286 pages
ISBN-13: 978-1544191799 (CreateSpace-Assigned)
ISBN-10: 1544191790
BISAC: Religion / Christian Life / Spiritual Growth

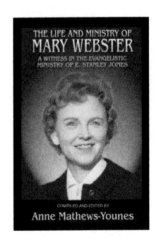

OTHER PUBLICATIONS

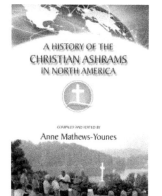

A History of the Christian Ashrams in North America
Compiled and Edited by Anne Mathews-Younes
List Price: $34.99
6" x 9" (15.24 x 22.86 cm)
528 pages
ISBN-13: 978-547229017 (CreateSpace-Assigned)
ISBN-10: 1547229012
BISAC: Religion / Christianity / History / General

Is The Kingdom of God Realism?
Authored by E. Stanley Jones, Foreword by Leonard Sweet, Afterword by Howard Snyder
List Price: $19.99
6" x 9" (15.24 x 22.86 cm)
428 pages
ISBN-13: 978-1976151514 (CreateSpace-Assigned)
ISBN-10: 1976151511
BISAC: Religion / Christianity / General

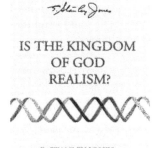

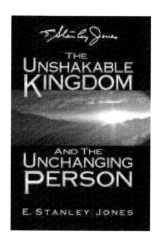

The Unshakable Kingdom and the Unchanging Person
Authored by E. Stanley Jones
List Price: $18.99
6" x 9" (15.24 x 22.86 cm)
408 pages
ISBN-13: 978-1974132935 (CreateSpace-Assigned)
ISBN-10: 1974132935
BISAC: Religion / Spirituality / General

OTHER PUBLICATIONS

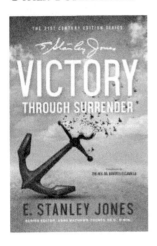

Victory Through Surrender
Authored by E. Stanley Jones, Preface by Anne Mathews-Younes
List Price: $12.99
6" x 9" (15.24 x 22.86 cm)
166 pages
ISBN-13: 978-1717548474
(CreateSpace-Assigned)
ISBN-10: 1717548474
BISAC: Religion / Christian Life / Professional Growth

A Love Affair With India: The Story of the Wife and Daughter of E. Stanley Jones
Authored by Martha Gunsalus Chamberlain, Preface by Anne Mathews-Younes
List Price: $14.99
6" x 9" (15.24 x 22.86 cm)
250 pages
ISBN-13: 978-1984960276
(CreateSpace-Assigned)
ISBN-10: 198496027X
BISAC: Biography & Autobiography

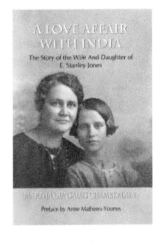

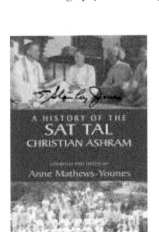

A History of the Sat Tal Christian Ashram (USA Edition)
Authored by Anne Mathews-Younes
List Price: $15.99
6" x 9" (15.24 x 22.86 cm)
238 pages
ISBN-13: 978-1722847524
(CreateSpace-Assigned)
ISBN-10: 1722847522
BISAC: Religion / Christianity / History /General

Other Publications

Living Upon the Way: Selected Sermons of E. Stanley Jones
Authored by Anne Mathews-Younes
List Price: $24.99
6" x 9" (15.24 x 22.86 cm)
454 pages
ISBN-13: 978-1724745736
(CreateSpace-Assigned)
ISBN-10: 1724745735
BISAC: Religion / Christianity / Sermons

Conversion
Authored by E. Stanley Jones
List Price: $15.99
6" x 9" (15.24 x 22.86 cm)
284 pages
ISBN-13: 978-1726458702
(CreateSpace-Assigned)
ISBN-10: 1726458709
BISAC: Religion / Christian living / Personal growth

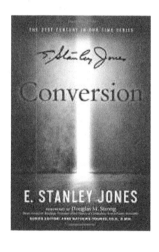

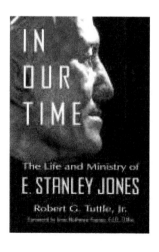

In Our Time: The Life and Ministry of E. Stanley Jones
Authored by Robert G. Tuttle, Jr
List Price: $22.99
6" x 1" x 9" (15.24 x 22.86 cm)
440 pages
ISBN-13: 978-1793813237
(KDP-Assigned)
ISBN-10: 179381323X
BISAC: Nonfiction / Biography and Autobiography / Religious

ALL PUBLICATIONS OF

The E. Stanley Jones Foundation

are available for purchase from:

www.estanleyjonesfoundation.com
and
www.amazon.com

Order your copies today!

Printed in Great Britain
by Amazon